KIMBERLY LISAGOR

AND HEATHER HANSEN

DISAPPEARING DESTINATIONS

KIMBERLY LISAGOR is a freelance journalist who has written about travel and the environment for *Outside*, *Mother Jones*, *Men's Journal*, *National Geographic Adventure*, *Modern Traveler*, *USA Weekend*, *The New York Times*, the *Los Angeles Times*, and others. She is the author of *Outside's Wilderness Lodge Vacations*, which won the Lowell Thomas Award for best guidebook and an Award of Excellence from the North American Travel Journalists Association. She lives in San Luis Obispo, California.

HEATHER HANSEN has worked on staff at *Boston* magazine, the *Sunday Independent* (Johannesburg, South Africa), and the *Provincetown Banner*. She won the *Harper's Magazine* award for Distinguished Magazine Writing in 1999 and has contributed to *Men's Journal*, *Modern Traveler*, *National Geographic Traveler*, the *San Francisco Chronicle*, *Smithsonian*, *Outside*, and others. She is a freelance journalist living in Boulder, Colorado.

DISAPPEARING DESTINATIONS

DISAPPEARING DESTINATIONS

37 PLACES IN PERIL
AND WHAT CAN BE DONE
TO HELP SAVE THEM

KIMBERLY LISAGOR

AND

HEATHER HANSEN

VINTAGE DEPARTURES
Vintage Books
A Division of Random House, Inc.
New York

FIRST VINTAGE DEPARTURES EDITION, APRIL 2008

Library of Congress Cataloging-in-Publication Data
Lisagor, Kimberly.
Disappearing destinations : 37 places in peril and what can be
done to help save them / by Kimberly Lisagor
and Heather Hansen.
p. cm.
ISBN: 978-0-307-27736-7
1. Endangered ecosystems.   2. Nature conservation.
3. Voyages and travels.   I. Hansen, Heather.   II. Title.
QH75.H3667 2008
333.72—dc22
2007033400

Book design by Rebecca Aidlin

www.vintagebooks.com

Printed in the United States of America
10 9 8 7 6 5 4 3 2 1

DEDICATION

*For Wes. May the world you'll explore hold
more wonders than we can imagine.*

*For the Baukneys and Hansens, who have always
encouraged curiosity and principle.*

For the defenders of our wild and sublime places.

A NOTE ON SOURCES

The organizations listed in the appendices are resources for readers who feel moved to act on behalf of these endangered destinations. They are among the hundreds of groups and individuals whose research was invaluable to the writing of this book. Our sources ranged from primatologists thrashing through forests counting apes to Nobel Prize–winning scientists who launched a global call to action by documenting the human causes of climate change. Our observations were built on the framework of their field studies, academic papers, and environmental impact reports. For a complete list of sources, visit endangeredplaces.com.

CONTENTS

FOREWORD

PROTECTING THE (GLOBAL) NEIGHBORHOOD

THE IMAGES FLASH PAST ME SOMETIMES, AS THEY DO IN
all our inner slide shows, and though, like most slide shows, they
bring delight and floods of happy memories, they also bring a
certain wistfulness, and unease. I see the winding, lamplit lanes
of Kathmandu, when I first viewed them, barely twenty years
ago, few motorbikes in sight, and the sight of the nearby mountains radiant. I see the temples of Angkor emerging from the
jungle in which they had long been shrouded, and the Taj Mahal
on the night I first visited—1974—when it was possible to enter
after nightfall and to see the building by day without a brown
shroud of smog. I even sometimes see the town of my birth,
Oxford, when it seemed a living historical memory, and not a
paved-over Universityland.

When I think of what's being lost in all these places, in only a
few years, I realize that some of it is in my head: nowhere looks
quite so startling as when first we met it, and for a certain kind of
traveler, every change is a change for the worse. In part, perhaps,
it's the very interest of people like me—our hunger to see the
wonders of the world—that has endangered certain treasures
through overcrowding. And yet beneath all the tricks of the
imagination, something else is true: many of the marvels of our
collective inheritance are disappearing, and because of human
neglect or corruption or greed. Kathmandu now is by some

counts the second most polluted city in the world. Angkor is the site of frantic construction crews building tourist hotels, which those of us who long to be tourists can hardly deny the locals, so grateful for opportunity after decades of hardship and war. And nearly everywhere that's precious across the world, as Kimberly Lisagor and Heather Hansen show us with such urgency and powerful reporting in these pages, is crying out for help. In our lives the most urgent challenge we face, often, is what we should do with the loved ones who are dying; in our travels the central question is what to do about beloved places that are fading before our eyes.

The first thing we can do, clearly, is to visit them, and the second—always helped by a visit—is to speak up and work for their survival. In a global village in which the treasure of any culture is the blessing of us all, it is our responsibility to protect everywhere, as we would a dying cousin down the road.

I can still remember—too vividly, perhaps—the first time I set foot in Lhasa, Tibet, in 1985. The "Forbidden City," as it's sometimes called, had only just opened up to the world, and the few of us who slipped in saw cultural habits unchanged in centuries. A cluster of whitewashed traditional houses, bright with awnings and flower boxes, sat under the many-windowed Potala Palace, and the sense of an attic door opening was palpable. In all its history, I had read, the heartstopping city had seen fewer than two thousand Westerners (one thousand of them in a single British military expedition). By the time I returned just six years later, the city was under martial law, and there were armed soldiers on the rooftops, surveillance cameras everywhere. By the next time I visited, at the beginning of this century, Lhasa was effectively an Eastern Atlantic City, gaudy with blue-glass shopping centers and high-rises, the Potala not even visible from most places and the few traditional buildings still in evidence referred to as "Old Town," as if they belonged to an artificially preserved theme park.

We marvel, rightly, at the acceleration of the new century we're entering, and a sense of speed, of ease and of mobility allows many of us in the privileged world to savor the planet as no generation has done before. Yet the shadow side of all these developments is the speed with which forests and glaciers that took centuries to form are being torn down or allowed to die. And those of us in the privileged world enjoy a particular responsibility that comes with our freedom because we have the potential and means to travel and to help these places, as most of our neighbors on the planet do not. I, on my travels, have often watched cities grow hazy or confused; what *Disappearing Destinations* shows us, with such richness and intensity, is how the same thing is happening, even more dramatically, to many natural wonders. And no clarity and health will come to the world around us until we start to protect and clear the open spaces of our minds and imaginations, and give globalism a conscience as well as eyes and legs.

All of us have our own examples, of course, and often they begin with our hometowns (Santa Barbara, where I grew up, had never seen generic malls or a smog layer until a few years ago). In Bagan, the heartstopping site of twenty-two hundred temples—white and earth-red and gold—set across the empty plains of Burma, a military dictatorship is busily destroying ancient buildings by "restoring" them with modern materials, and in nonsensical styles. Mount Everest is so cluttered with visitors and climbers today that traffic jams fill the slopes and what is a sacred presence to the people who live around it is turned into a status-symbol commodity. In Kyoto, near where I now live, a 1,200-year-old city that withstood earthquakes and fires and wars—it was even spared American bombs during the Second World War—is falling victim to grasping developers, who are razing centuries-old wooden buildings to make way for multistory, concrete apartment blocks.

As that example bears out, the sudden death of our history comes sometimes from natural causes or old age, but just as often from what we are doing, or failing to do. And what we do, we can potentially not do, or do better. Some sights (like the Buddhas of Bamiyan) are gone forever. Some places (I think of Bali or Beirut) seem permanently about to be spoiled, and yet have outlasted many obituaries. But dozens of others, described so well in these pages, are on the brink—on the equivalent of life-support systems—and it is up to us to mobilize our voices and hearts and energies, in part by remembering that the Yangtze River Valley, the Amazon, and the Great Barrier Reef are all now part of our community, our neighborhood, our backyard. Wake up and act now before the memories you cherish in your mind, and in your inner slide shows, turn into mere elegies, and relics of a world forever gone.

Pico Iyer
Jerusalem
January 2008

PICO IYER is the author of many books about travel, including *Video Night in Kathmandu*, *The Lady and the Monk*, and *The Global Soul*. His most recent book, *The Open Road*, looks at globalism through the eyes of the XIVth Dalai Lama.

DISAPPEARING
DESTINATIONS

INTRODUCTION

The real voyage of discovery consists not in seeing new landscapes,
but in having new eyes.
—MARCEL PROUST

THERE ARE CERTAIN TRUTHS WE HOLD ABOUT OUR WORLD:
Glaciers top Mount Kilimanjaro, the Amazon Basin is rain forest, the Rio Grande is a river (and it's grand), and the Great Barrier Reef is a wonder of the world—to name a few. As it turns out, these "truths" may not always be. Glaciers are melting, rain forests are succumbing to logging and development, rivers are drying up, and warming oceans are bleaching reefs.

All too often we assume that the places we know and love, or long to see, will remain essentially the same. But our environment is constantly in flux. Some changes happen slowly, others more spectacularly. Sometimes human impact is the catalyst. Other times it's the fury of nature reminding us who our mama really is. Most often it's a clashing of the two.

As travelers we are at an intersection in history, where place meets circumstance and where reality may not match our expectations for much longer.

It was with this realization that we set out to document places that will undergo dramatic transformations within our lifetime. Since then we have stood where Glacier National Park's last icy depressions can still be seen, cruised through the Yangtze River's Three Gorges amid construction of the great dam, and been awed by the fearless diversity on the shores of the Galápagos. This is not a complete catalogue of stunning places in transition; there are countless others. But all of the locations here were chosen because they are either unique and threatened or emblematic of other places facing similar struggles.

We hope this book will inspire you to see them for yourself. When you do so, please tread carefully, so as not to expedite their demise. See Appendix A at the end of the book for responsible travel resources and suggestions. Should you feel compelled to work toward slowing the pace of change, we have also included an appendix of advocacy organizations that can help you get involved.

Travel is more than just a visit to a destination. It's about seeing a place at a particular moment in time and understanding that it won't always look the same. Beyond that, it's about heeding your wanderlust with heightened awareness and a new sense of urgency.

See it now. The world isn't waiting.

NORTH
AMERICA

UNITED STATES

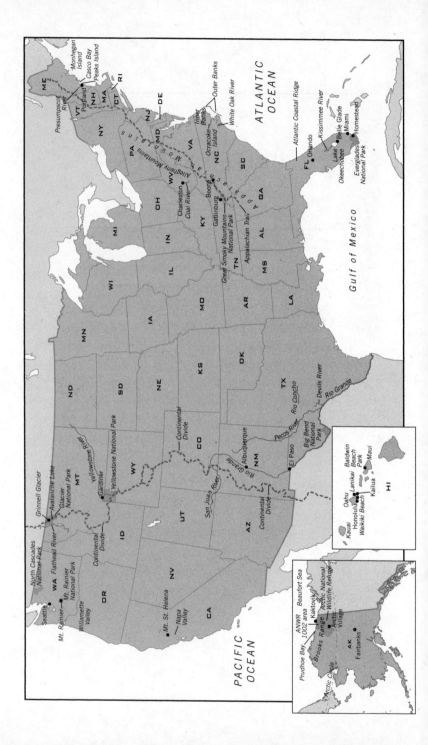

APPALACHIA

Hawks Nest State Park

SUMMER WAS CLINGING TO SOUTHERN WEST VIRGINIA halfway through September. It was still warm, but the really stagnant days had passed. There was a breeze, and the hardwood trees along the Coal River's banks had already begun their autumn show. Bill Currey and his buddies were moving their five kayaks slowly downriver on an eight-mile stretch in the Kanawha Valley. Beneath a baby-blue sky they bobbed and weaved through some light white water, occasionally pulling over to fish in some of the deep pools that form behind bedrock boulders. Currey, now with a snowy beard, has been plying the Coal River and its tributaries since his boyhood days in St. Albans, thirteen miles from the capital, Charleston. As president of the Coal River Group, a nonprofit focused on cleaning up and promoting the river, he is so thrilled to unveil his river that he's willing to divulge some of its secrets. But not too many. "That's a great fishing float. On an eight-mile trip we were catching, on any given day, about a fish per mile," he says. They reeled in a smallmouth bass, a walleye, and some Kentucky spotted bass. ("When you catch one, they get up on their tails and dance," says Currey.) "I can't be saying any more about fishing there or my buddies'll shoot me."

The Coal is made up of three branches—the Big, Little, and Lower Coal rivers—each stretching more than thirty miles. The Big and Little legs have their headwaters up over three thousand feet in the sandstone ridges of the Coal River, Cherry Pond, Guyandotte, and Kayford mountains. The Coal River in all drains about eight hundred square miles of West Virginia's rugged, rolling mountains. When the tributaries from those peaks come together, the river is at first rough and narrow but then opens up into smooth water that would welcome any beginning paddler. All one hundred miles of the river are included on the Walhonde Water Trail. The Walhonde was recently designated as the only river trail entirely within the state boundaries of West Virginia. It's the result of four years of faith and backbreaking labor by the Coal River Group. There are nineteen marked put-in sites along the river, and no matter which section you pick, you're in for a taste of legendary Appalachia. "On the upper ends it's more like a creek where the trees practically envelop it. It's so shady and the water is clear," Currey says. The traffic on the river is so light, and some of the communities so isolated, that river-runners themselves will often become the attraction. "People don't walk outside their back door and see bright-colored kayaks going by every day," says Currey. "So when we do go by some of the more isolated areas, kids will come out and wave from their yards and ask, 'Where'd you get them pretty boats at?' That area is so virgin in so many ways. It kind of blows you away."

Appalachia is still marked by such communities, spread out along the Coal River and beyond, where the word "stranger" has no meaning and where English and Scotch-Irish ballads plucked out on a dulcimer, banjo, or fiddle are still heard. Atop heavily misted peaks, purple monkshood and trumpet creeper bloom lavishly. Huckleberries, edible violets, peppermint, and sassafras wait to be sampled, and in antithetically named "hollows," fox and opossum roam and sourwood honey flows. West Virginia has historically been a land of locals, not of tourists, but that's beginning to change. Tourism is offering some much-needed economic diversity to the state where coal was once king. While mining no longer employs many of its residents, it's still environmentally devastating—particularly in the southwestern part of the state—and politically powerful. Locals like Currey believe that if given the chance, responsible tourism could be the area's "great green hope" and offer the reprieve from mining that the state desperately needs.

West Virginia is garnering the attention of a growing number of people from the alfresco set, most of whom are fleeing densely populated urban centers on the eastern seaboard. But the Coal River is a long way, geographically and culturally, from the feathers in the cap of the state's Division of Tourism, like Harpers Ferry, the New and Gauley rivers, and Monongahela National Forest. Despite its boomtown tourism potential, the western part of the state is relatively untouched by visitors. Southern West Virginia's naturally extreme topography, which has kept so much of it isolated for centuries, seems a natural draw for outdoor-recreation types. In that way, they'd fit right in with the locals. "We're outdoor people. We've grown up getting out on the river and into the woods," says Currey. Without the influence of outsiders, locals in the state's more remote areas have remained more of the mind and pace of the original West Virginians, who stood up against and seceded from Virginia because they didn't agree with its politics. "Mountaineers are always free" became their motto.

Maria Gunnoe is one of the descendants of Appalachia's original mountaineers, the Native Americans who thrived in the area and were joined later by liberated slaves and English, Irish, and Scottish immigrants. Maria's land is that of her granddaddy, and his daddy before him, whose wife was a Cherokee who fled the Trail of Tears and hid in these deep, bountiful recesses. Gunnoe lives in Bob White, not far from the serenity of the Coal River, where lush mountains seem to fold one over the other infinitely and where residents are custom-made for life in Appalachia. Among these isolated hills, their adaptability and self-sufficiency have made lives and land inseparable.

"My family spent four generations tending to this land to pass it on. We were God-fearing stewards of this land," Gunnoe says, surveying her forty acres, once lush with orchards. "I could walk through my yard at any given point and pull an apple off a tree, or a peach or a pear, and hazelnuts, walnuts, chestnuts—just an abundance of food that was there for the taking." But in the past few years that's all changed, due to a force that even her predecessors with all their tribulations couldn't have conceived of: mountaintop mining.

This newest method of coal extraction, called mountaintop removal/valley fill, is stripping Appalachia of its solace and natural richness. Residents of Bob White feel that like their namesake bird, the softly whirring bobwhite quail, they're being flushed from their habitat of steep mountain hollows. Gunnoe says that mountaintop mining is wresting away their safety, quiet, and subsistence. And it's yanking the heartstrings of those whose affection for and dependence on this land is no less vital than the blood in their veins. For them, mountaintop removal threatens to still the pulse of their Appalachia.

"Appalachia" refers to the dense, fertile belt that begins in Pennsylvania and stretches from the West Virginia border south along the spine of the southern Appalachian Mountains through

Virginia, Tennessee, Kentucky, North Carolina, and Georgia. These once-quiet rolling peaks, which begin where the glaciers of the last ice age halted, are carved from 350-million-year-old shale and limestone.

The staggering richness of the Appalachian Highlands ecosystem is renowned among the scientists, explorers, writers, and artists who have roamed there for centuries. In 1671, the frontiersman Robert Fallam said: "It was a pleasing tho dreadful sight, to see mountains and hills as if piled one upon the other." Botanist William Bartram, who traversed this wonderland in 1775, called the southern Appalachians a "sublime forest."

More recently, this area has been heralded as the most biologically diverse temperate region anywhere on earth. Around each curve here the vegetation alone astounds, from boreal, cove, pin oak, and hardwood forests—blooming dogwood, tulip poplar, and redbud are among the area's beauty queens—to heath and grassy balds. Some two thousand species of Appalachian flora

Highland Scenic Highway

have been identified, two hundred of which are said to be native to and entirely confined to this complex ecohub. Its multihued tangles of unkempt rhododendron, mountain laurel, and azalea are near mythical, its ginseng and morel mushrooms coveted worldwide.

This virtual island of biodiversity is a geological oddity. Life was chased southward by an advancing ice sheet ten thousand years ago, and where the glaciers stopped, the fifty-million-year-old mixed mesophytic forest remained—a vestige of the great forests that once dominated the northern hemisphere. These mountaintop forests packed with Fraser fir and fragrant balsam, like a vast green carpet tossed onto the earth and left lumpy and imperfect, give way to headwater streams and tributaries that strike out across the landscape like a thousand bolts of lightning. Those waters sustain life deep in the hollows, where the canopy is so thick that sunlight is seldom seen and where ferns and mosses flourish.

But what ice and rock failed to disrupt back then is now being scoured by coal collecting with a crude technique whose operations have become commonplace over the past decade. Mountaintop removal now accounts for nearly 95 percent of West Virginia surface mining and between 25 and 30 percent of all coal mining in the region.

To the dismay of locals, the Coalburg coal seam in southern West Virginia is where conditions are just right for mountaintop removal. Vast contiguous coalbeds deposited between 250 and 300 million years ago, with billions of tons of high-quality, low-sulfur spoils, lie just beneath the mountaintops. Downhill are steep valley creases where the trees and rocks blasted with dynamite from the apex are indelicately heaved. Where mountaintop removal thwacks and booms, green turns to gray, round to flat, and majestic to messy as bulldozers and oversized dragline scoopers roar to and fro in clouds of dirt and smoke.

Vivian Stockman, outreach coordinator for the Ohio Valley Environmental Coalition, often flies over mountaintop mining sites to document their irreparable transformation. "I came off of a recent flyover and I just had this thought flash through my head that this is what it must be like to view corpses," she says. "It really takes an emotional toll."

What Appalachia is being stripped of is not just its peaks and valleys (hundreds of thousands of forested acres so far), but its way of life. "The topography and the forest have shaped Appalachian culture," says Stockman. "It's a very sheltering and somewhat isolating landscape, and it's made people independent and rugged." While the rest of the world has looked upon Appalachia and generalized about its poverty and what it seems to lack, many have carried on, closely guarding a nearly bygone existence. "They didn't feel poor or cheated, because the woods and forests were a supplemental form of livelihood. The mountains are like a grocery store," Stockman says.

Maria Gunnoe, a self-described "hillbilly," sees mountaintop removal as a kind of cultural genocide that's stripping her area of tradition. Once-elaborate family feasts, stocked with the riches of their mountain outings, are no longer. Access to many wilderness areas has been restricted. "It's because the mine companies are stripping off the tops of mountains and they won't let you in," she says. In Bob White, like countless other towns in West Virginia, eastern Kentucky, Tennessee, and Virginia where mountaintop removal has taken hold, they're also facing an unraveling of their close-knit community. "I live in an area that for fifty square miles I know everybody," she says. "That's the kind of community that we are. Everybody watches over my kids and I watch over their kids. Those communities are just about a thing of the past."

Now hovering over them are three mountaintop mining sites within striking distance of Gunnoe's home and family. Dynamite blasting happens day and night, even on holidays. "My Christmas dinner jumped about two inches off the table," Gunnoe says. "What the blasting does is rumble up through the ground and it kind of shakes the earth, and then you hear the blast. So it scares the daylights out of you before you ever hear the blast. I just threw my hands up and said, 'It's official, merry Christmas.'"

Also at risk in Appalachia are the insects, crustaceans, mussels, worms, fish, and amphibians that thrive in the typical cobble, gravel, sand, and rocks of healthy streambeds. The US Fish and Wildlife Service biologist Cindy Tibbott says that in an area as thickly settled by critters as an Appalachian creek, some are bound to take a hit from pollution or degradation downstream from mining sites. She takes issue with coal companies that insist there's nothing being lost in valleys that are being crammed with blasted-off mountains. "They'll say, 'We're not filling in streams, these are dry ditches,'" says Tibbott. "I have stood in those streams that were proposed for filling and I've caught fish and seen salamanders scurrying in every direction. They are not dry ditches." They're living streams packed with aquatic life such as mayflies, stone flies, and caddis flies, spring peeper tadpoles, red-spotted newts, mountain chorus frogs, creek chub, bluegills, and blacknose dace. Tibbott is certain that rare and even undiscovered species are being lost beneath displaced mountain peaks. "We don't even know what's out there that we might be burying with these valley fills," she says.

The threatened cerulean warbler, adorned with shades of blue the sky would envy, is also declining in its last stronghold, the southern West Virginia highlands. The vast stretches of forest integral to its survival are being fragmented. "If they don't have that big of a piece of land that's forested they are not going to be successful in breeding," says Tibbott. "The mountaintop mining area happens to overlap with the core breeding area of a number of those forest interior species." When the warbler's favorite perches, including old hickory and sugar maples, are leveled, the area noisily mined, and adjacent valleys cluttered, it disappears. Mining companies are required to revegetate the area, but when they do, it's with alien green blades instead of stable, indigenous plant life. "All of the mines are reclaimed in some way," says Tibbott, "mostly to grassland with scattered shrubs or small trees. But creating huge areas of grassland is not a good thing for these species. If you're trying to get back a natural ecosystem, grasslands didn't occur on a large scale in southern West Virginia. But they do now."

But Tibbott's concerns, and those of many other like-minded scientists, supported by a mound of data as big as an Appalachian grayback boulder, were largely ignored by US Department of Interior officials when the largest evaluation of the effects of mountaintop removal to date was released in October 2005. The agency's task, says the report, was to make sure that the Clean Water Act and the Surface Mining Control and Reclamation Act were being upheld, and "to improve the regulatory process and effect better environmental protection for mountaintop mining and valley fill operations in steep slope Appalachia." But since the report was published, fast-tracking mining permits seems to have been the federal government's only priority. In an internal memo that is now evidence in the latest lawsuit being waged by coal country residents, the US Fish and Wildlife Service's Tibbott says, "It's hard to stay quiet about this when I really believe we're doing the public and the heart of the Clean Water Act a great disservice."

While the latest rounds of legal wrangling continue, trees across the top of Appalachia that once ignited with color in fall, were covered with hoarfrost in winter, and were thick with songbirds in spring continue to be razed to access what lies beneath. But Appalachia remains a first frontier and a last stronghold of an irreplaceable variety of human, geological, and biological history. Currey and Gunnoe believe that if outsiders would paddle the cool Coal River or hunt for wild mushrooms in shady hollows, the world might come to understand the value of what's being lost every day as more mountaintops succumb to mining. Even if she's ultimately driven from her land, Gunnoe will always recall that it was paradise once. Borrowing a sentiment from renowned labor organizer Mother Jones, she says, "When I die and go to heaven, I am going to tell almighty God about West Virginia."

ARCTIC NATIONAL WILDLIFE REFUGE, ALASKA

Mountains and meandering creeks, Arctic National Wildlife Refuge

WHEN THOUSANDS OF PORCUPINE CARIBOU TREK ACROSS the tundra and converge time and again in one particular spot above the Arctic Circle in northeast Alaska, it's the biggest show in town. Here, at their annual staging area, they come together from their wintering grounds and prepare for a northward surge. Before long, instinct and habit take over and they stir, usually in the last days of April, and begin the long walk to their ancestral calving grounds on the coastal plain of the Beaufort Sea. The heaving mammalian mass can be tracked easily, moving like a snow plow across the tundra, says Tara Wertz, a large-animal biologist with the US Fish and Wildlife Service. "When you have fifty thousand to eighty thousand animals moving across a landscape, it's almost as if the ground itself is moving. It's this undulating wave of life."

By June the herd will have walked hundreds of miles, crossing the peaks (which rise to nine thousand feet) and roaring rivers of the formidable Brooks Range. "Landforms don't seem to matter to them," says Wertz, who's hummed above them in a Cessna 206. "There can be this nice mountain pass and it's like they don't even recognize it's there. They're in a straight line headed for the coastal plain and nothing's gonna stop them. It truly is amazing," she says. "That must have been what the plains bison looked like sweeping across the prairie. It's unparalleled on the North American continent. You just don't see that type of congregation of animals anymore."

The caribou migration is but one inimitable feature of the 19.6-million-acre Arctic National Wildlife Refuge, which lies in Alaska's remote northeast corner. ANWR is so big that it actually encompasses six distinct climate zones, from the northern barrier islands on the coast of the Beaufort Sea, across the lush coastal plain, up into the foothills of the Brooks Range and through its alpine highlands and subalpine terrain, and deep into the boreal forest, which resembles much of interior Alaska. There's so much to see that it could easily take a lifetime, according to Carol Kasza, a founder of and guide with Fairbanks-based Arctic Treks. She first ventured into this area thirty years ago, and after many summers of introducing it to other people, it still seems new and remarkable to her. "Once you get up there it's pretty easy to fall in love with it. It doesn't take much."

Part of the thrill of going to ANWR is actually getting there. From Fairbanks it's 498 miles to Deadhorse, near the coast of the Arctic Ocean. The Dalton Highway runs due north for 414 of those miles. Markers along the only road north indicate the exciting northward push over the Yukon River, Continental Divide, and Arctic Circle. Those who take to the gravelly, washboard-grooved road by car or bicycle are warned that calling the Dalton a "highway" is a bit generous. It's just barely one lane in either direction, with sparse services along the way. Semitrucks roar down it, increasing its danger. Anyone undertaking this adventure should expect to take some rocks to the windshield, and should tote more than one spare tire and be prepared to use them. They should also be ready to stop at the many scenic overlooks, every thirty miles or so, to stare agape into the wild face of Alaska. For more than a hundred jaw-dropping miles, the Dalton nearly borders Gates of the Arctic National Park, to its west. During that stretch there are glacier-gouged valleys and icy summits, including 8,510-foot Mount Igikpak, the park's highest peak and the headwaters of the Noatak River. Landlubbers wanting to hand the wheel over to a professional might choose the Dalton Highway Express, which drops off backpackers anywhere along the "haul road," including ANWR, which borders the east side of the road for about three miles. The refuge itself is an entirely roadless wilderness the size of North Carolina that also lacks any marked foot trails (unless you count a gazillion game trails). This is desolate and unforgiving country requiring solo travelers to have superior orienteering and survival skills.

Most people reach ANWR by air, from Fairbanks to either Arctic Village, on the southern edge of the refuge, or Kaktovik, on its northern perimeter. Kasza says that while flying over the area, it begins to dawn on people how immense this part of the world is—ANWR alone is nine times the size of Yellowstone. "It takes people a while to grasp that scale of wilderness and untouched wild country," she says. "The mountains just go on and on and on, and it's phenomenally beautiful." Flying around Kaktovik is a study of the artistic Arctic landscape. The ocean is still frozen in June, and it looks like a meringue, with swoops of ice like frozen waves with brittle, frosty crests. The few leads of seawater that are beginning to break through are a sign of warmer days ahead. And the coastal plain is an irregular yet tidy expanse of geometric shapes, where snowmelt creates creek rings around bits of land. The green chunks are similar in size and appear to crowd the terrain all the way to the horizon.

From either of those Arctic outposts, bush planes buzz into and out of ANWR, most often landing on a gravel river bar or some dry, smooth patch of tundra. Only a select group of outfitters—twenty-six are listed on the Alaska Fish and Wildlife Service's website—is authorized to operate within the refuge. Many introduce newbies to the woolly diversity of ANWR on one- to two-week rafting trips down one of its remarkable rivers. More ground can be covered on the water, giving paddlers a taste of the refuge's diverse ecozones. On her North Slope river trips, Kasza runs four-person and twelve-person rafts from the mountains, through the foothills, and out onto the coastal plain. Most trips balance time on the water with hikes across the rolling tundra and lumpy tussocks, where wildlife is abundant but spread out. Some forty-five mammal species make their home in ANWR, including shaggy, Muppet-like musk oxen; sure-footed, cloud-white Dall sheep; fastidious polar bears; stealthy lynx; deliberate, majestic moose; and fierce grizzly bears. And then there are the hundreds of thousands of caribou.

As for a best "summer" month to visit the refuge, there really isn't one. Seasons in ANWR go by at warp speed, the tundra's vibrant colors and character changing with each passing day. "You can get a new season every month. June, July, and August are spring, summer, and fall up there," Kasza says. There's also no best place to go in ANWR. "What makes the Brooks Range and the refuge so unique is that it's all of a whole," she says. "You go to places in the lower forty-eight and there are little pockets of wild places left. But here, it doesn't matter where you are, it's all incredible."

ANWR makes quick advocates of its visitors. Many who have been won over by this landscape in person want to protect its wildness. And that's good, says Kasza: "We need all the help we can get to protect it from development." People have been standing up for ANWR for a long time. In 1925, Mardy Murie and her husband, Olaus Murie, of the US Biological Survey (now the US Fish and Wildlife Service), spent their honeymoon dog-sledding in Alaska's northern reaches, all the way up to the Sheenjek River basin, at the geographic center of the present-day ANWR. Mardy had been a resident of Alaska since she was nine years old and a defender of its backcountry solitude since childhood. The Muries' exploration and eloquent account of what they found in northern Alaska in Mardy's book *Two in the Far North* eventually helped earn ANWR protection in 1960. Up until her death in 2003, at age 101, Mardy stood by ANWR. In 2002, she told Congress, "Beauty is a resource in and of itself. Alaska must be allowed to be Alaska. That is her greatest economy. I hope the United States of America is not so rich that she can afford to let these wildernesses pass by. Or so poor she cannot afford to keep them."

ANWR was expanded to its current size in 1980 when President Carter more than doubled the 8.9 million acres that President Eisenhower had set aside as a refuge twenty years earlier, in his last moments as president. Carter perhaps foresaw the contention that would arise an area such as ANWR's coastal plain, which is so rich in oil and gas resources and in wildlife that a stipulation was put on expansion. That condition, section 1002 of the Alaska National Interest Lands Conservation Act, specifically protects the 1.5 million acres that hug roughly fifty miles of coastline, and allows drilling there only with a congressional act. "10-02" is the name now often used for the hotly contested coastal plain where pregnant, barren-ground porcupine caribou cows drop their calves, and under which the US Geological Survey estimates there is as much as ten billion barrels of oil. (At the current rate of twenty million barrels per day, Americans would use up ANWR's oil in less than two months.)

Not long after the area gained refuge status, people started arguing over its use. In 1987 President Reagan recommended leasing the coastal plain for energy exploration. But two years later when the tanker *Exxon Valdez* spilled eleven million gallons of oil into Prince William Sound (one of the largest spills in US history), public horror temporarily deflected exploration interests. In 1991 Native American opposition to disturbing the coastal plain foiled advancing energy interests, achieving a filibuster defeat in the Senate.

10-02 area of Arctic National Wildlife Refuge

The issue was quiet for four more years until an ANWR development rider was attached to a budget bill that then-president Clinton vetoed. Five years later, in 2000, President Bush included a push into ANWR on his campaign trail, calling it a "top energy priority" and emphasizing it again in his first State of the Union address in 2001. Congress grappled with the issue in 2002, 2003, 2005, and again in May 2006, each time voting down ANWR drilling by a slim majority. In January 2007 the Udall-Eisenhower Arctic Wilderness Act proposed to permanently prevent exploration or drilling in 10-02. After consideration by the House Committee on Natural Resources, it was passed on to the Subcommittee on National Parks, Forests, and Public Lands, which is now reviewing it.

Like any intense land feud, the ANWR debate has a surfeit of stakeholders. Those supporting the push into ANWR include the state of Alaska's leadership, energy companies, and nearly half of Congress. Drilling opponents include the Native American Gwich'in tribe; many of environmentalism's usual suspects, including the World Wildlife Fund and the Sierra Club; and the other half of Congress. Somewhere in between are the Kaktovik Inupiat, the Native American residents of the small rural village of Kaktovik, population 230, which lies smack in the middle of 10-02.

Long before Alaska was a state, the area now known as ANWR had been settled, explored, surveyed, and exploited for its freakish abundance of natural resources. In fact, people have been plodding around the farthest reaches of the North American continent since the first wave of humanity surged over the Bering land bridge between eight thousand and fourteen thousand years ago. Since that time what's now known as Arctic Alaska ceased to be barren or pristine but has maintained its status as a sometimes brutal, always spectacular place.

The Inupiat, or "real people," have been at home in far north

Alaska for three millennia. Their homeland, or Inuuniagviat Kaktovikmuit, stretches from the coast to about seventy miles inland, to the Continental Divide atop the Brooks Range. They have endured unspeakably harsh conditions, surviving by launching their tiny skiffs into the frigid Beaufort Sea to hunt their "great black whale," the bowhead, and polar bears. They have crisscrossed the plains in search of caribou and musk oxen, and trekked into the mountains in search of Dall sheep.

Over the past few centuries the Inupiat have faced and fought whalers, trappers, traders, and explorers. More recent invaders into their territory, which include many of the modern-day stakeholders, are no less appalling and scary to them. Regarding the interests of all these parties, the Inupiat are deeply conflicted. As part of the Kaktovik Impact Project, residents laid bare their damned-if-you-do, damned-if-you-don't position on ANWR, saying, "Our lands and water have received much attention from those who want to search here for oil and those who want to make it into a wilderness. We see both of these outside interests to be potentially destructive."

Most recently the Inupiat have been angered both by federal lawmakers, who, by drawing a line around ANWR, implied that the area was an empty wilderness, and by agencies like the US Fish and Wildlife Service, which manages the refuge. "Our rights to our continued wise and responsible use of our country and our resources within that federal claim are clearly at risk," say residents in the Kaktovik Impact Project report. "The most dangerous, in our view, to the things that matter to us, and surely the most insulting, is the notion that our homeland is empty or should be made so."

Perhaps more offensive to the Inupiat are those who traipse around ANWR as if providentially entitled. "We are also deeply concerned about the interest of urban recreationists in our country," says the report. These city slickers (which to the Inupiat means pretty much everyone below the Arctic Circle) descend upon their country to trek or paddle without understanding of, or respect for, the locals. "We want to make it very clear that our intense feeling about our land is a far cry from the odd lust of these urban wilderness buffs," say the Inupiat. "Indeed we see these people as dangerously naïve, with a strange, almost religious fanaticism that is . . . frightening."

The impression that outsiders make on the residents of Kaktovik is more than anecdotal, as the Inupiat own the surface rights to roughly one third of 10-02's coastal access. That makes them a crucial party in any attempt to explore or drill for oil there. While their interactions with the oil industry have been largely respectful, the Inupiat are also unconvinced that this is the lesser of the perceived evils. "But oil development is a large and potentially dangerous thing," say the Inupiat. "We are not in the mood to risk our future here. And we have no other future so we must be adamant."

To ANWR's south is another Native American tribe that fears for its future. The Gwich'in, a band of about eight thousand spread across fifteen small communities below the refuge and into Canada, have long been linked to the plain, though most have never even seen it. To them the area is Iizhik Gwats'an Gwandaii Goodlit, or the "sacred place where life begins," where the caribou, which eventually migrate south and are hunted by them, enter the world. "It's an incredibly important place for us," says Luci Beach, a Gwich'in whose family is halfway between Fort Yukon, Alaska, and Old Crow, Canada. She says that life as the Gwich'in know it would not be possible without ANWR's caribou. According to legend, the Gwich'in have been connected to the caribou from their creation as a people onward. Since that time, each retains a portion of the other's heart. "It's so sacred that we don't even go there," says Beach.

The Gwich'in still largely live by subsistence, with some 60 to

70 percent of their diet coming from the land, from hunting and fishing. "So this is an incredibly important part of what sustains us," says Beach. "We're not willing to take a gamble, because we've seen what's happened on the North Slope."

Alaska's North Slope, so called because of its location above the Brooks Range, is the coastal area that extends hundreds of miles west of 10-02. Prudhoe Bay, North America's largest oil field, is just sixty miles west of ANWR. Since 1968, the landscape around Prudhoe Bay, including offshore sites, has been prodded and drained by Exxon-Mobil, British Petroleum, and Anadarko Petroleum. The massive Trans-Alaska Pipeline originates there and conveys crude oil eight hundred miles south to Valdez, on Prince William Sound.

West of Prudhoe Bay is the 23.5-million-acre National Petroleum Reserve–Alaska, much of which is already open to oil development or soon will be. Hot on the heels of the latest congressional defeat of drilling in ANWR, the Department of the Interior opened roughly four hundred thousand additional acres of the reserve—called the Northeast Planning Area—including a controversial area around Teshekpuk Lake. Again caribou— this time the Central Arctic herd—are said to be at risk, as well as tundra swans, white-fronted geese, and brant geese, which munch on submerged plants in the deep lake. The Bureau of Land Reclamation, which technically leases the land, maintains that advances in drilling technology will allow for minimum impact. As for the geese, the bureau plans to keep an eye on them, too. The vast oil development complexes—the steel towers and roaring vehicles—west of ANWR are a glimpse at how 10-02 might be affected if drilling is ever green-lighted. The infrastructure, which spills inland from the coast like a full glass tipped over on a table, forever changed the area's life and aesthetic.

How the Central Arctic caribou herd have adapted to the

Prudhoe Bay development has been compared with what might happen to the Porcupine herd in 10-02. Since the Prudhoe Bay caribou adjusted to the drilling by finding other suitable birthing grounds, drilling proponents extrapolate that the porcupine herd will do the same. Not so, says Tara Wertz. While the Central Arctic caribou actually had some cushion, some alternate areas to relocate to that offered the same qualities that their original calving area did, "the Porcupine herd doesn't really have that option," says Wertz.

A direct impact of drilling on the coastal plain, and in 10-02 specifically, will be high calf mortality. When the caribou cannot give birth on the coastal plain, calf survival drops significantly. "The one thing that we've found that influences calf survival more that anything is where the caribou calve," says Wertz. When calves are born in 10-02, mother and babies tend to stay there, away from insects and predators, getting fat and strong for their walk hundreds of miles south to their wintering grounds. If they're not able to give birth on the coastal plain, the caribou still try to get there later because of its ideal conditions. But on the way to 10-02 many newborn calves are killed by predators or while crossing rivers swollen with spring runoff.

For now the possibility of oil development has been delayed but not eliminated. Many lawmakers, environmentalists, and indigenous groups agree that this moment is a respite, not a conclusion. "We were really concerned with this last go-round in the Senate," says Beach. "We were very relieved when that was over with and people's good sense came out. But we're gearing up for the next fight, because we know the proponents of development will be scheming on some new things to try." For her people, according to Sarah James, a Neets'aii Gwich'in elder from Arctic Village, Alaska, who grew up following the caribou migration, the issue is cut-and-dried. "We are caribou people and we have always been caribou people. Our life depends on it," she says.

If probing, drilling, and paving are eventually to make their way into 10-02, now is the moment to respectfully glimpse the area's vastness. ANWR is a place where natural and human history have become braided through time. Its complex arctic ecosystems are similarly and strongly woven, as creatures endure half the year in deep, cold darkness and revel in the other half when ANWR blooms in twenty-four hours of daylight with millions of acres of wildflowers.

THE CASCADES AND MOUNT RAINIER, WASHINGTON

South Sister from the Cascade Loop Highway

IN JULY, WHILE COUNTLESS STREAMS BRAID ACROSS THE landscape and subalpine meadows bloom, snow still lingers on the Nisqually Vista Trail on Mount Rainier's southern flank. Wildflowers like lavender lupine and yellow glacier lilies begin to emerge, offering a preview of the astounding color that will adorn this tundra region over the next several weeks. When Martha Longmire, the daughter-in-law of a local entrepreneur, first visited this spot in the late nineteenth century, she said, "This must be what paradise is like." And that's how this area got its official name. At around 5,400 feet, Paradise offers unobstructed views of Rainier's impressive bulk, its ice-carved flanks and the aqua-tinged Nisqually glacier, one of twenty-five frozen masses that crown the 14,410-foot peak. Massive piles of rocky moraine remain where the glacier has receded, and a torrent of water gushes from its terminus, forming the Nisqually River. The river flows through Mount Rainier National Park (roughly seventy miles southeast of Seattle) and eventually empties into Puget Sound.

The entire length of the Cascade range—the 725-mile stretch of peaks running from British Columbia to Northern California—is diverse, impressive, and bountiful, but Mount Rainier in central Washington is the highest and, arguably, most dramatic peak. "The Mountain," as Washingtonians refer to it, lies within and is completely surrounded by the national park. From all angles Rainier can be seen standing magnificently with twelve thousand feet of vertical relief, dwarfing its neighboring peaks. While all visitors in its vicinity do a fair amount of mountain watching, the park encompasses a wide range of fabulous features, from old-growth forests and towering waterfalls to narrow canyons and steaming geothermal pools.

Throughout history people have staked their survival on Rainier and its shorter but still lofty neighbors (nearby Mount Adams and even distant Mount St. Helens and Mount Hood can be seen by walking just an hour above Paradise). For at least eight thousand years Native Americans have trekked the steep volcanic slopes of the Cascades. Their stone tools have been found even at high altitudes. They fished in roaring rivers and massive lakes hidden among dense, aromatic forests, and they drank from melting snowpack. In the summer, Rainier's meadows and forests were critical hunting and gathering grounds for the Muckleshoot, Nisqually, Puyallup, Upper Cowlitz, and Yakama tribes. They sought berry fields thousands of feet up the mountain and killed bears, deer, elk, and mountain goats. For hundreds of years, at least, the mountain was called Ta-co-bet, Tahoma, and Takhoma, meaning "place where the waters begin," "snowy peak" and "big mountain," respectively.

In the nineteenth century fur traders roamed the area, followed by gold and silver miners. Around the same time that mining was big business, the first white homesteaders settled in the foothills to graze livestock and to log trees. In 1906, a group of Seattle-based climbers formed the Mountaineers, a club whose members still support the conservation and exploration of the vast, challenging Cascades. Today these mountains are still a climber's mecca, particularly Rainier, because of its reputation as the hardest endurance climb in the lower forty-eight (the first US team to summit Everest trained there). In 2005, 4,604 people summited Rainier, and almost that many tried and failed.

Mount Rainier is deceptively young. Its steepness, a characteristic of much older mountains, is due to glaciers carving relatively swiftly through its lava flows. While most people think of the omnipresent massif as a static peak, it's actually an active volcano. All of the Cascades lie within the Pacific "Ring of Fire." In the scale of geologic history, they blow their tops with some frequency, roughly twice per century. In the past one hundred years they have performed about average, erupting twice. Mount St. Helens erupted catastrophically in 1980 (killing fifty-seven people), and California's Lassen Peak eruption, which began in 1914, lasted three years. Rainier erupted most recently in the 1840s and, more powerfully 1,000 to 2,300 years ago. In some spots on the volcano, lava flowed for over nine miles from its crater.

In 2005, the US Geological Survey (USGS) named four Cascades peaks—Mount Rainier, Mount St. Helens, Mount Hood, and Mount Shasta—among the top five most threatening US volcanoes (Hawaii's Kilauea topped the list). The assessment was based on twenty-five factors, including how often the volcano has erupted in history and how dangerously, and the size of the population that is in imminent danger from eruption. Every US volcano's threat was ranked from "very low" to "very high." Of the eighteen volcanoes that are considered a very high threat, eleven are in the Cascades. Since the loss of life on Mount St. Helens, portable monitoring systems have been developed that can be brought to a volcano once it comes back to life. But volcanologists want permanent monitoring of the other peaks that have "sparse or antiquated" instruments. The USGS report revealed that right now, only about half of the most threatening US volcanoes are monitored even on a basic level. "We're minimally prepared right now," says Cynthia Gardner, the scientist in charge of the Cascades Volcano Observatory in Vancouver, Washington.

What makes possible volcanic events, which include both eruptions and large-scale landslides (known as debris avalanches or lahars), so potentially disastrous on Rainier is that its upper slopes are encased in roughly thirty square miles of snow and ice. This enormous frozen cache, which hangs from the mountain's peak like gargantuan folds of skin, would likely be melted by bubbling lava, triggering colossal landslides of slush, rocks, and trees. Sometimes lahars occur on unstable parts of Rainier even without the catalyst of an eruption. "One concern is

Mount Rainier from Mount St. Helens

whether we could get large flank failures at Mount Rainier, which has had quite a history of debris avalanches, spawning very-large-volume lahars," says Gardner.

Cloud-shrouded Rainier makes volcanologists particularly anxious because of the sheer number of people in that area who might be affected by a large-scale volcanic event. More than 1.5 million people live within a hundred miles of its pulsating core. One particular concern is the densely populated Puyallup Valley, which extends forty-four miles from Mount Rainier to Puget Sound. In the past ten thousand years many lahars have buried what are now well-populated areas, up to sixty-two miles from the mountain, with debris that once resided on Rainier. "At Mount Rainier we have a unique situation. We have a very large population in the Puyallup Valley living on deposits of past large lahars," says Gardner. "The concern is whether one of these could occur with little or no warning." Every river valley on Rainier's slopes has been mowed down by such speeding mud-flows at some point in history. Currently, all of its glaciers drain from the volcano into five major rivers—the Carbon, White, Cowlitz, Nisqually, and Puyallup—which have formed deep canyons over time. All but one of Rainier's rivers drains into Puget Sound near Tacoma.

There's a growing buzz in the scientific community that climate change may increase the likelihood of landslides on volcanoes. (While the link between global warming and eruptions hasn't been scientifically supported, the idea has some highly respected supporters among volcanologists. "There's some speculation that volcanic activity increased in the Cascades at the end of the last major ice age as the area and volume of glaciers decreased on volcanoes," says Gardner. "The idea is that you take off this overburden, this ice mass, and it's easier for magma to move up the conduit.") What is certain is that hydrological changes on steep slopes increase risk, says Jessica Larsen, volcanologist at the Alaska Volcano Observatory and at the Geophysical Institute at the University of Alaska in Fairbanks. She is particularly concerned with heavy rainfall on snow- and ice-covered volcanic slopes. "A significant increase in precipitation in a lahar-prone region could lead to an increase in the number and volume of lahars occurring on the slopes of a volcano, whether triggered directly by an eruption or not," she says.

This is not good news for the Cascades, where scientists across many disciplines agree that climate change, which includes temperature increases and precipitation fluctuations, is in full swing. During the twentieth century, the Pacific Northwest warmed 1.5 degrees Fahrenheit, more than the global average, and temperatures are still rising (now as much as 1 degree Fahrenheit per decade). And massive storms, once thought of as anomalies, are becoming part of a predictable trend. In 1995 and 1996 a series of powerful "pineapple express" storms—so called because they're the result of warm, wet air that comes from Hawaii—hit the Northwest. Soon after, the National Climatic Data Center offered a warning: as the climate continues to warm, these storms are expected to come more frequently. More recently, research released by the University of Washington's Climate Impacts Group reiterated that the western slope of the Cascades, which is already very wet seasonally, should expect larger and earlier storms.

Some of those "larger storms" hit hard in late 2006, causing record-setting damage to much of the central and northern Cascades. In federal parks and forests throughout the state, including North Cascades National Park, about one hundred miles north of Rainier, rain-swollen tributaries leveled trees and scoured trails. On Rainier, where the average November precipitation is seventeen inches, forty-one inches fell. (In Paradise alone, nearly eighteen inches of rain came down in thirty-six hours.) Warmer winter temperatures also caused precipitation that usually falls as snow to come as rain instead. Snow fell only above ten thousand feet, and because it was so warm, existing snow between seven thousand and ten thousand feet melted, worsening river runoff. As a result, the Nisqually River overran its banks and breached protective levees as it tore through the area.

Other rivers changed course entirely, cutting new creeks into the soft earth. A torrential flow on the Ohanapecosh River, on the southeast side of Rainier, seriously damaged several campgrounds and flooded a grove of old-growth Douglas firs, western red cedars, and western hemlocks. These stately trees, which have survived for more than a thousand years, are now fighting for their lives. Many footbridges were mangled or destroyed, and large sections of road were either wiped off the mountain entirely or so severely damaged that they remained closed through 2007. The glorious ninety-three-mile-long Wonderland Trail, which encircles the base of the mountain, was impassable in many spots, making the circumnavigation of Rainier impossible for the first time anyone could remember. During that time, the park suffered what officials called "unprecedented" damage. To the shock of Washingtonians who ski and snowshoe there all winter and spring, the entire park was closed for six months as officials assessed the destruction and stabilized thoroughfares.

Rainwater coursing down Rainier's river channels is only part of the problem. The Climate Impacts Group predicts that by the end of this century, snow will melt as much as three months earlier than it does now. On a massif such as Rainier, this is no small matter. From 1913 to 1994, the mountain lost an average of 21 percent of the overall area of its glaciers (25 percent of their total volume). Glaciers on the south side, such as Nisqually, generally shrank 10 percent faster than those on the north side. Since 1994, Rainier has lost an additional five square miles of ice. In Washington's stunning North Cascades National Park—the most densely glaciated area in the lower forty-eight—the loss is just as profound. Forty percent of its glaciers (which now number about three hundred) have melted since 1850, and 13 percent of that was in the last four decades alone.

Due to hotter summers and drier winters, the massive glaciers are also retreating. Receding glaciers scour the canyons in which they reside and dump additional rock into riverbeds, a process known as aggradation. The more a glacier melts, the more rock debris within it is freed and then deposited in its wake. That material is then carried down channels by meltwater and precipitation. The average rate of aggradation on Rainier is six to twelve inches per decade, but it's accelerating. During the 2006 downpours, some rivers saw overnight a rate of aggradation that should have taken decades. Tahoma Creek's bed, for example, is now four feet higher than it was before the flooding.

Following the 2006 storms, national park officials at Rainier are facing the fact that their mountain ecosystem may look and feel much different in coming years. A statement put out after the dramatic events said, "[We] will rely more and more on larger and stronger dikes, levees, and other flood control structures to separate the rivers from the roads. In the long term, park managers will have to consider how much effort is warranted to protect vulnerable facilities. Some roads may be closed permanently, or only repaired well enough to be passable until the next flood. Some structures may be relocated to places less prone to flooding, or perhaps removed from the park entirely."

Even before the record-setting storms of 2006, outdoors-lovers throughout the Cascades had been witnessing a transformation in the landscape. It was August 1978 when longtime Cascades climber Geof Childs first walked several miles from the end of Twisp River Road to North Lake, at the base of Gilbert Peak in the Sawtooth Range. The snowpack at the lake, the remnants of a former glacier, was impressive—over thirty feet high, one hundred fifty feet wide, and maybe three hundred feet deep. Twenty-seven years later the sight was greatly transformed, says Childs, who has guided in the North Cascades since the mid-seventies and still leads climbs for North Cascades Mountain Guides. By August 2005, the snowpack had shrunk to ten feet high, thirty feet wide, and thirty feet deep. "I may not be young anymore, but I certainly don't think of myself as being old, so to see the change in the snowpack was pretty stunning," he says.

Unfortunately for Childs, his observations are part of the Cascades' new climate reality, says Philip Mote, Washington State's climatologist. "We're not talking about climate change that's going to happen in 2050 and then we'll figure out how to cope with it," he says. "This is something that has already been happening over the past fifty years." Mote points to the "raft" of studies coming out recently that document the decline in snowpack, the shift toward earlier springs and plant blooming, and the changes in species range and activity in the Pacific Northwest. "The evidence is just adding up," he says. "We have a serious exposure to risk here and we have to figure out how to cope with that risk."

While climate change means too much water on the west side of the Cascades, the east side is suffering the opposite problem. The range normally casts a broad "rain shadow" across its eastern slope by capturing precipitation and leaving areas of eastern Washington desert-like from lack of moisture. Only extensive damming of the powerful Columbia River, which runs through the eastern part of the state, has made living there possible. The volume of the river depends on melting snowpack in the Cascades. Currently, the snow line there is at roughly three thousand feet. Within the next several decades, it's expected to rise more than a thousand feet, cutting in half the volume of water stored in snow. This is sobering news for thirsty people, crops, and power companies on the eastern slope, says Mote. "The degree to which the Northwest relies on snowmelt for summer water supply is quite high," he says. "Removing that reservoir bit by bit has profound impacts. Society is going to have to face squarely the reality of shrinking water supplies." A waning water supply is a fact that is just beginning to dawn on some residents, says Mote. "That discussion, that realization, that dialogue, is just now beginning," he says. "But it's past time to get serious."

For as much damage as the torrents of water did, it also reinforced love and respect for the mountain. "The flood recovery efforts have also helped us understand the place that Mount Rainier holds in the hearts of people across the nation," said park superintendent Dave Uberuaga. Visitors in the summer of 2007 stopped at the dry bed of Kautz Creek, in the southwest corner of the park, to get a firsthand look at some of recent changes to, and enduring grandeur of, the place. During the storms the Kautz drastically changed course and never returned to its original route. Beyond the former creek, whose banks are lined with three-hundred-foot-tall Douglas firs, Rainier glowed radiantly in the distance. Kautz glacier, which feeds the creek, could be seen clinging to the flanks of the mountain, curving elegantly toward the peak and out of sight.

CASCO BAY, MAINE

Outer Green Island

NO ONE KNOWS CASCO BAY LIKE CAPTAIN GENE Willard, the eighth-generation mariner whose great-great-uncle William launched the bay's first tugboat service in 1856. He has been shuttling commuters between the islands and the mainland since he was fourteen. Now forty-two, Willard commands the Casco Bay Lines ferry fleet and runs his own water taxi service—the only one that's open for business every day of the year. "I've got a great office," Willard jokes, "but sometimes when it's below zero and the wind is blowing thirty or forty knots out of the north, I think, what the hell am I doing? It's wicked cold and everything else, and how many people are out here on a twenty-four-foot boat in the middle of the night? I'm the only one."

Frigid nights aside, the captain relishes his time on the water. Most mornings, as seabirds soar overhead, Willard watches the muted orange sunlight creep up around the edges of the bay's 222 islands. He has hosted weddings and burials on the water, taken tourists on countless scenic excursions. He knows the favorite coves of harbor seals and a tree where a bald eagle nests, and he prides himself on being able to escort visitors to any native bird they want to see. Sometimes on clear days he taxis to rocky, rugged Monhegan Island and coasts along the fern-draped shoreline to watch the gannets fish, their big blue beaks and yellow heads plunging below the surface as they search for food. "This is the only life I know," he says, "but I couldn't imagine a better job."

The bay has changed quite a bit since Willard and his seven siblings were growing up on Peaks Island. Back then, the two-mile-long island, three miles off the coast of Portland, had about 350 residents, most of them homemakers, fishermen, and teachers. "Everyone was poor, but no one wanted anything," Willard says. "They had oceanfront property, but nobody wanted the view. We thought, the ocean's like a desert. Who wants to look at nothing?" These days, wealthy out-of-towners are willing to pay large sums for these "nothing" views. The island's year-round population has swelled to more than a thousand, and multi-million-dollar homes are cropping up all over the bay. "A lot of my business is moving contractors around," the captain says. Every one of Willard's brothers and sisters has been priced out of the region.

The consequences of the population boom aren't just economic. The increase in buildings, roads, and human activity is adding environmental stress to a region that's struggling to recover from its dirty past. Previous generations thought bodies of water such as Casco were large enough to dilute manufacturing byproducts. The glass, paper, and textile factories; tanneries; and metal foundries that established themselves near the Portland commercial hub in the late eighteenth century dumped unthinkable quantities of untreated waste and heavy metals into the watershed. The petroleum industry established tank farms in the 1920s, and Portland soon became New England's largest oil importing port. By 1965, the Presumpscot River, one of the major waterways that empty into Casco Bay, was so thick with toxic sludge that it looked like a "root beer float," according to Presumpscot River Watch documents. Exacerbating the problem were the thousands of residents who treated the rivers and ocean like a community toilet. Sewage treatment plants didn't come to the region until the Clean Water Act mandated them in 1977, along with industrial-waste-disposal measures.

Throughout the 1980s, the waterways cleared up visibly, and it was largely assumed that the new regulations had solved the pollution problem. Swimmers and clammers flocked to the beaches. Tourism thrived. The bay, which *looked* idyllic, became a popular seaside retreat for vacationers who sought solace among its clear, sparkling, island-dotted waters.

That's why a 1988 report by the Conservation Law Foundation and the Island Institute came as such a shock. "Troubled Waters: A Report on the Environmental Health of Casco Bay" named Casco as one of the most polluted estuaries in America. The levels of PCBs (polychlorinated biphenyls, introduced in the 1920s by power plants and hydraulic systems) and PAHs (polynucleated aromatic hydrocarbons, often-carcinogenic compounds likely leaked by the petroleum industry) measured high enough to be considered dangerous to the endemic plant and animal species, not to mention the humans who were splashing around in the bay and feasting on local shellfish. Researchers found lead, zinc, copper, and arsenic in disconcerting amounts as well. Despite appearances, Casco Bay was filthy.

Though some of its conclusions were later called into question, the report sparked an immediate and impassioned response. Friends of Casco Bay formed in 1989, followed in 1990 by a federally funded project that would become the Casco Bay Estuary Partnership. Both groups set out to educate the public, establish regular health reports for the bay, and work toward cleaning it up.

The Casco Bay watershed is now one of the most closely watched in the country. Since 1992, more than a hundred volunteers have helped Friends of Casco Bay gather more than 130,000 water-quality measurements. Recording the bay's salinity, dissolved oxygen, temperature, pH, and water clarity on a regular basis is like taking a human's body temperature, pulse, and blood pressure, says Friends of Casco Bay baykeeper Joe Payne, the area's official ombudsman and its most outspoken advocate. "It's like going to the doctor," he says. "If those things are okay, see you in a year."

Payne's organization provided much of the data that the Casco Bay Estuary Partnership used in a comprehensive progress report it published in 2005. The document contained some encouraging news. Improvements in storm water drainage systems had dramatically reduced the sewage overflows that had plagued Portland's coast during heavy rains. About three hundred acres of shellfish flats that were closed because of fecal contamination had been cleaned up and reopened—no small boon in a region where clamming brings in about $15 million a year. The amount of officially protected land had increased by almost half since 1997, guaranteeing migratory waterfowl uninterrupted access to 3,600 additional acres at ninety-five new sites. Eelgrass, a critical fish and shellfish habitat, had increased in

Outer Green Island

most parts of the bay. The level of toxic chemicals found in bay sediment—mostly leftovers from the industrial era—had gone down. Overall, the water quality was found to be "generally good," thanks in part to the introduction of a sewage pump-out service, which provided boaters with a legal alternative to dumping their holding tanks into the sea.

Casco Bay's protectors have succeeded in bandaging many of the bay's industrial wounds. But sprawl could prove to be an even greater enemy. Until the 1950s, almost all of the new residents who trickled into the region settled within Portland's city limits. Then suburbs started to become fashionable, and the population of the lower watershed increased by fifty thousand during the biggest surge, from 1970 to 1990. New homes, new roads, and new shopping centers are still infiltrating Portland's suburbs and rural areas at a steady rate. As the trend continues, the environmental stressors increase, negating some of the previous gains.

"At best we're holding the line," says Karen Young, director of the Casco Bay Estuary Partnership. "I think if we don't start developing smarter we're going to see declines in the future." A quarter of Maine's residents now live in the Casco Bay watershed, which makes up only 3 percent of the state's land mass. A 6 percent population increase is projected for the next decade. It used to be that industry was the greatest danger to Casco Bay; now it is less threatened by those who want to exploit it than by those who have come to enjoy it.

Many of the 2005 report's negative findings demonstrate what happens when development goes unchecked. Impervious surfaces like roads and parking lots, which cause rainwater and snowmelt to channel more pollutants into the waterways, now cover 5.9 percent of the watershed; studies have shown that a 6 percent cover can degrade the water quality of streams enough to affect aquatic life. In Casco Bay, that degradation has shown up in increased lead levels among the blue mussel population. Air pollution is another road-related problem. As cars travel those paved surfaces in greater numbers each year, the air quality deteriorates. Also, more pavement means less wildlife habitat. The vitality of endemic species such as the threatened wood thrush songbird depends on preserving large habitat blocks and the corridors that connect them. To date, nine of Casco Bay's forty-one municipalities have no remaining sections of undeveloped forest, grassland, or wetland larger than two thousand acres.

The Presumpscot River is emblematic of Casco Bay's evolving struggle. This is the estuary's largest source of freshwater, running twenty-seven miles from Sebago Lake to the bay. Nine dams once stifled its flow, making life difficult for the upstream-swimming salmon; now one of those dams has been removed and the others are becoming more strictly regulated. Pulp mills used to dump their waste in the water, but that practice was made illegal in 1999. Despite those changes, however, the majority of the river's tributaries still fail to pass state water-quality standards. Researchers with the Presumpscot River Watershed Coalition finger "non-point" pollution: storm water runoff from pavement, chemicals and bacteria from farming and landscaping, and sedimentation caused by construction too close to shore. As new buildings spread like weeds along the shoreline, along with the paved infrastructure needed to support them, they temper other water-quality improvements. These new problems, caused by large numbers of individuals, are harder to resolve than those attributed to single polluters.

For the bay's environmental advocates, hope hinges on the success of education and outreach programs designed to convince residents to make individual behavioral changes. One such endeavor is Friends of Casco Bay's environmental landscaping program, which encourages homeowners to curb their use of pesticides and fertilizers. Though most consumers don't realize it, common lawn-care products are packed with chemicals that make their way to the bay. Pesticide use among Maine's homeowners and renters is three times that of its agriculture businesses. Friends of Casco Bay bestows "BayScaper" status upon those who adopt an eco-friendly yard care regimen. Such approaches have a better chance of succeeding in Casco Bay than they might elsewhere, says Karen Young. "Mainers have a real land stewardship ethic," she says. "People really care about trying to preserve things the way they are."

Captain Willard is doing his part. He recently reduced the size of his boats to cut down on fuel consumption, and every day he sails, he conducts an unofficial water survey. Willard is optimistic about Casco's ability to persevere. The water looks cleaner to him than it did a few decades ago, and the wildlife population seems to be growing more diverse all the time. "There are thousands of harbor seals that we never had twenty years ago," he says. "They hang where everybody's fishing like they're looking for a free lunch or something. It's pretty cool." Likewise with the bird population. "In 1988 you didn't see any sea ducks in Casco Bay," he says. Now eider ducks often fly overhead in flocks so large they cast a shadow over his boat. As the captain shuttles increasing numbers of islanders around the bay, he points out the eiders and gannets and loons, making sure every new resident appreciates the landscape that it is now their responsibility to protect.

THE EVERGLADES, FLORIDA

Pinelands in Everglades National Park

ONE OF DAVID REINER'S FAVORITE WAYS TO SEE THE Everglades is by the glow of a full winter moon. He heads an hour west on the Tamiami Trail (US Route 41) from the neon dazzle of downtown Miami to the Shark Valley entrance of Everglades National Park. As the sun sinks into a sea of emerald sawgrass, Reiner takes to the limestone gravel trail on his bicycle for a fifteen-mile loop through the heart of the glades. The bug levels are down and the air is lighter than in summer, but the breeze still carries a rich, swampy scent. The Shark Valley trail is flanked by vast watery prairie, where snapping turtles clatter; great white herons crane their long, prima ballerina necks; and exotic Brazilian anhingas, with their blue-rimmed eyes and slicked-back black feathers, wade effortlessly through the blades. "As soon as your eyes get used to it, you can see the white specks of herons roosting in the trees. You can see alligators moving in the water. There's really a lot out there," says Reiner.

Shark Valley is on the national park's northern boundary, but it's actually the epicenter of the Everglades ecosystem. As president of Friends of the Everglades—Florida's preeminent conservation group—Reiner knows how special this area is. Among the breezy blades of sawgrass are hardwood hammocks, islands of sturdy mahogany, coco plum, and the gumbo-limbo, whose peeling bark reveals a dark trunk speckled with white that mimics a night sky crammed with stars. The aptly named "slough"—a twenty-five-mile-wide shallow river whose depth ranges from a couple of inches to a few feet—flows imperceptibly one hundred feet per day, from its northern headwaters at Lake Okeechobee, through Shark Valley and the rest of Everglades National Park, and southwest into the mangrove forest and coastal marshes of the Gulf of Mexico.

Seven miles along the Shark Valley loop, Reiner likes to climb a sixty-five-foot-high observation tower. From the top, level with circling vultures, one grassy acre appears to roll over another. "From up there, you can look out over the entire Everglades," he says. "And with the stars and the moon, the quiet and the rustle of the wind, it's just incredible." It never fails to impress him, because since the Everglades is a living, advancing river, it's ever changing. Greatness can emerge without notice, especially in the dark, when a blur of fur could be an endangered Florida panther pursuing its prey. At these moments, the Everglades has the feel of the deepest wilderness.

But in reality the clamor and continued growth on the Atlantic coast is dangerously close. Downtown Miami lies just thirty-five miles from Shark Valley, and just ten miles east of the park is Homestead. The bustling historic city of thirty-four thousand or so year-rounders is surrounded by farms that press right up against the national park. Mile after mile of tidy farm rows boast groves of citrus, papayas, and avocados. In winter, the land bursts with sweet corn, squash, cabbage, potatoes, and cucumbers. Farmland is relatively new to these parts. Before pioneering souls settled here in the late nineteenth century, Homestead was a muddy floodplain of the Everglades ecosystem.

In its heyday, which lasted five thousand years or so, the Everglades was twice the size it is today. It was three million acres of sawgrass, peat, mud, and water cradled in an oblong, shallow limestone bowl flanked on the west by the Big Cypress Ridge and on the east by the Atlantic Coastal Ridge. The ridges range in elevation from seven to fifteen feet above sea level.

Its headwaters, the Kissimmee River, flowed from just south of Orlando and drained into Lake Okeechobee, called *oki-chubi*, or "big water," by the native Seminole. When the lake rose to twenty feet above sea level or so, which happened often during the rainy season, it spilled over its southern banks and flowed southward toward the mangrove swamps at the southern tip of the peninsula. The Everglades was a forty- to fifty-mile-wide, one-hundred-thirty-mile-long, slow-moving river—vast, wild, and mysterious, with snarling mangroves, stalking wildcats, and thick clusters of birds that, when airborne, would stain the sun.

G. C. Matson and Samuel Sanford were so struck by their time in the Everglades that they wrote in their 1913 report for the US Geological Survey: "It is difficult for one who has not seen the Everglades to form even an approximate idea of that far-extending expanse of sedge, with its stretches of shallow water, its scattered clumps of bushes and its many islands. Photographs fail to convey the impressions of distance, or remoteness, and of virgin wildness which strikes the visitor who for the first time looks out across that vast expanse." Most other white people who first explored the area hundreds of years ago, mopping copious quantities of sweat from their brows, saw only buggy, croc-infested swampland. (Even John James Audubon, who visited south Florida in the 1830s, initially remarked that "all that is not mud, mud, mud" is "sand, sand, sand.")

But what seemed a perennially wet waste to many spelled opportunity for others. Around the same time that Matson and Sanford marveled at the sea of glades, some industrious farmers started draining, digging, and planting along the slightly raised natural levee on the southern end of Lake Okeechobee. Poor soil quality and climate made those early efforts all but fruitless. But as time passed and prospects and populations grew, the need to control southern Florida's water for drinking, irrigation, and development did too. The teeming lake was targeted first for damming and channeling, and before long, that desire to manipulate nature until it suited human needs spread in every direction the Everglades did.

Then, in 1928, a devastating hurricane, one of the worst natural disasters in US history, killed upwards of 2,500 people and galvanized federal support for controlling the headwaters of the Everglades. Pin-straight dikes and channels replaced untidy wildness, and residents breathed a sigh of relief that if the lake overflowed its banks again, it would be diverted with precision. The Tamiami Trail, the first and still the only route to cut straight across the 'glades, was finished that year, henceforth dividing the Everglades into two separate and unequal ecosystems. Soon after, in the 1930s, the 143-mile-long Hoover Dike was built by the Army Corp of Engineers to keep the often-inundated Lake Okeechobee from spilling over its southern banks. What had been the northern Everglades—swamp forest, wet prairie, sawgrass plains, and stands of cypress—passed away. In its place rose sprawling sugarcane fields, reliant on the rich, shallow layer of peat on top of limestone. The Everglades "Agricultural Area" spread west, east, and far south of Lake Okeechobee. Towns like Belle Glade (known then as Hillsboro), on the lake's southeastern shore, blossomed with homes and other infrastructure and basked in the sun of their newly cultivated wealth. Belle Glade's welcome sign still reads "Her soil is her

Snowy egret in Everglades National Park

fortune." In the 1830s, fewer than five hundred people lived south of Lake Okeechobee. By 2005, there were roughly 6.5 million.

To see Lake O (as it's known to locals) today, one wouldn't expect that it's even remotely related to the distant beauty of Everglades National Park. The walls that were built to contain it did their job, to a fault. Phosphates and other pollutants leached from fertilized, pesticized farmland are piling up on the lake's bottom, and Lake O's world-renowned bass fishery now teeters on the brink of total devastation. The lake's runoff still flows into the Everglades, as well as into the drinking water of the Micco-sukee reservation and the residents of the Atlantic coast. It's an issue that Reiner has been facing for years as he tries to force the South Florida Water Management District to clean the runoff before it is pumped into Lake O. The district is claiming that it isn't its responsibility to purify the water that it sends into the lake (it doesn't produce it, it just pumps it). To make matters worse, the US Army Corps of Engineers has been warning of weaknesses in the massive Hoover levee for more than twenty years. A breech in the dike would be a catastrophe for humans in the historic floodplain, as well as for the Everglades, which would be forced to absorb the tainted water.

Another unforeseen consequence of the dams and canals built to make the area more human-friendly was that they exacerbated the potential for drought and wildfires, which ravaged the land in the 1940s. They also failed to fortify the blooming population against catastrophic flooding in 1947, and again in 1948. The response by state and federal agencies was not to restrict growth but to further tighten the reins of southern Florida's hydrology. It was in that climate of control that Marjory Stoneman Douglas, a bulwark of Everglades environmentalism, began her landmark 1947 work, *The Everglades: River of Grass*, with "There are no other Everglades in the world." Expressing her frustration at the inexorable advance of development, Douglas said, "The future lies in the strength with which man can set his powers of creation against his impulses for destruction." The borders of Everglades National Park, ostensibly cordoning off the lower half of the swamp, were drawn that same year, officially expressing a will to protect what was left of the wholly unique ecosystem. In subsequent decades the park was expanded to its current size of 1.4 million acres. The park's record 1,534,328 visitors came in 1972, followed by a precipitous decline over the next decade, owing to the opening of Disney World in Orlando in 1971. But visitation has crept up steadily over the years. In 2005, 1,233,837 people spilled through the five park entrances, an increase of nearly 5 percent over the previous year.

What wasn't acknowledged eighty years ago when the Everglades was bisected was that by dividing it and greatly reducing the water that once flowed into it, they were severely altering the remaining ecosystem. Since the 1930s the wading bird population has declined by at least 80 percent, invasive plant species have crowded out many Everglades natives, and resident fauna haven't fared well. The Florida panther, which lost much of its wilderness habitat, and the West Indies manatee, which is often struck by boat propellers in shallow estuaries, slow-moving rivers, and saltwater bays, were driven to the verge of extinction. The panther population has rebounded only slightly from an all-time low of twenty cats to eighty in 2005.

Things looked like they might turn around for the wetlands several years ago when many locals took notice of the drastic decline in the quality of once world-class fishing, boating, and diving around the perimeter of the Florida peninsula. They began to demand protection for their swamp and coastal playgrounds, and in 2000, legislators made a first earnest move toward conserving the Everglades. That year Congress authorized the Comprehensive Everglades Restoration Plan. With an $8 billion price tag, it is the largest restoration plan in world history. While that bill is now already up to $10.5 billion, some estimates put the actual cost closer to ten times that amount.

Looking at a diagram of the plan is like staring at the strategy board in the Florida Gators locker room. Arrows point every which way, zigzagging across two dozen locations in southern Florida that are proposed targets of restoration. In short, the ambition is to restore the original hydrologic pattern of the "river of grass" by returning 1.7 billion gallons of water per day to the ecosystem that would have otherwise flowed through diversion channels to the Gulf of Mexico and Atlantic Ocean. To achieve this the Corps of Engineers, the group responsible for most of the public infrastructure that's altered the Everglades over the past century, will remove hundreds of miles of levees and canals and build new places for water to be stored during the wet season and portioned out during the dry one. They hope that reallocating the water, while continuing to prevent flooding in developed areas, will wean the glades off of life support.

But this multifaceted "restoration" plan is a misnomer to many people. Watchdogs such as Friends of the Everglades feel that the costly strategy amounts to further manipulation of the ecosystem. "Let's not replace natural function with man-engineered projects, which is what they're planning on doing with the Everglades restoration project," says Reiner. "Let's try to keep intact as much of the natural system as possible and repair it." Conservationists' concerns were reinforced when an independent study was done by the prestigious National Academy of Sciences in 2005. It said the government's first priority should be conserving what's left of the Everglades by buying "buffer" land between developed and wilderness areas. It concluded that simply concentrating on "getting the water right" by any means possible is shortsighted because it doesn't take into account other environmental threats like climate change, population growth, energy use, and land-use policies. Missing this point could mean that more of the Everglades could slip away in one area while attention is focused elsewhere.

The conflict between restoration and land-use policies that the National Academy report alluded to was not hypothetical. In June 2006 environmentalists successfully defeated a Corp of Engineers plan to allow 22,000 acres of Everglades wetlands to be mined for limestone. How the agency that's tasked with restoring the ecosystem could also be selling off areas crucial to that recovery boggles the minds of environmentalists. "There's a lot of politics at play," says Reiner. "There are a lot of large and well-financed landowners and business interests down here, and they can outspend us a hundred to one to sway public opinion. That's what's been happening."

So despite global attention and massive state and federal funding, the Everglades is still struggling. "More of the Everglades, even over the past five years, has been compromised," says Reiner. In some of his last conversations with Marjory Stoneman Douglas, he says she put Friends of the Everglades on a course to raise public awareness and bring environmental organizations together on a more effective path to wetlands renewal. "She wasn't easily snowed. She knew what was going on," says Reiner. "We knew that the restoration plan was heavily influenced by business and politics and development and agriculture, and that it wasn't going to be the real restoration." But he's still hopeful that more Floridians will wake up to the state of their environment as more frequent instances of degradation to their paradise occur, like mass sawgrass die-offs, beach closures due to high bacteria levels, fewer flocks of birds flying overhead, coral bleaching, and fish fatalities. "I really think that as things get worse—and they will—more people will get involved in trying to find a solution to saving the Everglades," says Reiner. "From the west coast to the east coast, from Lake Okeechobee to the Keys, the whole place is really worth saving."

For nowhere else on earth is there such a huge, flat expanse of limestone that, in combination with warm air and periods of wet and dry, creates one ecosystem with seven discrete habitats. From the freshwater marl prairies and sloughs to the coastal prairies, cypress clusters, pinelands, mangrove forests, and estuaries, the Everglades is southern Florida's life, its breath.

GLACIER NATIONAL PARK, MONTANA

Avalanche Lake, Glacier National Park

A POPULAR SUMMER WALK NEAR THE CENTER OF GLACIER National Park in northwest Montana heads southeast off Going-to-the-Sun Road toward Avalanche Lake. The path first winds gently through a cathedral of giant western red cedars. Then, under the shade of huge hemlocks with deeply grooved bark and black cottonwoods adorned with bright red catkins, you hear the gush of Avalanche Stream. Its unrelenting furor has cut a deep gash into the bedrock, known as Avalanche Gorge. As the trail continues to climb you can see erratics—boulders the size of minivans that were abandoned when vast glaciers receded from this area—coated with thick moss. The trail ends at the sandy, graveled shores of Avalanche Lake, so called for the frequent snowslides that roar down the steep slopes surrounding it. This subalpine tarn, or mountain lake, sits in a rock amphitheater called a cirque. This bowl, which was once filled with ice, is now the frigid lake. In late spring and summer the avalanches quiet down, and snowpack and glacial meltwater force dozens of rivulets over two-thousand-foot cliffs. Waterfalls plunge down the rock walls behind Avalanche Lake like long, flowing hair from its white glacial scalp, Sperry Glacier—the source of all this splendor and one of the park's remaining twenty-seven glaciers. (Based on data currently being analyzed, that number is expected to drop considerably.)

Since the 1.1 million acres that make up Glacier gained national park status in 1910, it has lost the bulk of its permanent ice. Some folks are surprised to learn that there are so few glaciers actually left in the park. In June 2006 visitors to the Jackson Glacier overlook, a stop along Going-to-the-Sun Road, identified most snowfields as glaciers, when in reality, once the summer sun beats down on the peaks for a while, the white will vanish, except for a speck that is actual glacier. It's easy to get confused from afar, but the reality is that Glacier's ice is melting rapidly. For years most estimates have had their extinction clocks set for the year 2030, but that notion may have been optimistic.

At a meeting of scientists from around the world in Mendoza, Argentina, in April 2006, Dan Fagre of the US Geological Survey, the man most familiar with the park's glaciers, said, "We have found that we're actually ahead of schedule. Our glaciers are melting faster than this model predicts." That model was completed in 2003, when most of the rest of the world learned of the imminent demise of Glacier's glaciers. In that report Fagre wrote, "For the park visitor, the disappearance of one of the park's charismatic features presents a great irony and aesthetic loss, because the park was established to protect a landscape that has now changed." At the Mendoza meeting Fagre again referred to the "aesthetic, spiritual, recreational" aspects of the human experience in the hills. "Mountains mean something to people, and embodied in that meaning is snow and ice and the whole hydrologic resource that these parks represent," he said. "People have a different relationship with the area once these are gone."

Contrary to popular belief, Glacier National Park was not named for the presence of glaciers but for the features they carved. The movement of rock and ice more than three thousand feet thick several thousand years ago chiseled bladelike arêtes, ice-chipped horned peaks, broad-bottomed valleys, and deep alpine lakes, and time refined them into what is now seen. Glacier is high, diverse country, from 3,150 feet on the Flathead River to 10,466 feet at the top of Mount Cleveland. Five other peaks in the park also rise above ten thousand feet, and in their rocky, glacial cirques and high alpine meadows are shaggy mountain goats, grazing bighorn sheep, stealthy mountain lions, skulking wolverines, chubby marmots, chirping pikas, lumbering grizzlies, and curious black bears. Throw in moose, golden eagles, wolves, and many hyperactive squirrels, and Glacier is as rare an intact ecosystem as they come.

Glacier's plenty can be indulged in year round. In fall, the warmth of the air and the amber of the setting sun seem to be absorbed by the leaves, which turn technicolor across the landscape. In winter, when snowdrifts sixty feet high can pile up on Going-to-the-Sun Road, it's a quiet, frigid, and unforgettable place to snowshoe and cross-country ski. In spring, when wildflowers begin to burst out in the valleys, the park begins to wake from hibernation. In summer most of the park's 1.5 million visitors arrive, roaming its one million acres by foot, bike, boat, horse, car, and camper, and they lay their heads down in thirteen campgrounds and a variety of historic lodges. The entire length of Going-to-the-Sun Road generally opens in the first two weeks of June (the latest opening date ever was June 28). The summer climate can vary from dry and sweltering to cool and rainy. Snow in the high country is possible year-round.

Long before white men had laid eyes on Glacier's landscape, the Blackfeet described the area as the "backbone of the world." Early European explorers, having seen nothing else like it in North America, called it "little Switzerland." It is now popularly known as the "crown of the continent" and is one of the few places on earth where there is a tri-oceanic divide. From the top of Triple Divide Peak the Atlantic, Hudson Bay, and Pacific creeks flow toward their namesake destinations via the mighty Missouri, Saskatchewan, and Columbia rivers.

For the lay traveler some of the best views of glaciers are right outside the historic Many Glacier Hotel in the park's northeast region. A barricade of rock, including Mount Gould, the Garden Wall, Grinnell Point, Swiftcurrent Mountain, Mount Wilbur, and the Iceberg-Ptarmigan Wall, rises beyond the far side of Swiftcurrent Lake. To the stark, formidable peaks cling the tiny Gem and North Swiftcurrent glaciers (possibly already gone), as well as the somewhat larger Grinnell Glacier. The retreat of these three patches of ice, which were once considered permanent, is emblematic of what's happening throughout the park.

By Dan Fagre's calculations the area's 150 glaciers began melting modestly sometime between 1850 and 1855. But by the middle of the twentieth century the loss was dramatic. As of 2006 only 18 percent of the park's glaciers remained; the rest are present only in grainy black-and-white photographs.

While the reason for the loss of ice in Glacier underwent a period of debate, it's now undisputed: global climate change. One of the things that makes the park so unique is that it's what Fagre calls an "unmodified natural system." It's a laboratory of nature, an area with strict boundaries and protections where it's clear that local phenomena are not causing glacial retreat. The

USGS estimates that over the past century the mean summer temperature in Glacier has gone up 3 degrees Fahrenheit. And it's getting warmer earlier in the year. While January 2006, when 7.66 inches of precipitation fell, was the wettest on record in the park (more than double the average of the decade before), it was also the warmest since 1953. Glaciers are literally going to the sun because not enough snow is falling to replenish them, and warmer temperatures for more days per year are now the norm.

Based on this understanding, a dozen conservation groups in the United States and Canada (Glacier makes up the southern portion of Waterton-Glacier International Peace Park, established in 1932) are sounding an alarm. In 2006 they petitioned UNESCO's World Heritage Committee to add Waterton-Glacier to its list of sites in danger. Kassie Siegel of the Center for Biological Diversity, one of the groups that is asking UNESCO to look at the issue, says that the move is meant to raise awareness about the effects of climate change in North

Glacier National Park

America and to force some action to stabilize it. "There's a huge disconnect in this country right now between current policy and what scientists are telling us, which is very sharp warnings that we need greenhouse gas emissions reductions of 80 percent or more from the US and other industrialized countries to avoid the worst impacts of climate change," says Siegel. "We need to bridge this gap." If the committee agrees with Siegel and the others, and Waterton-Glacier is labeled as threatened, the United States and Canada would be strongly encouraged by UNESCO to protect the park.

Siegel is concerned not just about the loss of Glacier's eponymous ice but about the increasing stress on species and the ecosystem. At present, and unlike in the remainder of the lower forty-eight, the native species that have always been in Glacier are still there; only bison and caribou have been extirpated since Lewis and Clark came near here in 1806. But warming is expected to disrupt that balance. "Global warming may seriously affect our ability to protect the species and habitats that are now encompassed by national parks, forests, wilderness areas, and other nature reserves. Many species in Glacier may be particularly sensitive to climate change," a National Park Service memo says.

The dominoes of ecosystem change are already dropping. Alpine lakes are warming, to the detriment of the plants and animals that reside there. With less glacial runoff, stream temperatures are also increasing and their courses are changing. Entire aquatic systems will continue to be in jeopardy because insects and invertebrates that rely on cold water will decline, striking a blow to the fish, especially rainbow and brown trout, that rely on them. Each one-degree increase in temperature also raises the tree line a few hundred feet, forcing species that are supremely adapted to mountaintops toward extinction. Pika, a timid member of the rabbit family, are a probable first casualty. "They're one of the 'canary in the coal mine' species," says Siegel. "They are cold, alpine-adapted, Pleistocene-relic species. Pikas can't go up any more once they reach the top of the mountain they're on." A changing alpine "ecotone," or ecological frontier, will also threaten rare alpine plants, which are at the southern border of their geographical range, and ultimately diminish the biodiversity of Glacier's fauna. For now there are 1,400 plant species in the park; twenty-eight of them are found nowhere else in the state.

In the longer term, perhaps by 2100, Fagre has predicted that climate change will greatly alter the look of Glacier National Park. In his animated time-lapse map of the park, which is available on the USGS website, lodgepole pine and Douglas fir creep above the present tree line, up over the continent's crown. Sub-alpine meadows yield to forest (which is already occurring) and current stands of lodgepole pine and western red cedar, like the beauties crowding around Avalanche Gorge, are overrun with spruce and hemlock. The hotter and drier conditions that lead to such transformation also change the fire regime. The number and intensity of fires is predicted to rise.

Changes in the park's ecology were first brought to the attention of the average American a decade ago when then–vice president Al Gore stood at Many Glacier Hotel and quipped, "To borrow a phrase from a well-known pop musician, this could become the Park Formerly Known as Glacier." In his jeans and polo shirt, Gore had trekked up to the terminus of Grinnell Glacier, which, at the time, was one third the size it had been at its maximum extent in 1850. Over 90 percent of it is now gone.

Steve Thompson, who heads the National Parks Conservation Association's Glacier branch, climbed up to Grinnell with Gore on that hot September day in 1997. He's as concerned now as he was then about the loss of remnant glaciers in the park, and about what "cascade effect" climate change might have on the region. "We've got a huge, complex problem here," he says. But at present Thompson is just as bothered by a more immediate threat to the park that's flying under most people's radar: coal mining in the Transboundary Flathead River Valley, the headwaters of several major Glacier National Park rivers. The Flathead crosses the border into Montana and forms forty-seven miles of the western boundary of the park.

For many years Thompson and his friends and colleagues—conservationists, hunters, anglers, and business folk—have worked hard and prosperously to preserve the integrity of the Transboundary Flathead's water. Coal mining schemes on the Canadian side have come and gone over the years, and Thompson has fought them all, but the latest round has him terrified. It also has all of those groups, who ordinarily disagree on a good many other topics, coming together to tussle with Canadian coal interests. Thompson talks of the full-speed efforts of two companies with international tentacles: Cline Mining Corporation and Western Canadian Coal. Cline has already pushed several miles of new roads through the Foisey Creek drainage, the forest of the Flathead River headwaters, during exploration. The permitting process is well under way, and according to company documents, they expect to start digging this year. The company is currently permitted to extract twenty thousand tons of coal and hopes to ultimately unearth two million tons over the next twenty years.

Thompson says that while there is partnership between the two countries on the preservation of Waterton-Glacier, what lies outside of those protected areas (only one third of the Flathead Valley is currently preserved) seems fair game in the coal-friendly Canadian political climate. "We're dealing with a streamlined regulatory process in British Columbia, a pro-mining government," he says. "BC is advertising itself as open for business for this type of extractive industry." As the director of the Flathead

Coalition, Thompson is pushing for a halt to the mining until some baseline environmental data can be established.

The mining operations will drive out outfitters who make their living in the area, says Thompson, and it will affect the purity of water as it flows into Glacier National Park, threatening countless species that rely on it. (As for Waterton, whose boundary lies just east of the proposed mine site on the Canadian side, park superintendent Rod Blair expressed grave concern in 2007 that the scope of the environmental assessment was not broad enough to evaluate the impact that the drilling would have on the entire Crown of the Continent ecosystem.) The Flathead's vast floodplain provides habitat critical to maintaining the biodiversity of the park and larger Flathead Valley, especially in the face of growing stresses brought on by climate change, which is why the Outdoor Recreation Council of British Columbia labeled the Flathead the country's most endangered river in 2007. "It's got everything," says Thompson. "This tremendous water value, native fish, and grizzly bears roam all over the valley. It's where the wolves first naturally returned. This is not an appropriate place for mining or drilling."

If it's the case that, as John Muir said, "In wildness is the preservation of the world," then Thompson thinks it's time the world turns its attention to the Flathead. The river is wholly undammed and it rises and falls with Mother Nature's whims. There are no cities, factories, or other point sources of pollution along the turquoise-hued Flathead. Not a single person lives along it year-round on the Canadian side, and few do in the US portion. "It's one of the wildest places that you can find, one of the wildest valleys in the temperate zones of North America," he says, and one of the continent's last truly free rivers.

GREAT SMOKY MOUNTAINS NATIONAL PARK

Great Smoky Mountains National Park

FROM THE TOWER ATOP 6,643-FOOT CLINGMAN'S DOME, the highest point in Great Smoky Mountains National Park, you can get one heck of a panoramic snapshot of North Carolina and Tennessee. Hemlocks, spruce, and fir cover the mountains for miles, shading the southern stretch of the Appalachian Trail, which crosses the park on its 2,160-mile journey from Georgia to Maine. In the valleys, a thick blue mist blankets the treetops—that's how the Smoky Mountains got their name.

On summer days when the haze is tinted brown from air polution, however, the moniker takes on a whole new meaning. America's most visited national park has also become its smoggiest, with air quality often reaching dangerous levels.

"There are times when the air is so bad up there it can actually damage your health," says Erik Plakanis, co-owner of A Walk in the Woods, a nature guiding service in Gatlinburg, Tennessee. Plakanis and his wife, Vesna, both experienced naturalists with an encyclopedic knowledge of the park's history and ecology, have led extended hikes and backpacking trips in the Smokies for more than a decade.

Several years ago Plakanis had a firsthand lesson on the effects of bad air. He was leading a backpacking trip in the higher elevations of the park—a scenic, three-day traverse of a narrow ridgeline that rises and falls through old-growth forest—when suddenly he lost his breath. He took a short rest, then walked another hundred yards or so before he started gasping for air again. "I couldn't catch my breath," he says. "I knew something bad was going on but I didn't know what." It wasn't until nighttime brought the temperature down that his breathing returned to normal. "About midnight the weather broke and it was like a hand was lifted from my chest," he says. Finally able to breathe comfortably again, Plakanis finished the trip.

On his return, he tracked down an air-quality report and found that the ozone level for that day had risen 14 percent over the level deemed unhealthy by the Environmental Protection Agency. Ground-level ozone is not the same as the atmospheric ozone layer that protects us from ultraviolet rays; it is a harmful gas that forms when the nitrogen oxides released by cars, factories, and power plants combine with sunlight. High levels of ozone can cause coughing, sinus inflammation, chest pain, and even lung damage. "I had a full-fledged asthma attack, and I have healthy lungs," Plakanis says. Soon afterward, A Walk in the Woods implemented a new policy: on poor-air-quality days, scheduled hiking and backpacking trips to the higher elevations of the national park would be canceled.

Poor air quality in the southern Appalachians is a relatively recent phenomenon. Regional airport records show that average summertime visibility has decreased 80 percent since 1948, when visitors who hiked to lookouts could expect crisp landscape views. Today the colors are muted, and you can actually inhale more pollutants on a stroll through the Smokies than you would walking around Knoxville or Atlanta.

The problem isn't coming from the park itself. It floats in on wind currents from the surrounding areas. Fossil fuel emissions like sulfur dioxide and nitrogen oxide travel from as far away as the Ohio and Mississippi valleys. The mountain ridges that capture and concentrate the Smokies' stunning blue mist also trap this bad air.

Power plants are to blame for 77 percent of the sulfur dioxide pollution, according to National Park Service air quality reports. Identifying a key culprit has helped legislators narrow the focus of clean-air measures. In 2001 the Tennessee Valley Authority announced a plan to install sulfur dioxide controls called "scrubbers" on the park's two closest power plants by 2010, a move that is expected to curb emissions from those plants by more than 90 percent. In 2002 North Carolina passed the Clean Smokestack Act, which will reduce nitrogen oxide emissions from the state's electricity utilities by 77 percent by 2009 and eliminate 73 percent of their sulfur dioxide output by 2013. Some progress has already been made, but federal standards have not kept pace with state initiatives. The Clean Air Interstate Rule that the EPA passed in 2005 has loopholes, like the one that exempts Georgia from certain summertime emissions. In the meantime, pollution continues to blow across state lines.

The park service now monitors Great Smoky air quality continuously and posts the current ozone levels on its website, www .nps.gov/grsm, alongside images from the webcams stationed at Look Rock, on the northwest edge of the park, and Purchase Knob, in the southeast. Before venturing out, you can catch an online preview of the mountain vistas, along with color-coded ozone and particulate matter counts. You can also download an annual air quality report that examines long-term trends and makes predictions for the future. The 2006 report gave smog watchers a rare breath of fresh air—pollution levels had dropped or stabilized in the previous two years because of favorable weather conditions and new mitigation measures implemented by power plants throughout the eastern United States. In their forecast, the feds dared to wax bullish: "We are optimistic that air quality will continue to improve over the next 10–12 years at GRSM because of new air quality regulations and other related actions."

Even so, the Smokies are hardly out of the woods. The laws that protect the park are tenuous—the National Park Service recently dodged an attempt by the Department of the Interior to rewrite its management policies in a way that would have reduced the government's ability to regulate polluters. Park officials who spend a lot of time in the field receive positive reports with measured enthusiasm. "We're seeing a little bit of a change, but we're still woefully over where we should be," says park botanist Janet Rock, who has watched pollution wreak havoc on the Smokies' plant life for eighteen years. The airborne crud that makes humans cough and wheeze can devastate simpler organisms and alter entire ecosystems over time. Even with air quality starting to improve, the natural landscape could continue to deteriorate.

Rock and her cohorts have identified thirty-two plant species that are sensitive to ozone. Pollution can trigger acute cell death within hours of exposure. The veins of the park's milkweed plants blanch and their leaves blister on high-ozone days. Deep-green blackberry leaves turn purple when they're under attack. Over time, even low doses can hurt the leaves of the sassafras and tuliptrees, which fleck and wither with sustained stress. Among the most sensitive species, the damage is pervasive—up to 90 percent of the park's milkweed plants and black cherry trees show signs of ozone-caused damage.

Ozone is not the only enemy. There's also acid rain. The Great Smoky Mountains have the highest sulfur and nitrogen deposit levels of any monitored national park. On average, its rainfall has a pH of 4.5—that's at least five times more acidic than normal rainfall. And the clouds that sometimes cloak the forested peaks during the growing season have been measured at 2.0, the same pH of the chemical peels used by dermatologists to burn the wrinkles off of aging faces. The acid's impact on a forest ecosystem is devastating. It saturates the soil with nitrogen, crowding out essential nutrients like calcium, and causes plants to excrete aluminum, which pollutes mountain streams and threatens water-dwelling critters.

No one knows how long the domino effect will last and whether the forest can make a complete recovery, even if air quality continues to improve. What park scientists do know is that foreign insect species have launched successful invasions in recent years, exposing the Smokies to ailments such as hemlock woolly adelgid and beech bark disease. Researchers have theorized that heavy doses of pollution weaken the immunity of plants and trees, making them more vulnerable and initiating dramatic, long-term changes to the forest landscape.

At elevations above five thousand feet, where the pollutants are more concentrated and their effects more dramatic, the shift has already begun. "We are right now witnessing what may be the greatest change in our Appalachian forest in recorded history," Erik Plakanis says. "We're going to lose thirty to seventy percent of the hemlock trees in just a few years, and they're the second-most-common trees in the park. It will be hard to find a living hemlock in the eastern US in twenty years."

For now, however, Great Smoky Mountains remains one of America's most biologically diverse parks, where you might happen upon a two-foot-long salamander as you're wandering along a mountain stream or spot a black bear snacking on berries. The park's seven-hundred-plus miles of streams host fifty native species, including a protected brook trout population. Rhododendron, azalea, and mountain laurel blanket the high-elevation heath meadows known as "balds," and fifty or so types of ferns line the waterways.

The signature Smokies experience is walking beneath the towering old-growth trees that were rescued from logging when the park was created in 1934. In the Greenbrier region, northeast of the park's Gatlinburg Welcome Center, you can hike amid red maples, northern red oaks, and eastern hemlock to Ramsay Cascades, a ninety-foot waterfall that tumbles down moss-slicked boulders to a shallow pool. The eight-mile out-and-back trail through Greenbrier is steep and rocky enough to deter the day-tripping masses—a necessity if you're looking for solitude in a park that logs nine million visits each year. "I've always been drawn to Greenbrier," says Plakanis, who likes to point out the old-growth forest's edible and medicinal plants while leading hikers to Ramsay Cascades. "It's as close as you can get to true wilderness in the eastern US."

The significance of the Great Smoky Mountains ecosystem is recognized worldwide—it became an International Biosphere Reserve in 1976 and a UNESCO World Heritage Site in 1983. Unfortunately, such designations don't necessarily guarantee its protection.

Appalachian Voices, an environmental advocacy group based in Boone, North Carolina, drew national attention to the air-quality problem in 2002 when it produced a report called Code Red that identified the national parks with the most polluted air. Great Smoky Mountains, of course, topped the list. "I spent my whole childhood playing and hiking in the park," says executive director Mary Ann Hitt, whose father was the park's chief scientist throughout the late 1980s and early 1990s. Her primary concern is air pollution and its impact on ecosystems in the Smokies and beyond. "People think of the mountains, and they think of fresh mountain air and clean flowing springs, and a place that is a reprieve from the woes of urban living. People think there's a force field around it," she says. "Even with a national park, you can't stop the air from blowing in."

INNER AND OUTER BANKS, NORTH CAROLINA

ON NORTH CAROLINA'S WHITE OAK RIVER, FRANK TURSI had a day that he won't soon forget. Tursi was in his kayak, paddling down near the mouth of the blackwater river just behind bulky Jones Island, when he found himself flowing amid a pod of some twenty-five porpoises, some bigger than his boat. "They would come up around me, blowing—phhhh!—and I would feel the spray on my face. I was actually able to reach out and feel them brush up against my hand," he says. Having spent over three decades roaming the state's rivers, estuaries, inlets, and sounds—which he now patrols as a coastkeeper for the North Carolina Coastal Federation—Tursi has seen a lot of wild and wonderful spots, but the White Oak is still his favorite.

From its headwaters thirty miles inland in the Hofmann Forest, the White Oak flows narrowly at first, just inches deep, through swampland, then opens wide as it nears the Atlantic Ocean. Its banks are rich with southern bottomland hardwoods such as Carolina ash, tupelo gum, and, closer to the ocean, salt-tolerant red maples. Bald eagles nest along the White Oak and alligators troll these waters. After cutting through the salt marsh cordgrass of the White Oak estuary, the river flows through the Bogue Inlet, flanked by two of this area's world-famous barrier islands. On the left is Bogue Banks and on the right, Bear Island.

At this juncture, the growing dichotomoty and vulnerability of North Carolina's coastal personality is clear. Bear Island, which is part of Hammocks Beach State Park, remains entirely undeveloped. Fifty-foot-high dunes a half-mile wide stretch for five miles. Deer tracks cut up and over the sand heaps and through hearty patches of dune grass. On the east end of the island, all that remains after a thrashing by a hurricane are low dunes and a graveyard of stumps and tree trunks. From here, across the inlet, the distant rooflines of Bogue Banks are visible. But this view is new. It seems to most locals like Bogue Banks grew a skyline overnight. All along the twenty-six-mile barrier island, modest motels, campgrounds, piers, public-access beaches, and vacant lots are being gobbled up by developers. In their place, multistory, multi-million-dollar condominium complexes are being built despite a pattern of increased storms.

Bogue Banks is known to some as the southern terminus of North Carolina's Outer Banks (others argue it ends north at Cape Lookout or extends farther south to Cape Fear). It's one of the barrier islands that cling to North Carolina's coast all the way to the Virginia border. As their name suggests, the long, narrow bands of sand bravely face the Atlantic and protect the calm inlets and inland coast from the ocean's perpetual fury. Anyone who crosses from one island to the next, by bridge or ferry, soon realizes that the Banks are, in many ways, a universe unto themselves. Time slows and pretense dissolves. But there's a drama on these islands, and their dynamic and treacherous geological nature, in which their existence is constantly in flux, is rivaled only by their colorful human element. Ocracoke Island was once the base camp of the pirate Edward Teach, a.k.a. Blackbeard. And Orville Wright and his brother took their first flight on the Outer Banks. Orville, in particular, was in awe of the rare beauty of this place, which is shaped by wind, water, and time, and where the horizon has hosted the closing of countless days. "The sunsets here are the prettiest I have ever seen," he wrote in 1900.

Most of the roughly seven million visitors to the Banks today pass the site of the Wright brothers' first flight at Kill Devil Hills (not four miles north at Kitty Hawk, as many think). From the stone monolith, high on the grassy dune, they consider the Wrights' plucky plunge, if only briefly, before moving on to the Outer Banks' main event: the beach. The sands of the northern barrier islands are popular for accomplishing little more than building a sand castle. Some might be lucky enough to be roused from a waterfront nap on Cape Lookout National Seashore's Shackleford Banks by the clopping hooves of the "Banker ponies," a herd of wild Spanish mustangs that swam ashore here from a shipwreck hundreds of years ago. In places like Nags Head, a lively old village that has been catering to travelers for a century, visitors might even rub elbows with some of the thirty thousand locals (conspicuous with OBX on their license plates).

From here the Cape Hatteras National Seashore stretches for seventy-two miles to Ocracoke Island. The rough-and-ready expanse of shore, protected from development in perpetuity, is a magnet for sea-glass hunting, surfing, swimming, scuba diving, birdwatching, and hang gliding, among other activities. To beachcomb on the Outer Banks is to be in the company of ghost crabs tiptoeing across the sand and pelicans plummeting for sea trout or bluefish. On the channel side of the islands, over dunes and past trees gnarled from wind and salt water, clamming and crabbing is just another way to while away a morning. Not far from the din of waves smacking the shore, hikes through maritime forest reveal some of the Banks' vivacious nature, including red wildflowers and holly berries that stand out against dark oak and cedar.

At the island's elbow, where the sand tilts southeast following the shore, lies Cape Hatteras Lighthouse, the world's largest brick beacon and a reminder of the thousands of shipwrecks embedded in the ocean floor in this "graveyard of the Atlantic." Visitors to the black-and-white-striped light station several years ago would have seen the 193-foot giant (its height has been widely mispublished as 208 feet) more than a half-mile closer to the sea. In an extraordinary feat of human engineering, the lighthouse was slid on rails, little by little, for twenty-three days, to its new residence. It had to be moved back from the brink because of the constant erosion of coastal North Carolina. During Hurricane Isabel, Hatteras Island was actually split in two. The storm surged repeatedly over the island, creating a new three-thousand-foot-long, thirty-foot-deep inlet. Not long after the weather blew out to sea, the Army Corps of Engineers swept in to refill the hole with sand.

East Carolina University geologist Stan Riggs is all too familiar with the perils and particulars of the barrier island systems. For thirty-five years, Riggs has been up and down the Banks, onshore and off. He says it surprises most people to learn that the land upon which sand was deposited, through a unique combination of currents and storms, to form the precious Outer Banks was originally part of a coast that's now submerged. During field studies, Riggs has found ancient forests and mastodon bones buried out near the present-day continental shelf. He discovered that the shoreline used to be 60 miles east and 425 feet lower. After the last ice age, about 18,000 years ago, glacial melt deepened and warming temperatures expanded the Atlantic, a process that continues today.

One major misconception about the barrier islands, he says, is that they're dainty ribbons of sand. "They're not fragile at all," he says. "They're an incredibly tough, dynamic environment." And, contrary to popular thinking, says Riggs, "they're formed by storms and need them to maintain themselves and evolve through time as sea level rises." The Banks are constantly evolving, and over time they have come and gone, formed and collapsed, and formed again. Riggs has seen clear evidence of that. Right now, he says, "As we speak, we're watching them collapse again."

Enter humans. Riggs says we think of these barrier islands as fragile because, "humans do not like change. Our society, our rules, our land ownership doesn't allow for it because we have absolute property boundaries and absolute structures that we want to stay there, so the conflict becomes pretty severe." That mind-set is the basis for the struggle between geological might and human engineering that's ongoing on the Outer Banks. Sandbags are stacked up against storm surges and homes are erected on high pilings, and whatever a storm does wreck— roads, houses, shops—humans generally rush in to replace. The artificial rebuilding of Hatteras Island post-Isabel—a massive undertaking—and the near-continuous bulldozing and repaving of Highway 12, the only road down the length of the islands, are recent examples of the human desire to battle nature. But it's not a system that's meant to be regulated, and the more humans try to prevent the Banks from evolving, from pursuing their natural course, the more damage we're doing. "Barrier islands are a very complex and dynamic system, and as a species, we have not made an effort to try to understand and live with that," says Riggs. "We've always had this attitude of conquer and control."

And because human memory is sometimes short, a thirty-year lull in the storm cycle that typically lashes North Carolina, from the mid-1960s to the early 1990s, wasn't regarded as temporary. Instead it was considered the new norm and massive development was undertaken on the Outer Banks. Now that the respite has passed, people mourn multi-million-dollar homes that have collapsed like a house of cards in the path of a hurricane. They have built artificial dunes and piled up massive sandbags, all considered "soft" barriers, but hardly so, according to Riggs. All of this is serving to undermine the highly mobile system and is actually exacerbating the erosion of the Outer Banks.

It's hard to say whether there's any hope for the barrier islands as we now know them. But the pattern of current storms and quickening pace of climate change lead to bleak predictions. And some islands south of Bogue Banks and Bear Island could be particularly hard hit, says Riggs. "If we were to get a sequence of hurricanes like the Gulf of Mexico got in the summer of 2005, the Outer Banks wouldn't be there," he says. "Places like Topsail Island, Onslow Beach, Figure Eight Island, forget those places, they're gone." Riggs published a series of highly unpopular "collapse maps" recently that showed what will happen over time to the barrier islands. Their scale was originally in increments of centuries and millennia. Riggs then shrank those to decades. "I'm about to change that again because things are happening so fast out there," he says. "A single storm could now produce what would have taken decades before. There's already about twenty to thirty miles of the Outer Banks that are gone. We're in a very anomalous period of time and it's not going to stay so nice. Whether humans change the Outer Banks or it changes naturally, it will change."

As if there were no lessons to be learned from the scramble to keep the Outer Banks habitable, coastal North Carolina is facing a new challenge that troubles both Riggs and Tursi. Once-rural "Inner Banks" communities are the new target for large-scale development. The term "Inner Banks" refers to North Carolina's mainland shores, which face lazy rivers and tranquil sounds, and consists of twenty mostly economically disadvantaged counties. "The inland communities have been very much like the rest of North Carolina," says Tursi, who lives on a branch of the White Oak River. "They're rural in nature, a lot of farming, and until recently a very large, healthy fishing industry, including boatbuilding and net mending. These weren't tourist destinations. But now they're being descended upon."

When the millions of seasonal tourists swoop down onto the Outer Banks, Inner Banks communities have been a predictably quiet refuge from the crowds. But once-hushed fishing villages are beginning to transform before locals' eyes. Take Whichard's Beach, down the Tar River, not far from where Riggs lives. Until recently, it was owned by a bunch of locals, who sold it to a Florida developer for $9.5 million. That developer then loaded prospective buyers onto a bus and drove them around dozens of lots selling for a half-million dollars apiece. "They sold the whole thing off in an afternoon," he says. "Those developers took their money and then left the state. They're in and out of here so fast." Where an open-air pavilion once stood will some-day be a thirteen-story condo building, and so on. According to a *News and Observer* tally taken in the summer of 2006, more than thirty-four thousand homes in roughly one hundred subdivisions and condo complexes are in the works for the Inner Banks, and more are expected.

As a coastkeeper, it's Tursi's job to maintain a close watch on the condition of his beat, surveying the area's environmental well-being. He doesn't much like what he sees. "A lot of my territory is rural but quickly developing," he says. Tursi is out nearly every day on wheels or water monitoring the toll that development is taking on the Carolinas' newest cash coast. "This is a very frustrating job because this is not a level playing field. The rules are skewed in favor of more growth, more development," he says. Many of the volunteers that Tursi takes on patrol are fishermen who know the waters by intuition alone. "They've fished with their daddies and granddaddies, so they know what happens when you start developing a shoreline, and what happens to their shellfish and shrimp," he says. "As a result, they work very hard to try to protect it." But it seems a losing battle. Storm water runs off of newly paved areas, picking up an abundance of chemical and biological toxins and carrying them to the sea. As water quality declines, the harvest of edible shellfish becomes increasingly sporadic. Fishermen, already on hard times because of fuel costs and international competition, are being pressed to sell their ancestral digs to the highest bidder. "Here a developer comes along and is offering you a million dollars for your two or three acres," says Tursi. "You won't turn that down."

Since the beach communities of the Outer Banks were completely maxed out long ago, the inland shoreline is the new and improved Banks. "The baby boomers, the largest demographic in history, is getting ready to retire, and in most cases, they're looking for a place on the water," says Tursi. "It's clear from all the marketing we've seen, and from people in the real estate business, North Carolina is the target." In the census projections for the state, the population is predicted to increase dramatically by 2030. "A lot of that growth will be in the inland communities," he says. And while the price tags on these lots might give sticker shock to a rural North Carolinian, they're a bargain by the standards of people coming from pricier zip codes, mostly in the Northeast.

Perhaps the greatest danger of swift and large-scale development, to old and new Inner Banks dwellers alike, is the physical one. From Stan Riggs's perspective, geology and meteorology are unforgiving of building at water's edge. In the three decades that he's been looking at the Tar River, a quarter mile downhill from his windows, it's gotten much closer. His property is eroding upwards of three feet per year. "It's not much," says Riggs, "but when my kids inherit it, I told them, 'Don't sell it, it will be waterfront.' I've been on this farm for thirty years. I've been watching it and it's very real. It's happening." What's happening on Riggs's property is indicative of what's happening all along the Inner Banks. "We have four thousand miles of inland shoreline and estuaries, and it's all eroding. All of it," says Riggs. "Land loss out there is incredible, sometimes as much as fifty to one hundred feet in a single storm." This process is made much worse when, with the intent of protecting their investments or prettying them, people tinker with the natural system.

"The minute someone buys something out there and wants to develop it, the first thing they do is cut down all the vegetation, which increases the rate of erosion," says Riggs. "Then they want a bulkhead because they don't want to lose their valuable property, their lot that they paid half a million dollars for. But the minute you harden the shoreline, you stop the whole process." That process is the balance of wetland, swamp, and marsh that regulates the tides and, to a large degree, the safety of shoreline residents. Riggs estimates that between 30 and 40 percent of Inner Banks shores have already been bulkheaded, and they continue to be at a rate of roughly fifty miles a year. "In another ten to twenty years we're looking at the whole coast being bulkheaded," he says. "At that point, the evolutionary succession is dead."

The influx of tax revenue from the building boom into some of North Carolina's poorest communities has been cited as a silver lining, as has the prospect of new businesses and jobs. But that's not enough to offset what's really at stake on the Inner Banks, say locals such as Tursi. Culture is at risk and ecology is imperiled. "What's at stake here is not so much oyster and clams, it's that guy who goes out there every single day trying to eke out a living harvesting clams or oysters out of the water," says Tursi. "As North Carolinians, we all lose. I don't want to see the coast turn into endless mile after endless mile of gated communities and golf courses designed by some famous golfer. Is that who we are as a people? Damn, I hope not."

When he's out on the water, Tursi is the epitome of who North Carolinians are now, and who they will continue to be for as long as circumstances allow. He marvels at the dunes and grasses as he cruises the barrier isles, he chats up the fishermen as they clean their daily catch, and he keeps an eye out for the porpoises that ushered him down the White Oak River long ago, lightening his worries with their frolic.

NAPA VALLEY, CALIFORNIA

Vineyard, Sonoma

MAY 24, 1976. FOR THE FRENCH WINE INDUSTRY, IT was a day of infamy. A panel of the country's foremost wine experts gathered at the Intercontinental Hotel in Paris for what would have been a pleasant afternoon of sipping, if only the judges' palates had demonstrated more patriotic preferences. The blind tasting competition, organized by a British wine seller hoping to capitalize on America's bicentennial, pitted French wines against a selection from California. To everyone's surprise,

Napa Valley wines won first place among both the whites (1973 Chateau Montelena Chardonnay) and the reds (1973 Stag's Leap Cabernet Sauvignon). The judges were as shocked as anyone—only one of them had ever tried a California wine before that day.

France might have succeeded in brushing the incident under the tapis if a lone reporter, George Taber, had not been in attendance. The article he went on to write for *Time* magazine, "The Judgment of Paris," ended France's era of uncontested dominance and catapulted Napa into fine-wine fame.

More than 260 wineries now inhabit the narrow, thirty-mile-long valley, and a multi-million-dollar tourism industry has emerged. Since that fateful day three decades ago, the great wines have attracted great chefs, and the region has become an international epicurean mecca. Napa Valley is now California's most popular travel destination, after Disneyland.

But its reign could be coming to an end. If recent scientific predictions hold true, rising global temperatures will soon alter the growing climate that's long been key to Napa's success. In the future, a blind taste test could put wines from cooler locales like Canada and England on top. "I never like to say that Napa will be no more," says Dr. Gregory Jones, an associate professor and research climatologist at Southern Oregon University, "but Napa is at the upper limit of the fairly hot climates in terms of grape growing." In other words, America's most storied vineyards could be churning out jug wine by the century's end.

Grapes are fickle fruits; they require hot days and cool nights throughout the growing season (April to October in the northern hemisphere; October to April in the southern hemisphere), and the environment in which they'll grow comfortably has a very narrow window. Within that range, Jones says, individual varietals have even narrower preferences. A region's average temperature during the growing season gives a good indication of which types of grapes it can accommodate best. Pinot Noir and Riesling, for instance, thrive in cooler zones like the Burgundy region of France, where the seasonal average is about 59 degrees Fahrenheit. Merlot and Syrah prefer places such as Napa, which typically averages 63. In locations where the average exceeds 66 degrees, few varietals perform well. That's where you're most likely to find table grapes and raisins (or no grapes at all).

While advances in vineyard science and enology have made it possible to produce mediocre wine in a wider range of climates, premium grapes demand specific natural conditions like those Napa Valley has enjoyed for a very long time. Wild grapes thrived here long before early-nineteenth-century homesteaders started cultivating them, thanks in part to the fertile blend of volcanic and oceanic soils that were mixed together during thousands of years of California quakes. The valley's geography is just right, too: dry heat hovers between the surrounding Vaca and Mayacamas mountains during the day, and cool breezes from the Pacific blow in at night. The consistent daily temperature swing allows the grapes to ripen slowly and steadily, producing perfectly balanced fruit.

"We all know that temperature is the most important climate component affecting grape composition and wine quality," vineyard consultant and wine columnist Dr. Richard Smart wrote in the January/February 2005 issue of *Practical Winery and Vineyard*. "There is a strong relationship between temperature and optimal quality of any given variety." Exactly how climate change will impact wine quality is a question that Smart, Jones, and other scientists have only recently begun to explore in depth. But the long-term impact of climate change on warm wine-producing regions such as Napa, Chianti, and the Rhône Valley is clear, Smart says: "They will lose their existing reputations."

Over the last half century, climate change has been a boon to growers in cool to intermediate climates. One of the first studies on climate and wine was published in a meteorology journal in 1983. The authors predicted that wine quality in the Champagne and Bordeaux regions of France would improve as warming weather extended their growing season. In the following years, their predictions proved correct.

Nearly two decades later, Jones and his colleagues set out to quantify that correlation by documenting the exact relationship between the temperatures and the *Wine Spectator* vintage ratings in those two regions and twenty-five others in Western Europe, the US West, and Chile. They found statistically significant warming trends in seventeen of those places, including Northern California, where the average temperature increased 1.23 degrees Celsius between 1950 and 1999. They also found that warmer weather meant empirically better wine: Each temperature increase of one degree Celsius translated to a 9.4-point increase on the one-hundred-point vintage rating scale.

Sonoma, California

But only to a point. As the warming approached a certain threshold, the change in quality leveled off. The critical cutoff, which they dubbed the "climate quality optimum," was 63 degrees—exactly where Napa is now. If the trajectory continues, Northern California will warm by two or three degrees Fahrenheit in the next fifty years. That's more than enough to affect grape quality. "Plants respond to their temperature environment in one of two ways," Jones says. "If it's way too hot for them physiologically, then they will shut down and not produce at all. If it is warmer than what they normally experience but not overwhelming physiologically, then they will go through their growth stages more rapidly. For grapevines, what we have seen is earlier bud break, bloom, and ripening for most varieties in most locations." Grapes from those vines tend to lack balance in terms of sugar, acid, and flavor, he says. "You can't tell me that doesn't change the way you do business."

You might think Napa's winemakers would be shaking in their stompers at the revelations of Jones et al. Not so. Though several producers have quietly voiced their unease, very few have factored potential warming into their long-range plans. Those who have chosen to act are doing so primarily at the winemaking level—removing alcohol when there is too much, for instance, or using yeast to artificially alter fermentation. But most Napa winemakers are ignoring the issue. Eventually they will simply have to grow different grapes or relocate altogether, Jones says. "One problem with climate change is that it's a slow process. We tend to act on immediate impacts and we don't act on slow processes." If the climate models are correct, he says, "in 2050, 2075, 2100, we're going to be severely challenged in terms of doing the same thing." But 2050 is a long way off, and today business is booming.

For visitors, the pastoral ethos of day-to-day living is part of Napa's appeal. When you're roaming the vines, it's easy to live in the moment. Biking and walking paths crisscross the towns and the open space between them. Pristine hillsides surround the patchwork of vineyards in golden grasses at harvest time and poppies in the spring. Natural hot springs bubble up from underground, feeding the decadent day spas that have cropped up all over the valley. And the nineteenth-century wineries that produced the winning vintages in the 1976 Paris Tasting have only gotten better. You can tour Stag's Leap only by special arrangement, but Chateau Montelena is open to visitors daily. One of Napa's prettiest sipping settings, the winery is housed in a stone hillside castle at the foot of Mount St. Helena. The building may someday be seen as an icon of the "old" wine country.

When Napa relinquishes its crown, the "new" wine country could appear in any number of up-and-coming regions, like the Okanagan Valley in British Columbia; Sussex and Kent in southern England; Puget Sound in Washington; and Tasmania in Australia. Places that have traditionally been limited to cooler-climate grapes are branching out and producing better wines than in decades past.

Signs of the shift are already appearing in winemaker Harry Peterson Nedry's northern Oregon vineyards. "Here in the Northwest we're having greater regularity of very good vintages," says Nedry, who founded Chehalem winery in the Willamette Valley in 1990 and sits on the board of WineAmerica, the national trade group for US wineries. "We used to have three or four out of ten that sucked. Now we're having like eight or nine out of ten that are great. I think that tells us a lot."

Nedry spent twenty-six years in the high-tech manufacturing industry before turning his passion for wine into a new career in 1980. From the beginning, he has enjoyed the challenge of cultivating the notoriously temperamental Pinot Noir. In recent years, his efforts have yielded increasingly positive results. "We can attribute that to some knowledge on our part. But a great deal of it has to be given to Mother Nature and what she has been giving us."

Grape growers who have enjoyed improved crops in the recent warmer years are fooling themselves if they think things will stay the same, Nedry says. "This is like a freight train that starts getting momentum. You might like the speed it's at part-way through your trip, but if it continues to gain speed it's like hell at the end." Conversations with Jones and other experts about wine and climate change have led Nedry to expect that his beloved Pinot's days in the Willamette Valley are numbered. "Sooner or later, we're going to be seeing a shift in what we grow," he says. "This is going to change from Pinot Noir to probably Syrah country within what's left of my lifetime." Since Nedry doesn't particularly like Syrah, he is buying time by moving some of his Pinot vines uphill to cooler temperatures, several hundred feet above the rest. He has also started experimenting with what he calls "futuristic whites," grapes such as Grüner Veltliner and Riesling, which he expects to flourish in years to come.

In a recent Chehalem newsletter, he told subscribers about the winery's decision to plant some new varietals. "We experiment partly because we're restless and curious—OK, because I'm restless," he wrote. "But partly, we look to change because we have to. I'm in the no-nonsense, scientific camp on the reality of Global Climate Change and bear a sense of urgency that things need now to be done—or eventually we're done."

Napa vintner Rob Sinskey couldn't agree more. He is the general manager of Robert Sinskey Vineyards, a certified organic winery that gets its electricity from solar panels and runs its vehicles on biodiesel fuel. His highly regarded wines are served at some of Napa's finest eateries and are distributed throughout the United States and Asia. Not surprisingly, Sinskey has given plenty of thought to climate change and grapes. "We have a theory that organic methodology helps the vines deal with the weather," he says. "The vines can put more energy into the grape cycle rather than caring for the canopy." Compared to their artificially fertilized neighbors, Sinskey's compost-fed vineyards look somewhat thin and yellow—a sign that nutrients that would otherwise be diverted to create a showy canopy are staying in the soil, he says. The result is a more weather-resistant plant and healthier, heartier grapes. "When you have a heat spike where other vines shut down," he says, "ours seem to weather the storm."

But the motivation behind the winery's green philosophy has more to do with the causes of global warming than its effects. Sinskey sees organic winemaking as an opportunity to show his peers that they can take a more direct role in slowing the industry's demise by tackling climate change itself. "If we can make people in the wine industry understand that you can make a better wine being environmentally sound," he says, "then perhaps we can get some of these educated people to respect the planet a little more in their daily practices."

OAHU, HAWAII

Mokulua Islands from the Oahu mainland

FROM THE VANTAGE POINT OF KAILUA BEACH ON OAHU'S eastern shore, the Mokulua Islands look like two dollops of wet clay afloat in a sparkling green sea. It's a vista that begs for exploration, and if you heed the call by kayak, paddling against the wind until the dollops solidify into two volcanic cones, you'll find solitude and an easy landing on a picnic-perfect beach. Between those islets and the toasted-sugar sand across the bay, windsurfers graze the tips of translucent ripples, snorkelers hover above sea turtles, and boogie boarders tumble with the crashing waves.

This version of Oahu belies the island's reputation as a paved-over paradise. Far from the congestion of Honolulu and the high-rise clutter of Waikiki, the Mokuluas and Kailua Bay serve as reminders that Hawaii's most populated isle still has plenty of natural appeal.

What's left, however, is fragile. As you paddle back toward shore, you'll see one clear sign of trouble. Kailua Beach ends abruptly at the north end of Lanikai, which not long ago was home to another expanse of sand. Now it is a fortress of seawalls—sandbags or boulders piled head-high, or taller concrete barriers—that were built to keep the ocean from encroaching on beachfront properties. "The seawalls themselves are land-protection structures, but they're not beach-protection structures," says Dr. Bruce Richmond, a geologist with the USGS Pacific Science Center. "When you put a seawall in, eventually you will lose the beach in front of it." Indeed, Lanikai's seawalls succeeded in protecting its homes, but in doing so they destroyed two thirds of its beach.

As the natural process of coastal erosion comes into conflict with the human process of coastal development, sandy shorelines all over Hawaii—and throughout the world—are suffering a similar fate. Beaches are dynamic; buildings are not. When the forces of the ocean cause beaches to migrate landward, the static objects near the coastline risk getting swallowed by the sea. "The natural tendency of homeowners is to protect their home," Richmond says. And so they build seawalls in an effort to keep the ocean at bay. On an undeveloped eroding shoreline, the size of the beach stays fairly constant as it moves. But seawalls disrupt the sand's inland migration, causing the beach to shrink and eventually disappear.

"Every place where we have developed the coastline and there is a pattern of chronic erosion, either beach has been lost, or it is narrowed, or it's headed in that direction," says Dr. Chip Fletcher, a geology and geophysics professor at the University of Hawaii at Manoa. One fourth of Oahu's beaches and more than a third of Maui's have fallen victim to seawalls in the last fifty years. "It is my fear that decades from now—fifty years, one hundred years—the Hawaiian Islands and many other coastal locations around the world are going to be down to the last vestiges of their beaches."

The ocean has an undeniable draw. Eighty percent of the US population lives within fifty miles of the coast. And in Hawaii, where no piece of land is more than twenty-nine miles from the water, everyone lives near the beach. Seven and a half million tourists come to the Hawaiian Islands each year to lounge on the warm sand beneath the swaying palms, surf frothing at their feet. Hawaii's air, heavy with the scent of tuberose and plumeria, carries the aroma of vacation. It's no wonder that so many visitors return again and again, and that so many mainlanders in recent years have made Hawaii their home.

America's coastal migration trend started just after World War II, "when a whole generation of young people were able to travel around the world at the government's expense as part of the armed forces and saw the oceans for the first time," Fletcher says. "They came out of the farmlands and they saw the beautiful coastlines, and they decided to relocate." In the nearly fifty years Hawaii has been a US state, its population has nearly doubled to 1.2 million (the population of the United States grew by 70 percent during the same period), and it continues to grow by tens of thousands each year. Three quarters of that population lives on the island of Oahu, which makes up less than a tenth of Hawaii's landmass. Oahu is also the center of tourist activity, hosting about half of the island chain's visitors.

More people means more accommodations for residents and tourists, and waterfront development has boomed—mostly without regard to erosion. "What's happened in Hawaii is that we've overdeveloped our coastal zone," Fletcher says. "We've allowed development in the form of buildings that are large, that are immovable, that are permanent structures adjacent to shorelines that are migrating. And as the erosion moves toward the building and threatens the building, Hawaii has allowed for seawalls to be built."

Hawaii native Christie Botelho has watched the beach loss progress over the past few decades. When she was growing up on Oahu in the 1970s and 1980s, she and her friends would spend every weekend outside the Outrigger Canoe Club on Waikiki Beach. As their parents watched from the sand, they'd swim out to a small catamaran that was anchored offshore, then ride the waves home.

Botelho now lives in California, but she still visits Oahu every two years with her husband. She doesn't take him swimming near the clubhouse, however. "There's nothing there. The ocean comes all the way up to the building," she says. More than a third of Waikiki is now armored with seawalls; much of the remaining beach vanishes beneath the surf during high tide. "I'm curious to see where they launch their canoes now, because the beach there is pretty much gone."

Long before Botelho was born, the beach at Waikiki was lined with sand dunes instead of buildings and walls. Those dunes played a crucial role in maintaining the health of the beach. When the ocean was calm and waves were small, the dunes would swell with accumulated sand. During storms, when large waves pounded the coastline, the dunes would spread their excess to the ocean floor, protecting the beach by causing waves to break farther from shore. Waikiki's sand dunes, like others on the island, have long since been mined for concrete aggregate or flattened for construction. All of Hawaii's shorelines were once lined with dunes, and most have suffered similar fates. Quite a few were destroyed in repeated attempts to restore the ever-shrinking Waikiki, the center of Hawaii's lucrative tourism industry, by transporting truckloads of sand from lesser-known beaches. The transplants never lasted very long, and the damaged dunes never recovered.

Oahu's dunes are almost completely gone. So are the dunes in Maui, where 70 percent of the 318,000 tons of sand excavated each year is shipped to Oahu. County officials estimate that the island's last removable sand will be gone by 2013. Maui's mining

Lanikai Beach before seawall construction

history predates the construction boom. Sugar plantations used the lime-rich sand to condition their cane fields in the nineteenth and early twentieth centuries. At Baldwin Beach Park, on Maui's north shore, a footpath leads to one of the original lime kiln sites. A public park since 1963, Baldwin is known for its long white beach flanked with ironwoods and palms. But the ocean has crept closer in recent years. In July 2006, the county was forced to close the park for two weeks in order to remove a dozen twenty- to forty-foot-tall ironwood trees that were in danger of collapsing because the ocean had eroded the sand beneath their roots. The following month, powerful waves threatened to destroy an outdoor shower and a lifeguard tower on the park's east end, prompting officials to consider another closure. The county parks director, who grew up on Maui, told local reporters it was the worst erosion season he'd ever seen.

In Hawaii, where almost half the land lies within five miles of the coast, rising seas are also wreaking havoc, as low-lying areas routinely flood, saltwater creeps into aquifers, waves crash onto coastal highways during storms, and beaches and bluffs erode. The world's seas rose four to eight inches during the twentieth century as increased greenhouse gases warmed the oceans and melted glaciers and sea ice. The rate of warming was much faster toward the end of that century, and it continues to increase. Between 1993 and 2005, the seas rose at a rate of one foot per century. Researchers published an alarming prediction in the journal *Science* in March 2006, stating that the sea level would rise another twenty feet by 2100 because of the rapid melting of the Greenland and Antarctic ice sheets. "It must be recognized that the impacts of sea-level rise within our lifetime in Hawaii are certainly going to be significant and to ignore the threat may lead to irreversible effects," Fletcher, the University of Hawaii professor, wrote in his book, *On the Shores of Paradise*. "Sometimes one has to wonder what early island planners could have been thinking when they decided to allow homes within forty feet of the reach of the waves, important highways built literally at water's edge, and seawalls to be used on our fragile beaches."

At Kailua Beach, the Oahu kayaking and windsurfing mecca across the bay from the Mokulua Islands, nature has offered some insurance against the shortsighted development policies of decades past. Unlike most Hawaiian beaches, Kailua gets its sand from an offshore channel that has pulled the beach seaward over time, even as its neighbors have migrated inland. This "accretion" pattern has actually led to the formation of new dunes—a very rare sight on these islands. As Lanikai, the seawall-lined beach to the south, continues to vanish, Kailua could actually flourish—with proper care. Two threats remain: aggressive salt-resistant plants such as morning glory and naupaka are spreading across the sand, narrowing the beach from the inland side, and the possibility of development still looms. As the modest homes of the old neighborhoods succumb to real estate pressures and disrepair, fancy new mansions replace them, edging ever closer to shore. "These homeowners will demand seawalls when erosion strikes—and it will strike as sea level rises over coming decades," Fletcher says. "And those seawalls will kill Kailua Beach."

Beach management policies vary from island to island because of a peculiar division of coastal jurisdiction between the state and the counties. The dividing line, or "shoreline," is the highest point touched by breaking waves, not including storm waves. Everything inland from that point is managed by the counties; everything seaward is managed by the state. There is hope among conservationists that today's county planners will start prioritizing Hawaii's remaining beaches over its buildings. Policy seems to be moving in that direction in Maui County, where new setback rules factor in the rate of erosion, not just the distance from the coast. Kauai County, too, is considering adding an erosion clause to its construction codes. Not so in Honolulu County, which encompasses all of Oahu. On this island, where souvenir shops sell postcards with pictures of pristine beaches that have long since disappeared, the population continues to swell and tourists from around the world spread their towels on precious sand that is in increasingly short supply.

At least some of those tourists will leave Oahu with a better understanding of its fragility. Kailua-based eco-outfitter Mokulua Kayak Guides runs daily paddling and snorkeling excursions that serve to educate travelers about the environment as they have fun exploring it. Groups are limited to nine people per day, the price of the trip includes a 5 percent conservation fee that goes to the Hawaiian Wildlife Society, and the guides are disciples of the "tread lightly" school of adventure tourism.

"Hawaii in general is so amazing, and this area is a neat little part of that system," says guide and cofounder Robbie Schultz, who leads kayak trips from Kailua Beach to the Mokulua Islands. On a typical five-hour tour, he guides visitors on the hourlong paddle across the bay. They spend the better part of the day exploring island tidepools and, in the summertime, watching the wedge-tailed shearwaters. The offshore islets are seabird sanctuaries, and these open-ocean birds come to the islands once a year to lay their eggs and nest in the sandy soil. On the way home, the kayakers visit a coral head known as the Turtle Cleaning Station, where fish congregate to nibble algae from sea turtle shells. They snorkel in the clear water, where multicolored wrasses, tangs, and triggerfish dart in and out of the algae-crusted coral folds. And as they paddle back toward Kailua Beach, they can't help but contrast its sandy coastline with that of the beach next door, the ever-shrinking Lanikai. "You see the retaining walls built on either side and see that slowly the beach is just washing away," Schultz says. It's a lesson in erosion that will outlast their vacations, if not the beach itself.

THE RIO GRANDE

Rio Grande near Taos, New Mexico

EDWARD ABBEY ONCE PADDLED A PONTOON BOAT DOWN a scenic southern stretch of the Rio Grande just outside Big Bend National Park in Texas. The trip became a story, "On the River Again," about succumbing to the mesmerizing flow of the waterway that cut through his beloved Southwest. "We float on the dreamlike river down into a subterranean country of water and walls," Abbey wrote, "with fluted gray limestone at the river's edge, tumbled boulders, banks of sand where the mesquite grows (leafing out in spring green), clusters of bamboo twenty feet tall, thorny acacia in golden bloom spicing the air with a fragrance like that of apple blossoms, everything illuminated by a soft, filtered, indirect, refracted light." The famously curmudgeonly author was so taken with the Rio Grande that he called it "a tunnel of love."

Back then, this enchanted tunnel was one long, contiguous river. At its headwaters in southwestern Colorado, snowmelt spilled over the eastern edge of the Continental Divide and trickled through the San Juan Mountains into New Mexico. It ran uninterrupted for 1,960 miles, wetting the grasslands and scrub of the great Chihuahuan Desert through Texas en route to its final destination, the Gulf of Mexico.

Today the Rio Grande is essentially two rivers. Just south of El Paso, it disappears beneath a thirsty patch of salt cedar and travels underground for a couple hundred miles. Then it resurfaces where it meets the Rio Concho, which flows north from the pine and oak forests of the Sierra Madre Occidental Mountains in Mexico and infuses the Grande with enough water to push it through Big Bend toward the Gulf—though no longer all the way there. Earlier this decade, the river stopped emptying into the sea; it simply seeped into the delta sand and faded away.

The beautiful Rio Grande could still inspire poetic outpourings from visiting paddlers. But the great river is slowly shrinking. Growing cities have sucked up its dwindling water supply, non-native plants have spread out of control, and one dry winter after another has brought little relief. By most accounts, the decline is expected to continue. Officials are still granting water permits to developers, even though demand exceeds supply. Invasive salt cedar is still being left to choke out native vegetation. And experts say the last decade's paltry amount of precipitation is a return to normal levels, not a temporary drought. "The Rio Grande is a very old river, and it's getting worn out," says Brian Shields, executive director of Amigos Bravos, an environmental watchdog group for the Rio Grande watershed. "Will Rogers called it 'the only river I know of that is in need of irrigating,' and that's what it is."

For now, the Colorado headwaters still produce a healthy surge of snowmelt. And you can still drive alongside the thin green line of cottonwoods that parallels parts of Interstate 25 in northern New Mexico, where the viridescent stripe of color stands in stark contrast to the brown and blood-red rocks of the surrounding mountains. You can also explore the river from the water, though the rafting season is getting ever shorter—especially in the southern stretch that travels through Big Bend.

No one knows that better than Mike Long. For more than twenty years the adventure guide has eked out a living on the lower river, shuttling adventure seekers through the skinny limestone canyons of the Big Bend region on rafts and canoes. A decade ago, when he started his own multisport outfitter business, Desert Sports, in Terlingua, Texas, a long period of uncharacteristically wet winters was coming to an end, and water levels were not much of a concern. Things are different now. "For about the last ten to twelve years, the river's gone from being raftable year-round to what is apparently becoming very seasonal, and more than seasonal, it's becoming very erratic," he says. "It's hard to predict when we will have a good river."

Water permitting, Long's favorite trip is a weeklong paddle through the Lower Canyons, where the warm river twists and turns through deep rocky chasms and expanses of desert that explode with wildflowers in the spring. It's an eighty-five-mile journey through a hot spring–rich section of the park where the limestone walls can tower 1,800 feet overhead. "It's probably the closest thing we've got to a real wilderness situation," he says. "It's pretty awesome."

Booking rafting excursions has become increasingly tricky, however. Long doesn't take reservations unless he's pretty sure a trip will run, but in the summertime, that's not so easy to predict. "There was a time period last summer where we would be low-water canoeing one day and nearly flood-stage rafting the next," he says. The water level in the lower river depends on local rainfall and releases from upstream dams, which can happen without warning. The frequency and quantity of those releases are determined by a complicated morass of interstate and international agreements that have evolved over the last hundred-plus years. Long keeps a close watch on the International Boundary and Water Commission website, which posts real-time stream flow data and daily water flow reports. But sometimes it's impossible to determine the day's itinerary until the morning of a trip. In recent years, the outfitter's on-the-water adventures have gone from mostly rafting to mostly canoe trips, which are less dependent on water quantity. Long has also started promoting other activities like mountain biking and hiking, which have been on the company's multisport trip roster

Rio Grande near Embudo, New Mexico

from the start but have never been as popular as the water sports. "We've really had to try to reemphasize the off-river stuff," he says.

The trouble began in the late 1800s, when an agriculture boom in southern Colorado and northern New Mexico caused water shortages in Texas and northern Mexico, where the river serves as the international boundary for more than a thousand miles. A 1906 treaty obligated the United States to provide its southern neighbor with 60,000 acre-feet of water per year at the International Dam near El Paso, Texas. That helped ease international tensions, but it did little to stem the stateside squabbling—southern New Mexico and Texas were then relinquishing their water to the north and to the south. In 1938, the U.S. Congress gave New Mexico some relief by approving the Rio Grande Compact, a treaty signed by Colorado, New Mexico, and Texas that guaranteed an average 750,000 annual acre-feet to the Elephant Butte Reservoir in southern New Mexico, which was built in 1916. One representative from each state, plus a federal official, made up the commission that still oversees the allocations from the headwaters to Fort Quitman, Texas, just south of the reservoir. That's about the point where the Rio Grande becomes the "forgotten river" that disappears beneath the salt cedar.

Below Fort Quitman, the Rio Grande enters the jurisdiction of the International Boundary and Water Commission, which manages the water rights from there to the Gulf. Tributaries that feed the lower river include the dwindling Pecos and Devil's rivers in the United States and six Mexican tributaries; the largest of them is Rio Concho. According to a 1944 treaty, at least a third of the Mexican water, plus all of the water entering the river from American tributaries, belongs to the United States. But water diversions and drought conditions in Mexico have drastically reduced the amount of inflow from the Concho, and the US rivers aren't hearty enough to pick up the slack. That leaves the Rio Grande through much of Texas at the mercy of the weather. "Right now it depends pretty much on local rainfall," Long says.

Every now and then, however, the old treaty delivers a pleasant surprise that has the river gushing with some of its former glory. A series of gauging stations in the United States and Mexico monitor the river's flow, which is controlled in part by dams on both sides of the border. One summer day, officials on the Concho released about five hundred cubic feet per second into the Rio Grande, and Long suddenly had rafting trips to offer. "No one knew it was coming," he says. "It took weeks before anyone could figure out why exactly it was happening, but we were out enjoying it while it was here."

In the Rio Grande, water quality is also a problem. Mining pollution in the north and waste from American and Mexican cities and factories in the south, in addition to the concerns about water being diverted from the river, led the conservation group American Rivers to name the Rio Grande "America's Most Endangered River" in 1993. The river has since graced the organization's "Most Endangered" list three times, for reasons of both quantity and quality. The report that American Rivers issued in 2000 warned, "If significant changes to river management are not made soon, the Rio Grande will lose its ability to sustain the fish, birds, wildlife, and people that depend on it." The following year, the river dried up before reaching the Gulf for the first time in its history. In 2003, the river ran dry in parts of Big Bend National Park for the first time since the 1950s. And even though water diversions already claimed 95 percent of the river's yearly output, the city of Albuquerque introduced plans to remove as much as a hundred thousand acre-feet of additional water per year from the Rio Grande and San Juan rivers.

Supplying water to Albuquerque is a problem that has confounded New Mexico officials for decades. In 1956, the state engineer announced that no new water rights would be issued. Existing rights could be transferred between owners, but the limited water supply meant that the age of new appropriations was over. However, the state continued to issue permits for new domestic wells and still does so at the rate of about three thousand per year. Conservationists say officials have been slow to acknowledge the link between groundwater pumping and surface-water depletion. The wells are draining the river from beneath, like tiny drains in a giant bathtub.

From the 10,378-foot Sandia Peak in the mountains above Albuquerque, where juniper and pine cling to the towering striated cliffs, you can look down on the development projects that are spreading through the parched valleys. This is one of the fastest-growing regions in America and one of the biggest per capita water consumers in the Southwest. There is immense political pressure to build, and despite the reality of the limited supply, water permits continue to be granted.

"There's plenty of paper water," says Shields, the Amigos Bravos director. "They seem to be giving out more and more permits for pumping water out of the ground. As long as that happens I think the Rio Grande is going to be a dry ditch. There's not a lot of future that I can see."

The Middle Rio Grande Water Assembly is a group of New Mexicans who banded together in 1996 to develop a regional water plan that addresses the disparity between the needs of the area's eight hundred thousand residents and the amount of available water. According to their research, average annual water use is 15 to 20 percent higher than what is sustainable. "We have on average a deficit of about seventy thousand acre-feet per year; it just depends on the year," president Ed Payne says. "Why the state engineer continues to issue permits is a question that we're asking at this point."

In 2003, the Office of the State Engineer and Interstate Stream Commission published a strategic plan that acknowledged the problem: "The flows of New Mexico's two major rivers—the Rio Grande and the Pecos River—are barely adequate to meet both New Mexico's existing needs and its interstate stream compact delivery obligations. The state's continuing ability to meet those compact obligations is a delicate balance." And yet, the growth continues.

The Water Assembly's plan calls for widespread conservation measures, more accurate water measurement that factors in groundwater as well as surface water, more efficient agricultural irrigation, improved water quality and testing, habitat restoration, improved water storage, water desalination, and increased public education. In 2003, the plan was officially accepted by the New Mexico Interstate Stream Commission, which oversees the region's water rights. Each of the nineteen local governments followed suit. But implementation has been slow. "I think, short-term, things are going to get much worse," Payne says. "We're pretty out of control at this point."

A paddler on a winter float trip in the Lower Canyons might not know the river is in such dire straits. In the part of Texas where the river makes its "big bend," its southeast flow turning sharply northeast, lies the only portion of the Rio Grande that is federally protected as a Wild and Scenic River. Though the flow and water quality remain somewhat vulnerable to the management decisions beyond its borders, 69 miles of river that form the southern boundary of Big Bend National Park and an additional 127 miles that continue downstream are permanently free from local water diversions and development. M. T. Chandler, a surveyor who traveled this region in 1852, described it as "a section of country which for ruggedness and wildness of scenery is perhaps unparalleled." The naked rock along its banks has buckled, cracked, and folded over the past hundred million years to form the stark, seemingly endless canyons whose muted edges fade into distant, quivering heat waves. Tiny pink blooms erupt from the tops of flowering cacti, and the spiny tips of waxy century plants fan outward from their sturdy cores. Garter snakes slither to the water's edge to hunt for frogs. Coyotes bark and howl. Jackrabbits dart between the creosotes and cottonwoods, nibbling on grasses and hiding from the many predators that would gladly nibble on them. The river rages and boils with rapids that can surge to Class Vs in a good hard rain, then flattens to a slow, peaceful gurgle that complements the subtle sounds of the surrounding desert.

The National Park Service says it designated the Rio Grande a Wild and Scenic River in 1978 to protect the scenery, wildlife, and recreation opportunities along this unique stretch of water, and "to preserve the free-flowing condition" of the river forever. But the Wild and Scenic River is intimately connected to the rest of the Rio Grande, from the San Juan Mountains snowmelt to the Albuquerque basin to the sandy delta at the Gulf. The park service can keep its promise for only as long as there is a river to protect.

YELLOWSTONE NATIONAL PARK

Grand Canyon of the Yellowstone, Yellowstone National Park

RIDE HORSEBACK ALONGSIDE JETT HITT, UP FROM THE confluence of the Blacktail Creek and the Yellowstone River, onto a grassy plateau with the Gallatin Range as a backdrop, and he'll likely tip his hat and tell you the story of how the Everts thistle got its name. In 1870, would-be cowboy Truman Everts (who up to that point was a more successful thinker than explorer, says Hitt) accompanied the Washburn Expedition into northwest Wyoming and the territory that was to become Yellowstone National Park. After getting separated from his party and horse, which was loaded with his supplies, Everts sustained himself on the partially edible, celery-like elk thistle. When he was found thirty-seven days later—barely alive—he was mistaken for a scrawny black bear and shot at. "Old Truman had been crawling on all fours," says Hitt, shaking his head and grimacing. It seems the hairy, waiflike man was half crazed from his ordeal, which included being spooked by the area's skilled predators and scalded after slumbering too close to one of the park's ten thousand or so geothermal features.

Everts experienced firsthand what surveyors and scientists were just beginning to understand: the area is a volcanic hot spot. At the center of the park is a thirty- by forty-five-mile volcanic basin that formed 640,000 years ago when the area collapsed during its last volcanic mega-eruption. The distant edges of the caldera rise clifflike from the floor of the depression. This is the Norris Geyser Basin and the heart of Yellowstone. It's one of the world's most massive and active volcanoes. The Black Growler Steam Vent belches loudly; Emerald Spring's boiling pool is home to namesake thermophiles that thrive on sulfur; and Steamboat Geyser has been known to spew a lean line of superheated water over three hundred feet high. Piles of bison and elk scat are evidence of some of the creatures that tread confidently here. Indeed, at Norris, what John Muir called Yellowstone's "Wonderland" engulfs you.

For centuries Native Americans, artists, scientists, explorers, and visitors have been going on about Yellowstone's weird, wonderful landscape. The work of those artists, like photographer William Henry Jackson and painter Thomas Moran, ultimately brought the area to the attention of Congress and bolstered its designation in 1872 as the country's first national park. They had a sense of what is now well known: no other place on earth is even remotely like Yellowstone. Sure, Iceland and New Zealand have geysers, but not many compared to those in the park, and neither has boiling pools of acid and seething pots of mud. Yellowstone also boasts its own Grand Canyon, where waterfalls as tall as skyscrapers cut through lava flows, and dense lodgepole forests open to subalpine meadows crowded with glacier lily and fireweed. Two mountain ranges flank the park, and twin magma chambers course and swell beneath its surface.

Its surreal scenery is rivaled only by its wildlife: grizzlies laze and forage on the banks of the Yellowstone River, packs of wolves hunt stealthily in the Lamar Valley, herds of bison graze lush slopes within view of Old Faithful, schools of cutthroat trout struggle upstream through DeHardy's Rapids on their journey to Yellowstone Lake, and flocks of white pelicans swarm near the Fishing Bridge to intercept them.

As the first of its kind, Yellowstone was the gold standard that all national parks were to match. By design these open spaces were meant to be carefully guarded, not as museums of nature, but as public playgrounds where ecosystems might also be maintained. The founding mandate of Yellowstone is chiseled right on the rock arch over the southern entrance in Gardiner, Montana. The narrow gateway, whose cornerstone was laid by President Theodore Roosevelt in 1903, reads: "For the benefit and enjoyment of the people." The message was clear—as solid as stone—that the borders of our first public "pleasuring-ground" were not meant to be impervious; all were welcome. But even a century ago Roosevelt had a sense of the imposition people were on that landscape. He ditched the three thousand people who showed up at the dedication ceremony, even leaving behind his doctor and Secret Service detail, in order to wander unfettered in the wild solitude of Yellowstone.

Follow Jett Hitt on horseback through that same backcountry, on a trail dotted with magenta bitterroot blooms, and he'll likely give the impression that the park and the people who seek to know it, or control it, still walk a precarious line in one of the world's most beautiful and beguiling wilderness areas. In Yellowstone, there is no longer any such place as the "middle of nowhere." For the small percentage of visitors who actually leave the park's asphalt—some estimates put it at as little as 1 percent—there is at least an edge of nowhere, but it hasn't been pristine in some time.

Since humans first trod on this land (or at least since Truman Everts fought its demons), Yellowstone's relationship with humans has been nearly as explosive as its geology. Soon after it was named America's first national park, the cavalry had to be sent in to guard its resources from poaching and trampling. When tourism picked up in the 1880s, "Keep off, out, away"–type signs were posted in hopes of preventing injury from the park's perilous geysers and from free-roaming wildlife, whose ire, if sparked, was often fatal. Despite the bold, obvious warnings, some of the visiting throngs still met their end in the park either by scalding, mauling, or goring. By 1915 the debate about allowing automobiles into Yellowstone was at its peak. That year, in the spring issue of the *Yellowstone News*, a correspondent wrote, "Both practical and sentimental reasons can be urged against the admission of the automobile to Yellowstone National Park . . . Otherwise we will tell travelers the legends of the big game one used to see before this bedlam drove these wild animals into the deepest recesses of the mighty forests."

It wasn't until thirteen years after Roosevelt's visit, when the National Park Service itself was founded, that the concept of conservation of those spaces, for their own sake, was made manifest. For over ninety years the task of the park service has been to "conserve the scenery and the natural and historic objects and the wild life therein and to provide for the enjoyment for the same in such manner and by such means as will leave them unimpaired for the enjoyment of future generations." Since then, the park service's dual mandate—to protect Yellowstone both from and for people—has been in grave conflict. Less than two decades after the conservation ethic was established, Yellowstone's dynamic ecosystem was showing signs of stress, from both tourism and evolving wildlife management policies. A 1934 report called "Wildlife Management in the National Parks" concluded, "It is probable that the white-tailed deer, cougar, lynx, wolf and possibly wolverine and fisher are gone from the Yellowstone fauna." Over the years park wardens undertook activities that now seem unthinkable, including hand-feeding elk to bolster a waning population and—perhaps even more bizarre—encouraging grizzlies to forage in garbage dumps for the entertainment of bleachers full of visitors (which ceased only in 1970). The World Heritage Committee was so concerned for the health of Yellowstone that it placed the park on its World Heritage in Danger list. It removed Yellowstone from the list in 2003, reportedly amid political pressure, but many threats endure.

Today, as Yellowstone's borders become increasingly porous, its status and popularity, charisma, and vital wilds are at a familiar but more critical crossroads. Despite the fierce dedication of its rangers to protect Yellowstone, several forces—including budget shortfalls, faltering wildlife and land management, and private interests pressing in on its borders—are weakening the park's perimeter and purpose.

While ascending on horseback from Gardiner to the steaming travertine terraces of Mammoth Hot Springs, Roosevelt likely couldn't have imagined that roughly three million visitors per year would one day pass through Yellowstone's gates. But if he arrived here today he would have certainly left behind the ones who gab on cell phones; those who walk clear past "Do not enter" signage for a better photo of the falls, bears, geysers, and so on; and those who harass wildlife. Many of the millions of Yellowstone's fly-bys, the ones who fail to leave their vehicles but for an occasional photo op, also fail to realize that those bison, elk, and grizzlies in the crosshairs of their binoculars are also in the middle of several major human debates.

The highest-profile wildlife policy change that Yellowstone faces is that after thirty-two years of protection, its grizzly bears were booted off the Endangered Species list in the spring of 2007. In that time the population has rebounded softly from 132 to 312 (there was never an accurate count) in 1975, to 500 today. That's long and strong enough, said Deputy Interior Secretary Lynn Scarlett, who made the announcement while also expressing confidence in local and state governments to adequately manage the protection of grizzlies.

Heidi Godwin, the Sierra Club's Grizzly Bear Project coordinator, disagrees. She says that delisting the grizzly will mean a significant loss of habitat. The eighteen million acres of the Greater Yellowstone ecosystem that are home to Yellowstone's grizzlies include a decent swath of private land, some of which is a hotbed of grizzly hostility. Godwin points to Fremont County, southeast of Yellowstone. "What they're saying is if you take it off the list we're going to kill every bear in Fremont County. If we find it, we're going to kill it. That's not management. That's annihilation," says Godwin. Habitat and human tolerance are equal parts of the grizzly survival formula; one without the other will lead to grizzly eradication. Without human acceptance, grizzlies will decline through pure human force, and without sufficient habitat, they'll lose what remaining wildlife corridors there are and become genetically isolated.

Opponents of the federal delisting also argue that the action is shortsighted because of other stresses on the grizzly population—such as climate change—that have not yet been fully realized. Godwin points to the infestation of blister rust and mountain pine beetles in white pine bark, a result of warming temperatures. White pine seeds are a critical component of the grizzlies' diet, as are cutthroat trout, whose numbers are also declining. "It's not a question whether that food source will be around for a long time, it's when it's going to be gone," says Godwin.

If grizzly numbers do tank, the US Fish and Wildlife Service plans to import some into Yellowstone from up north. "The assumption is that you're going to plunk this bear down into a foreign ecosystem and it's going to survive and procreate," says Godwin. But the Yellowstone bears' northern cousins are skilled at finding huckleberries and roots, which, while abundant in their habitat, are seldom seen in Wyoming. In such a scheme, transplanted bears will automatically be at risk. "That bear is immediately going to get pushed to the bottom of the pecking order, to the more marginal landscape where there's less available food," says Godwin. "Then the chances are good that that bear is going to travel to a lower elevation and come into contact with people."

Eight conservation groups plan to sue to put grizzlies back on the Endangered Species list. "Do I want the grizzly bear on the endangered species list forever? *Hell* no," says Godwin. "That's not what it's about. There's some serious problems that need to be addressed before this thing is ready to fly on its own." She says delisting grizzlies now is like going directly from the emergency room of a hospital to the parking lot. "The American public has invested so much time, money, and energy into bringing the grizzly bear back to where it is in Yellowstone. Why gamble?"

Far less publicized than grizzly delisting is the great bison debacle of 2005–2006, the winter in which officials attempted to keep bison from leaving the park to try to protect them. Those bison that were not successfully "hazed" back into Yellowstone and crossed that invisible border from federally protected to public enemy number one were corralled, and of those, nearly a thousand were sent to slaughter. Tim Stevens, of the National Park Conservation Association, a nonprofit parks watchdog, explains what happened. "Bison were moving out of the park or massing to move out of the park," he says. "And for political and not necessarily biological reasons, and because of the strict backward nature of the bison management plan, the park service was required to capture and ship [them] off to slaughter." If the bison had made it out of the park, which the iconic western beast is inclined to do when it's cold to find better grazing, there was a chance that they would encounter cattle from the vast ranchlands in Wyoming and Montana that border the park, a possibility that strikes fear in the heart of even the hardiest rancher.

Bison carry brucellosis, a disease that has cattle ranchers shaking in their boots. While bison are unaffected by the disease, it can be transmitted to cattle, causing females to auto-abort. Stevens says that the Bison Management Plan currently in place is fundamentally flawed because "there's no tolerance for the bison outside of the park even in places were there's absolutely no chance for bison to commingle with livestock."

According to a source within the National Park Service, while some Yellowstone rangers were devastated by the loss of nearly 1,000 of the 4,900 bison in the park, they maintain that the herd is still oversized. Even if that is true, says Stevens, the actual number of bison is irrelevant. "Regardless of if you have twenty-five bison or twenty-five thousand bison, the fact of the matter is that the winter [grazing] range in Yellowstone for bison and other wildlife is very limited," he says. Montana's governor, Brian Schweitzer, has said that such a winter will never be repeated in Yellowstone. He is committed to leasing grazing lands outside the park to allow the bulky, impressive herds to forage successfully in the winter, but that's an expensive proposition. "I'm hopeful that an agreement will be in place by the time winter rolls around again," says Tim Stevens. "But I could be wrong."

Behind closed doors another potential management catastrophe is brewing, says Jeff Ruch, executive director of Public Employees for Environmental Responsibility, a nonprofit that has been closely watching the growing relationship between national parks and the telecommunications industry. In March 2006, his organization got hold of some notes from an unadvertised meeting between Yellowstone officials and a handful of companies that would like to bring more radio, TV, cell phone, and wi-fi access to the park. Ruch says that the meetings, having never been properly disclosed to the public, are illegal. If most Americans knew about the plan, Ruch feels they would be

Norris Geyser Basin, Yellowstone National Park

opposed. "As for the notion that American people want it," says Ruch, "I don't think the American people have been asked. The park service is giving away assets without any consideration or involvement of the public." The documents that Ruch's group acquired suggest that up to ten telecom entities would be able to provide service in the park. Two thirds of Yellowstone already has cell coverage, courtesy of six cell towers, one of which is on Mount Gardiner, a distinctly nonorganic backdrop for Old Faithful (it's no wonder one of the most frequently asked questions in the park is "When do you turn on Old Faithful?"). "Who made that decision? It turns out that nobody did. It's a product of institutional drift, thoughtlessness, and management inertia," says Ruch. Planting a larger technological footprint on Yellowstone will destroy more than a few vistas, says Ruch, who fears that it foreshadows the death of solitude in Yellowstone. "It's a form of commercialization of the park and it transforms what the park is," he says. "Part of the way they're selling the parks is 'come and get away from it all,' but with the other hand they're making it so that you can never get away, so that you can be in the middle of God's country and hear someone ordering a pizza or making a stock transaction."

Proponents of quiet have also tussled for years over the park's policy on snowmobiles. The argument had been curtailed at the end of the Clinton administration when plans were made to phase out the use of snowmobiles in the park. But the concern of local industry and outfitters that might suffer financial losses, and the outrage of those who take to heart that Gardiner arch motto, "For the benefit and enjoyment of the people," swayed the Bush administration to reopen the issue. Snowmobile skeptics worry that the machines are, at the very least, an acoustic nuisance in their tranquil winter park and, at worst, may be harmful to the movements and hearing of park wildlife, staff, and visitors. "We continue to be very concerned about motorized vehicles, specifically snowmobiles," says Bill Knight of the National Park Conservation Association's State of the Parks program. There are two antisnowmobile arguments, Knight says. "One is that they're not conducive to the well-being of the ecosystem," he says. While researchers aren't sure whether or not animal behavior is affected by the sound of snowmobiles, they know that they're impacted by emissions. "[Snowmobiles] are getting a little better with their new technologies, but there are still pollution vectors." The second argument against snow machines is that Americans by and large do not want them in the park. "When you poll Americans in general, and when you poll even the Yellowstone visitor base about those kinds of motorized vehicle activities in national parks," he says, "they dominantly say, 'No, that's not an appropriate use.' Public sentiment is against the use of them." But the industry lobby is persuasive. "The book hasn't been written yet," says Knight. "The final chapter is not yet known."

The sounds of Yellowstone, in all seasons, are still among its many strengths, says Jett Hitt. Having steered Jitterbug, his red roan filly, through thousands of miles of Yellowstone's back-country, Hitt has learned what sounds solitude makes. Away from the buzz and whine of snowmobiles, or of hemi engines towing oversized campers, he's really heard Yellowstone: crackling thunder, howling wolf packs, gurgling mud pots, and hissing geysers. The park still has a wild heart, full of drama and radiance, and it speaks to those who'll lend their ears. While Hitt's been a lot of places, he says, "None has ever spoken as definitively as Yellowstone."

CANADA

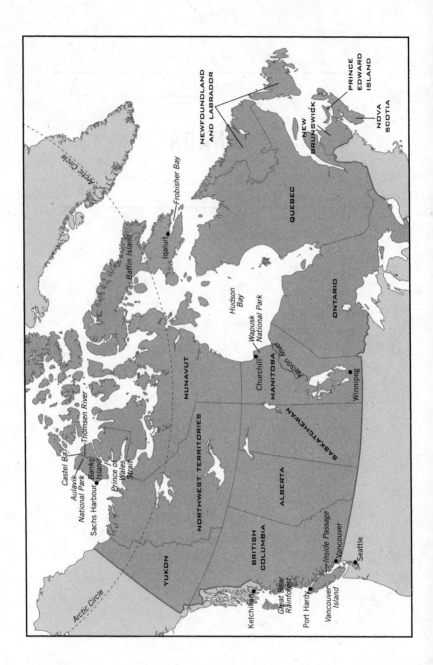

BANKS ISLAND, NORTHWEST TERRITORIES

FOUR HUNDRED MILES ABOVE THE ARCTIC CIRCLE, IN Canada's Northwest Territories, is one of the world's most remote wildlife-viewing destinations. Flying is the only way outsiders get to Banks Island, and it's a bumpy three-hour ride on a Twin Otter from the mainland. But those who have been lucky enough to walk or paddle among its pristine Arctic lowlands know it's worth the haul.

Known to the Inuit as Ikaahuk, or, roughly, "the place where you cross to," Banks Island was first traversed by paleo-Eskimo hunters roughly 3,800 years ago. These first known inhabitants of the Canadian Arctic were followed by other nomads also hunting caribou and musk ox. From 1000 to 1600, the Thule people occupied the island and were focused on harvesting bowhead whales. Archaeologists who have found remnants of dwellings, flint scrapers, and bone harpoon heads theorize that drastic cooling in the seventeenth century forced the Inuit from Banks until conditions improved over a century later. The Inuinnait, descendents of the Thule, returned to the island and were active there throughout the nineteenth century. From the early to mid twentieth century, many people risked crossing the unpredictable Prince of Wales Strait from nearby Victoria Island to Banks seasonally to trap foxes.

One highlight of Banks is Aulavik National Park, on the island's north side. The park, which is about the size of Maine, protects 4,739 square miles (roughly one fifth of the entire island) and is thick with wild critters. Aulavik is also the world's largest polar desert, a distinction that belies the prosperity of its

150 plant species, a remarkable concentration given their harsh home. Creamy mountain avens, pink lousewort, and purple oxytrope burgeon despite occasional gale-force winds, snow, and subfreezing temperatures that can occur even in late July, when dusk never succumbs to darkness.

Although Aulavik means "place where people travel to," fewer than a hundred people per year have visited there since its founding in 1992. While Parks Canada allows guideless exploration of the park, it warns that there's not a single visitor facility there. If they're self-guided, most people charter a plane from Inuvik, 466 miles southwest of the park's southern boundary, and get dropped off somewhere in Aulavik. (They also schedule a pickup time and place.) The other option is to take a guided trip with a licensed outfitter. Currently the only guide service listed on the Parks Canada website is the Alberta-based Whitney & Smith Legendary Expeditions, which does two fifteen-day trips per summer, kayaking ninety easy miles of the Thomsen River, with opportunities for daily hikes to explore the park's geology, flora, animals, and archaeology.

Most people float along the remote, crystalline Thomsen River for at least a little while during their stay on Banks. The river is the most northerly navigable river in North America, and it snakes gradually across the island. From its headwaters on the southeast side of the windswept island, the Thomsen pulses gently for 180 miles north, bisecting the island. Its shorelines sprawl lazily in wide, verdant valleys—twelve thousand square miles of them in all. The sandy banks of the river boast a profusion of wildflowers, like Jacob's ladder and arctic poppy, which absorb twenty-four hours of midsummer daylight, transforming Banks Island into a high-Arctic Garden of Eden. The sandstone and shale shoulders of the river sprawl to oxbow lakes and watery meadows, which rise to rolling hills blanketed with tundra flora. There, among the grasses and sedges, the island's tallest plant, the arctic willow, occasionally grows knee-high.

The Thomsen is a teeming wildlife corridor. Vigilant rafters or canoers paddling down it may see a wolf pack denning, an artic fox skulking, rough-legged hawks and gyrfalcons riding the wind, and brown and collared lemmings scurrying nervously. The endangered Peary caribou, classified as such in 1991 due to a sharp drop in population (two thousand remain), are few but memorable. Their creamy coffee coats turn nearly stark white in the winter to camouflage them from predators.

The most dramatic sight along the Thomsen passageway is the scraggly musk ox. With curved horns like mastodon tusks, it looks almost prehistoric. Unlike the Peary caribou, these shaggy beasts have boomed in the past three to four decades. At most recent count, there were 68,608 adult musk oxen on Banks, the most productive place for them on earth. Now, at an estimated population of 80,000, they are the largest herd in the world. Clumps of compact musk oxen can be seen driving through the cold on Banks, their breath blasting from their broad noses like exhaust from a locomotive. The *oomingmak*, or "bearded one," as they are known to the native Inuit, has a furry muzzle and thick pelt that's engineered with lengthy "guard" hairs and dense underwool to help it withstand the brutal Arctic winters.

Remnants of the last ice age are evident in most of Aulavik—drumlins, eskers, and terminal moraines are scattered across the terrain. But in the extreme northwest corner of the park these features are conspicuously absent, evidence that the glaciers stopped advancing in this stark, humble margin of North America. Everywhere in the park, 350-million-year-old rock formations whisper of Banks Island's former life as a marine reef off the coast of an ancient seashore. The area east of Thomsen River is rich with fossilized snails (gastropods), shells (brachiopods), and corals. Mounds of petrified wood are also scattered across the island, reminders of the pine, spruce, and juniper forests that blanketed Banks in warmer days forty million years ago.

Nowadays smaller rivers and tributaries spider across the landscape like delicate, glistening webs. In addition to the mighty mammals that drink from it, the Thomsen watershed itself hosts six freshwater species, including the nine-spine stickleback and four-horn sculpin. Among the birds, only ptarmigan and ravens are year-round residents of Aulavik, but it's a birders' nirvana. At least forty-three bird species visit each year, thirty-two of which are known to breed there, including yellow-billed loons, black-bellied plovers, and, on the lush north shore, lesser snow geese and sandhill cranes. That north end of Banks is where the Thomsen finally empties into Castel Bay, which cuts nine miles inland. There frigid water frequented by polar bears, ringed seals, bearded seals, beluga whales, bowhead whales, laps at the base of abrupt thousand-foot cliffs.

But the gentle, perpetual flow of the Thomsen could cease as higher winter temperatures decrease the snowpack that feeds Arctic lakes and streams. And the species that carefully congregate along the lengthy river—from phlox to fox to falcon—are so specifically adapted to their current climate that they too could disappear along with the water. Permafrost, the thick layer of permanently frozen ground that underlies all of Banks Island, is also now melting. This may, for a short time, maintain the volume of the Thomsen by offsetting a decline in the snowpack. But it also tranforms the landscape into numerous bogs and unstable hummocks, making travel across the tundra nearly impossible for two- and four-legged creatures alike.

In the past century the western Arctic has gotten at least 1 degree Fahrenheit warmer—a negligible increase, on the face of it. But most of that warming occurred in the last twenty years, and that rate of warming promises to intensify. For each degree's increase in air temperature, species are expected to be forced to migrate an average of ninety-three miles northward. This will cause major disruption, driving musk oxen and caribou farther north over the cliffs of Castel Bay, possibly to extinction.

Those with an ancestral memory of this land have already seen significant changes, and in some cases, downright bizarre ones. For instance, robins, barn swallows, and salmon have recently taken up residence on Banks Island. This left the native Inuvialuit literally speechless, because in Inuvialuktun, there simply is no word for "robin." The bird was referred to descriptively as the "bird with the red breast."

As part of their Inuit Knowledge Project, Parks Canada is using traditional knowledge to augment scientific studies of climate change in the Arctic. "What we hear through the aboriginal communities is about all of the other effects, like bird species turning up that haven't been seen before in the Arctic and new plants expanding northward of their range," says David Welch, head of environmental quality for Parks Canada. "They are the eyes and ears to tell us about new things that are happening before scientists can get in there and study it."

How the past climate contrasts with current observations is well-known to the 119 Inuvialuit who inhabit Sachs Harbour, the only community on Banks Island. The quiet town, surrounded by dramatic cliffs topped with snow-covered plateaus, is nestled in an arc on the waterfront facing south into the Amundsen Gulf in the southwest corner of the island, 125 miles below the headwaters of the Thomsen River. It is the most northerly community in Canada's Northwest Territories. The Inuvialuit here sustain themselves traditionally by hunting, fishing, and trapping. Historically, they have survived by navigating harsh but somewhat predictable conditions with Inuit *Qaujimajatuqangit,* or "that which is long known by Inuit," passed on generationally. Because they depend on their environment for survival, they are acutely aware of changes in it. Sharing their Qaujimajatuqangit with outsiders has cast a light on how the lives and landscape of the Inuvialuit are being gravely unsettled by climate change.

Sachs Harbour residents testify to their crises in *Sila Alango-*

tok ("Inuit Observations on Climate Change") a documentary made in 2000 with the help of the Winnipeg-based International Institute for Sustainable Development. Rosemarie Kuptana, who was born on the frozen Prince of Wales Strait while her parents were seal hunting, says that survival for her people has always meant adapting to and enduring extreme conditions. But warming has unleashed disorder and confusion. "What's scary is that there's uncertainty because we don't know when to travel on the ice," she says in the film. "Our food sources are getting farther and farther away. We can't read the weather like we used to. It's changing our way of life."

Ice is integral to the Inuvialuit lifestyle. Nowadays Ski-Doos, the snow machines that are the main mode of transportation over land and frozen ice, can still be seen zipping around Sachs Harbour, often pulling wooden box sleds filled with kids, their heads bobbing up and down. But taking their Ski-Doos out onto ice to hunt, as their ancestors used dogsleds in generations prior, is now too risky for even the most experienced hunters. What used to be solid ice sheets are now cracking, and great gaps are yawning in between. The winds are also stronger, changing water currents and stranding hunters on breakaway ice floes. In years past, ice floes withstood summer warming, allowing seals to birth and nurse their pups there and providing a steady food supply for the Inuvialuit, who hunt the adult seals. But no longer.

River ice is now breaking up much earlier than expected, often stranding hunters. When the rivers melt they become raging torrents, making them impossible to cross. This change has denied the Inuvialuit the joyful tradition of resettling in spring hunting camps, where they visit neighbors and tell stories. "It affects your soul, as a people," says Kuptana. Travel is further impeded by land that is listing and slumping from warming. As permafrost across the island melts, it's undermining the foundations of structures in Sachs Harbour. Resident John Keogak, who has been tracking the changes in permafrost along the coast for nearly twenty years, worries that warming will ultimately drive away his people. "It doesn't look good. I think we'll have to evacuate the community and we'll have to move somewhere else," he says.

Climatologists expect annual precipitation to increase 25 percent on Banks Island over the next several decades. Residents have already experienced more rain and thunderstorms, which had never before appeared this far north. The Inuvialuit report that wildlife is stressed and spooked by the thunderstorms, that musk oxen will dart one way and then another when storms rumble overhead. "It's now impossible to tell when the seasons will change and what they will bring," says Kuptana. More rain on Banks will also disrupt the delicate dynamics of the polar desert in Aulavik National Park as it transforms into boggy peatlands. And more freezing rain in the winter is bad news for foragers like musk oxen and caribou, which will be unable to break the ice layer covering lichens, grasses, and sedges that they rely on for survival.

"There will be enormous hydrological changes in areas currently dominated by snowfall, and minimal evaporation, or runoff, during winter months," says Parks Canada's David Welch. Shorter winter spans, flanked by lengthening periods of warmth, will eventually lessen, and perhaps completely eliminate, the snowpack that feeds the Thomsen River. "Runoff will shift from spring peaks to a more even year-round flow so that less water will be available during summer irrigation and navigation seasons," says Welch.

Without the strong, steady Thomsen or rich, enduring culture of the Inuit, Banks Island will be a very different place. From the cliffs of Sachs Harbour today, the sun is eyed cautiously by the Inuvialuit as it settles on the horizon in bands of gold atop orange. In time they'll know if their fate will resemble that of the other cultures, like the ones that hastily left behind hearths and tent rings here thousands of years ago, when climate change drove them from this rugged but delicate island.

HUDSON BAY, MANITOBA AND NUNAVUT

Hudson Bay, Canada

IT MAY BE THE LEAST GLAMOROUS VACATION CONCEIV-able: sixteen-hour days draped in mosquito netting, plodding through Canada's subarctic peatlands in the name of science. But that doesn't deter the Earthwatch Institute's volunteers, who flock to Churchill, Manitoba, like its two hundred species of migratory birds. Some even trek from tropical latitudes to work with Peter Kershaw, a biogeographer from the University of Alberta, who spends several weeks a year working out of the Churchill Northern Studies Center, monitoring the area's immense stores of greenhouse gases, which are housed in its peatlands. "They come from all over the world—people from Brazil who have never seen snow before. I even had someone from Botswana once," says Kershaw. "There are people who would look on it as absolute drudgery. I look on it as, hey, it's minus thirty-five today, it's warmer by five degrees than yesterday."

As harsh as some moments may be—spectacular swarms of

mosquitoes and flesh-hungry deer flies, roaming polar bears, and temperatures of minus 40 degrees—others are the stuff of Arctic imagination: energetic pods of beluga whales, mother polar bears lumbering across the tundra with cubs in pursuit, or the aurora borealis and its luminous, ethereal curtains of color drawn surreally across the night sky.

Kershaw's team converges just south of the coastal community of Churchill, enduring cruel conditions in order to take the pulse of this rapidly changing Arctic ecosystem. The area is a maze of bogs, ice wedges, and frozen peat. "That whole region is the largest peatland in North America," he says. "It's massive." Scientists like Kershaw are focusing on peat melt because when that wet organic material warms and then rots it releases methane and carbon dixide, both powerful greenhouse gases. Determining how quickly the area's permafrost—the layer of permanently frozen ground that can be as deep as fifty meters near Churchill—is thawing and at what rate the peat will decay is so important to Kershaw that he's willing to suffer through frost "nips" on his nose and chin just to collect the most recent data.

Churchill lies atop tundra on the northern border of the boreal forest, at the geographical center of North America and along the west coast of Hudson Bay. Around its entire perimeter, the bay is revealing changes that have been brought on by the rise in global temperature over the past century. That grave shift in conditions includes pack ice freezing later and melting earlier than usual, and dissolving permafrost that makes travel unpredictable and dangerous. These changes are outpacing the ability of many of Hudson Bay's otherwise expertly adapted residents—including indigenous Canadians (Inuit, Cree, and Déné) and this planet's largest land carnivore, the polar bear—to live off the land.

Hudson Bay owes its existence to the climate change that

occurred during the last Ice Age. Its basin was formed as the weight of an ice sheet pressed downward. When that ice receded and melted, the basin filled with water. The smooth, shallow bottom is still rebounding from the ice sheet's retreat, growing shallower and revealing new shoreline. The "bay" is actually a huge inland sea, 850 miles long and 650 miles wide. It's fed by many rivers, including the torrential Hudson and Nelson, near Churchill. On its northeast edge the bay forces its way through the Hudson Strait and into the Atlantic. Its low salinity and far-below-zero temperatures used to keep it ice-covered from October until June.

But Hudson Bay is now open to shipping an extra week every year, and as early as 2010, there may be regular summer shipping even in the far north. Some scientists predict that the bay will be ice-free year-round by 2050, greatly boosting Arctic shipping from Churchill.

The land where Churchill is located rose from the bay only about eight hundred years ago. The surrounding peatlands are just as young, but despite its youth and forbidding climate, it's rich in human tradition. Four thousand years ago, paleo-Eskimos settled on the coast of Hudson Bay. They were followed by the Dorset Eskimo, the Déné, and about a thousand years ago, the advanced and highly adaptable Thule, ancestors of the Inuit. The bay got its modern name from the explorer Henry Hudson, who traversed it in 1610 in an unsuccessful bid to reach the Northwest Passage. For centuries Churchill was a popular trading post where the area's coveted animal pelts were sent abroad.

Churchill is still known for its skins, but today they remain on the backs of live polar, brown, and black bears; caribou; arctic foxes; and harp seals, which come together in the uniquely mixed environment of tundra, forest, and ice. Its throngs of beluga whales (locally called "sea canaries" because they migrate by the thousands) head to the warm mouth of the Churchill River to feed after the bay's spring ice breakup.

But the town is most famous for its polar bears, which, after waiting out the summer on land, hungrily make their way onto the recently formed pack ice to hunt seals in the fall. More than fifteen thousand visitors converge in Churchill in September and October and crowd onto tall (their tires are over six feet high), NASA-like tundra buggies to hunt the fast, agile bears with their cameras. There isn't a single paved road into town, so all travelers arrive by train or plane. VIA Rail's Hudson Bay train, which huffs and puffs from Winnipeg into Churchill three times a week, takes thirty-six hours and is among the most popular journeys. The town keeps a twenty-four-hour lookout during the polar bear migration; visitors to this barren landscape heed red-and-yellow triangular signs on the edges of town advising "Polar Bear Alert" and "Don't Walk in This Area," and they hear warning shots ringing out in the night. Bears who continue into Churchill unfazed are tranquilized and transported by helicopter out of the vicinity.

Several hundred bears spend their four-month summer fast twenty-eight miles southeast of Churchill in a national park that borders Hudson Bay, aptly named Wapusk, meaning "white bear" in Cree. The park shelters one of the world's largest maternity denning areas for polar bears. Because Wapusk is so wild, remote, and unforgiving, it is visited by fewer than a hundred tourists a year, who generally hire guides authorized, but not required, by Parks Canada. Current plans include improving access to the park and requiring travelers to have approved operators. As of now, Frontiers North is the only company that has a tundra lodge inside the park (it's actually mobile so they can stake out the best sites for observing the bears). Just outside the park's border is Wat'chee Lodge, where indigenous Arctic guides use their expertise to track North America's largest land mammals.

But Wapusk's remoteness can do little to protect its namesake inhabitants from the greatest threat they've ever faced. "Climate change is one of the major factors that could impact the ecological balance in the park," says Cam Elliott, Wapusk's superintendent and a biologist with twenty years' experience at high latitudes. That will occur on a number of fronts, but the most widely known impact at this point, and the best-studied, is the impact on polar bears. Elliott says that recent variability in the freezing of Hudson Bay is causing chaos in the habits and habitat of the bears, which depend on the stability of sea ice. "What we have measured is an advancing time period for the onset of the spring melt, and right now, that melt is about three weeks earlier than it was twenty-five years ago," he says. "This is happening at the same period of time that the polar bears have to fatten up on the ice prior to coming ashore."

Polar bears, icons of the Arctic (a word that comes from an ancient Greek term meaning "land of the great bear"), are now coming off Hudson Bay earlier and therefore much skinnier. They are now about 15 percent thinner than they were thirty years ago, which means male bears have dropped about 150 pounds. Fewer young and old bears are surviving. From 1995 to 2005 the Hudson Bay population shrank 22 percent, from 1,200 to 935 bears. The future portends more of the same for the "great, lonely roamer," called *nanuk* by the Inuit who hunted them and respected them as wise, strong, and second only to humans. "At present our investigations would indicate that change is happening too rapidly for the bears to adapt," says Elliott. "In the short term, nothing can be done. We are powerless to affect change locally; this is a global problem. There's going to be no magic bullet in this. The only way to change this is on a global level, to halt climate change."

That's what Sheila Watt-Cloutier, Inuit activist and 2007 Nobel Peace Prize winner (Al Gore shares the nomination), is working toward. She and her family live northeast of Churchill, on the southern tip of Baffin Island, at the mouth of Frobisher

Bay. Watt-Cloutier, who chaired the Inuit Circumpolar Council from 2002 to 2006, has called attention to the dangers facing the Inuit way of life and their connnection to the fossil-fuel-burning habits of cultures to the south. In 2007, she testified in front of the Inter-American Commission on Human Rights that climate change violates the human rights of indigenous people and that US greenhouse gas emissions, in particular, are to blame. Watt-Cloutier says global climate change threatens every aspect of their culture of cold, which relies on frozen land, pack ice, snow, and the animals that frequent them. "It's really a story about a people. It's really a human story that's happening up here," she says.

The Inuit and Cree of Hudson Bay use their traditional knowledge, passed down from generation to generation, to forecast daily and seasonal weather. They read the snow, ice, wind, sea currents, stars, northern lights, clouds, and animal activity year-round to plan hunts. If a caribou or seal shakes its head, the Inuit expect bad weather will follow. The same is true if migrating snow geese reverse course, don't move at all, or if many flocks gather. Birds high in the sky foretell fair weather.

For generations, nature's signals have also notified indigenous groups in the Arctic of the coming winter. Fall is upon them when caribou scrape the velvet from their antlers and battle for supremacy, and when arctic char migrate upriver. Winter is imminent when belugas and seals move on and walrus move in. Understanding the cold and ice is so crucial to their survival that there are no fewer than two dozen Inuktitut words to describe the condition of ice. *Sikutait* describes ice that is transitioning from thin to landfast and is not yet safe to travel upon. *Uiguak* is smooth and solid, *akgutinik* is slushy, and *tavak* is hard ice that forms the hunters' winter highway.

Looking out the plate-glass window of her home in Iqaluit, the capital of Canada's Nunavut province, Watt-Cloutier can see onto the *tavak* of Frobisher Bay. The fjord was named for English explorer Martin Frobisher, who sailed down the passage in 1576, believing it would lead to Asia. But Frobisher never even made it to Iqaluit. Instead he met the Inuit in the narrow, island-studded inlet. For several days the two traded cautiously until Frobisher employed an Inuit man to guide them through the swirling currents to the western terminus of the fjord. Five of his crew went ashore with the man to retrieve his kayak and were never again seen.

Iqaluit, which lies at the head of the 186-mile-long inlet, can be reached only by air. It's a compact and fascinating mix of trendy and traditional. Of the town's six thousand or so residents, 60 percent are Inuit, but you're as likely to be greeted on the street with "Good morning" as "*Ullaakkut.*" The town is growing rapidly, with more hotels and restaurants popping up each year. Within walking distance of downtown is Sylvia Grinnell Territorial Park, where caribou and arctic fox roam and blueberries flourish. Walk forty-five minutes northwest of the village and you'll find the one-thousand-year-old ruins of a Thule settlement. To the south is the lovely, remote village of Lake Harbour, also called Kimmirut, or "the heel," named for a huge hunk of limestone that resembles the back of a foot. The area is known for its remarkable fifty-foot tides, as well as the walls of ice that form when the waves freeze in winter. Cape Dorset, to the west of Iqaluit, is the famous center of Inuit artisans who work in stone, bone, and ivory.

For Watt-Cloutier, another bright, calm Arctic day has passed. The sun is setting on the red roofs and low, gleaming white buildings of the village. It's January, 4:30 P.M., and the rolling snow-covered hills and distant, abrupt gray peaks and glacial domes reflect what's left of the cool salmon sun. The headlights of Ski-Doos flicker as they bump and weave over the pack ice, announcing the return of the hunters. "When the hunters come home, whether it's in boats in the summer or Ski-Doos at the end of the winter day, I have an immediate connection to my heritage, to the hunter, and I can't help but just smile."

But as the Artic continues to warm—the effects are acute here, where temperatures are rising at twice the rate of the world average—that connection is cracking like spring ice. Throughout the circumpolar north, from Lake El'gygytgyn, in Russia's farthest northeast region, to Greenland, Inuit elders and hunters have spoken of environmental abnormalities. The recently published Arctic Climate Impact Assessment lays out indigenous peoples' observations and the research of more than three hundred scientists from fifteen countries. It concludes that the Arctic is changing, rapidly. It warns that what happens in the Arctic will not stay solely in the Arctic, but is a sign of what's in store for points south.

Watt-Cloutier has a front-row seat to the upheaval in her "terra incognita." In spring 2006, what should have been snow came as rain in Iqaluit. They're accustomed to minus 22 degrees Fahrenheit at that time, but it was 47 degrees, and that is changing everything. In 2007, record winds tore roofs off buildings. "We don't worry just about the future; we worry about every day now," she says. Three years ago an experienced Iqaluit hunter fell through the ice and had to have his legs amputated. "He couldn't see or read the condition of the ice since it's much thinner and open in areas that never used to be," says Watt-Cloutier. With accidents becoming more frequent, hunters are left second-guessing themselves. "What has been here for millennia, in terms of traditional knowledge, is being weakened as a result of these changes," she says. The historical know-how that's passed on from generation to generation is given a climate-change disclaimer. "They say, 'But it may not be that way today,' " says Watt-Cloutier.

She also attributes the growing number of suicides among

young Inuit to the confusion and despair brought on by climate change. "The tumultuous change has contributed to the social and community upheaval," she says. "We struggle enormously at the spirit level, trying to address these issues of what to do in terms of community and family and so on."

Watt-Cloutier fights for all of the north's 155,000 Inuit, but mostly she toils for her eight-year-old grandson, because hunting is not just about nutritious "country" food and warm clothes but about character and maturity. "He has a young father who himself is a survivor, hunting as much as he can," she says. "He's teaching his little boy the skills that are required to survive, not just the technical skills of aiming the gun and skinning the seal and cutting up the meat, but patience and courage and being bold under pressure, how to withstand stress and how not to be impulsive." As Watt-Cloutier looks beyond her living room window, across the frozen bay and into the future, her hope rests on the wings of the ptarmigan fluttering over the tundra. "I have a partnership with this view. I say, 'You protect me, hold me, and I will protect you,'" she says. "This view in front of me is so beautiful, majestic, and powerful, you can palpably feel it."

For his part, Peter Kershaw will return next year to Churchill, to check up on the inimitable Arctic. After a day of traveling in sleds to collect data, he and his volunteers spend the night beneath a sky surging with colorful waves of the aurora borealis. Each will build a *quinzhee*, a kind of snow cave, or an igloo out on the open tundra and sleep snuggly as the winds howl and the temperature drops to around minus 30 degrees Celsius. Not far from there polar bears roam whatever pack ice Hudson Bay has to offer and hover near the breathing holes of ringed seals for their next meal, as they've done for thousands of years.

INSIDE PASSAGE, BRITISH COLUMBIA

Inside Passage

THERE'S A SECRET SPOT, HUNDREDS OF MILES FROM ANY major port, where Bill Bailey likes to anchor his historic wooden ship in a jade-green lagoon at the edge of a white sand beach. It's a quiet place where the hoary-bearded sea captain and his dozen or so passengers can shake out their sea legs en route from Washington to Alaska, a thousand-mile journey amid the wild islands and narrow channels of Canada's Inside Passage. Bailey seldom encounters other humans on this beach, but it is hardly devoid of life. "The last time we were there we could hear a wolf howling in the distance," he says. "And as we came in and anchored, there were wolf tracks on the beach. You could hear him off in the forest, calling."

Travelers choose small ships like Bailey's *M/V Catalyst* because they stop at places like this. Unlike the enormous cruise liners that blast through the passage in a day and a half in their rush to reach bustling Ketchikan, Bailey's seventy-five-year-old former research vessel meanders along the lush British Columbia coastline for ten days, exploring weather holes where fishermen have sought shelter from winter storms, retracing the routes of early Russian and Spanish explorers, and allowing its passengers to disembark for a spontaneous kayak trip up a sedge-lined river or a hike through a cedar-and-spruce forest to a First Nations village. "We very seldom share the same waterways as the cruise ships do. They can't maneuver well enough to handle some of the really narrow places we go," Bailey says. "We get off the beaten track as much as possible and wander through the inland fjords, or we'll go out to some of the open-ocean barrier islands and hang out there for a day. Our goal on our trips is not to be where there's another boat."

Indeed, *Catalyst* travelers rarely see the larger vessels that pass them in the night, navigating the deeper waters of the inland sea that separates Vancouver Island from the mainland. But every year, cruise ships transport more than a million passengers from Seattle or Vancouver to the Alaskan ports, where they spend hundreds of millions of dollars shopping, eating, and touring. "That's one of the ironies of the cruise ship business," Bailey says. "They'll travel at night to make sure they're in a port where they can sell you a diamond tennis bracelet the next day." In doing so, they bypass some of the most scenic stretches of Canada's west coast, where brown bears hunt for salmon in the river mouths, sea otters splash around in glassy coves, and fog-tipped evergreens climb the hillsides to distant, snow-topped peaks.

Travelers aboard the smaller ships consider it a blessing that British Columbia's Inside Passage has been spared the crowded port towns and daytime cruise ship traffic that plague coastlines farther north. Environmentalists would too, if not for one problem: they have reason to suspect those stealthy passersby of leaving behind one hell of a toxic mess.

Cruise ships generate a tremendous amount of waste. In a typical weeklong journey, a single ship's toilets swallow about 210,000 gallons of sewage, according to the US Bureau of Transportation Statistics. That's nothing compared to the amount of gray water sent swirling down sink and shower drains and washing machine hoses—more than a million gallons, all of it tainted with soaps and solvents and other nefarious substances. Solid waste like paper, plastic, and empty bottles and cans adds up to about eight tons. Then there are the miscellaneous hazmats: a hundred and ten gallons of photo shop chemicals; five gallons of dry-cleaning perchloroethylene; ten gallons of used paint; and a smattering of discarded lightbulbs, batteries, and other noxious trash. Last but not least, a substance that begs for a euphemism: the petroleum-tinged liquid called "oily bilge water," about twenty-five thousand gallons of which collects at the base of the boat.

The rules governing how cruise ships dispose of their waste vary from country to country and state to state, but all of them are somewhat stomach turning. Alaska's are some of the most stringent in the world (even treated sewage must be contained until the ship is 1.15 miles from shore and traveling at a speed of at least six knots); Canada's pale in comparison. Enforcement of those laws also varies. Alaska requires the cruise industry to pay for regular testing of its treated waste. Canada has voluntary guidelines, but there is no legal incentive to comply.

"There is no monitoring of ships in BC's Inside Passage, so we really don't know the depth of the environmental threat," says Dr. Ross Klein, a sociologist at Memorial University of Newfoundland. In a report he produced for the Canadian Centre for Policy Alternatives in 2005, Klein examined the differences between cruise ship laws in Canada and the United States and the problems that result. "This creates a curious situation," he wrote. "Ships visiting Alaska and using Seattle as a homeport are held to lower standards in Canada than in either state. They can discharge in Canada's waters what they are not allowed to discharge elsewhere." The result, he wrote, is that British Columbia's coast is poised to become "the toilet of the Pacific Northwest."

The Inside Passage is home to a menagerie of underwater wildlife. Giant Pacific octopi sweep their sixteen-foot-long arms across the ocean floor, suctioning scallops and clams as they go. Humpback whales hoist their heavy bodies above the water, crashing down with a thunderous splash. Pods of orcas blow plumes of water into the air as they cruise along the shores to forage for salmon. Sea lions and harbor seals poke their glossy heads above the surface of the waters, while several thousand invertebrate species dwell below.

Though the impact of water pollution on the resident critters isn't always visible right away, repeated discharges degrade their habitat over time. High coliform bacteria levels cause excess algae growth, which smothers the marine plants that release

Inside Passage

oxygen into the water. Low oxygen levels cause widespread fish kills, reducing the supply for animals higher up the food chain. Pollutants also make shellfish inedible. And plastic trash that ends up in the water can kill the birds and marine mammals that swallow it or get tangled in it.

Because of the lack of enforcement, it is impossible to measure the amount of waste that cruise ships deposit along Canada's beautiful coastline. But some of the documented incidents in Alaska and Washington are harrowing. In August 2002, a Holland America ship discharged an estimated forty thousand gallons of sewage sludge into the Juneau harbor; the cruise line blamed the violation on "human error" and was fined $2 million in December 2004. In May 2003, a Norwegian Cruise Line ship dumped sixteen thousand gallons of raw sewage into Washington's Strait of Juan de Fuca; the case is still in court, pending a decision on the cruise line's argument that the state officials who cited them did not have jurisdiction to do so. One of the most notorious cruise ship pollution tales included multiple oil discharges by Royal Caribbean Cruises throughout the 1990s. In 1999 the cruise line was fined $18 million and placed on a five-year probation for routinely discharging oily bilge water and contaminated gray water, and for lying to Coast Guard officials about its practices. Nine Royal Caribbean ships were involved in the case.

Since then, the company has undergone a significant image overhaul. Its website now has a multipage environmental section that outlines its green philosophy and lists its eco-recognitions and outreach programs. "Clean oceans are good for the environment, good for our guests and good for our business," writes Royal Caribbean CEO Richard Fain. "We take our responsibility to the environment very seriously, and we feel it's inextricably linked with our continued success as an industry-leading cruise line." Each Royal Caribbean ship now has a full-time environmental officer whose job is to oversee waste management practices and to train crew members to comply. And all of its official policies and procedures now meet or exceed international standards. The most recent improvement is the addition of a cleaning system called CleanSea on several of its ships, at a cost of 9.2 million Canadian dollars. "Royal Caribbean decided, with the negative PR they were having, they would become the leader in the cruising industry in adopting state-of-the-art wastewater treatment," says Brodie Guy, waste management systems marketing manager at Hydroxyl Systems, the Canadian company that developed CleanSea. "Alaska state has the toughest standards in the world, so far as what kind of contaminant levels you're allowed to discharge, and Royal Caribbean is committed to beating them by fifty percent."

Others doubt that the cruise line's recent actions represent a true mentality shift. "If RCCL had made this announcement four or five years ago, when they first talked about and made commitments to retrofitting their ships, then I'd say that it is a positive sign," Klein says. He suspects the changes were motivated by appearance, politics, and the anticipation of future regulations that might require better treatment systems anyway.

Regardless, the new technology is a vast improvement over the industry standard. All cruise ships have some sort of waste treatment system, but few have been proven effective. Many of the older ships simply treat their sewage and gray water with large quantities of chlorine before flushing the waste out to sea. "That might solve one problem, but it creates another problem," Guy says. "It's going to kill everything that comes in contact with the water that's discharged." On ships with CleanSea, waste goes through a multistep process that includes pH balancing, treatment with pollution-eating bacteria, and ultraviolet irradiation. Similar systems are used on ten of British Columbia's ferries and at industrial facilities throughout the United States.

One of the smaller businesses to implement a sewage treatment system produced by Hydroxyl is Nimmo Bay Resort, a high-end wilderness lodge in a secluded BC bay just across the Passage from Port Hardy. All along the Great Bear Rainforest coastline, tall, straight stands of Sitka spruce and stately red cedars grow thick on the islands and inlets, and red alders form bright green leafy trails that trace the paths of rivers and streams. Grizzlies feast on sedge grass and berries until the salmon come in. Elusive wolves creep stealthily through the woods in search of prey. Harbor seals sun themselves on floating logs, and mohawked female mergansers carry babies on their backs as they glide across the gleaming bays.

At Nimmo Bay, the well-heeled guests arrive by helicopter, swooping down on the evergreen-fringed cottages that serve as their base for chopper-assisted fly-fishing, rafting, hiking, and kayaking excursions in the surrounding wilderness. Every detail here is given careful consideration—from the delicate Riedel wine glasses to the iPods in the choppers—and the resort's environmental program is no exception. The buildings were constructed on floats so as not to harm the surrounding forest; an on-site waterfall with a high-impulse turbine supplies most of the property's energy needs; and the treatment of sewage and gray water is so thorough that the effluent is actually drinkable. "All that waste is going back into the environment bacteria-free," says owner Craig Murray, who has been known to take inquiring guests on what he calls the "poo tour," a behind-the-scenes look at the lodge's state-of-the-art waste treatment system. The lodge's clients invariably support such measures and sometimes even insist on them. "People want to feel as if they're not contributing to the degradation of the environment when they go to enjoy themselves."

Nimmo Bay's procedures far exceed the Canadian standards—like cruise ships, wilderness lodges are rarely held accountable for their environmental indiscretions. But Murray hopes that will change. "If you're in a sensitive environment, then it's up to you and the people you deal with to maintain that," he says. "Out there in the wilderness they just don't do that. At what point in time do the oceans need some assistance? When do we stop this?"

As the cruise ship industry grows, so do concerns about its impact on sensitive environments like the Inside Passage. Between 1996 and 2006, the number of North American cruise passengers doubled, from five million to ten million, and the number of boats increased accordingly. Ship size has increased, too—during that same decade, the capacity of the largest ships went from 1,800 passengers to 3,600. Thirty-two new cruise vessels are expected to hit the water by 2010; the largest of them will hold 5,400 travelers.

In the United States, legislators and private citizens are taking steps to increase cruise industry accountability and decrease ecosystem damage. Alaska voters passed a cruise ship initiative in August 2006 that imposes a $50-per-passenger tax, part of which will fund environmental monitoring. In Washington, DC, the Clean Cruise Ship Act, which would close federal loopholes that allow for legal dumping, is slowly making its way through Congress. And in the Pacific Northwest, small-ship operators such as Bill Bailey are working to minimize their own impact. The *M/V Catalyst* separates its recyclables to deposit in each port and will soon start experimenting with biodiesel fuel. Another small-ship company, AdventureSmith, has implemented a carbon-offset program that balances its fuel emissions with investments in renewable energy projects. Because these cruisers have a more intimate relationship with the pristine fjords and inlets that make the Inside Passage a destination worth exploring, they're determined to help it stay that way.

THE CARIBBEAN

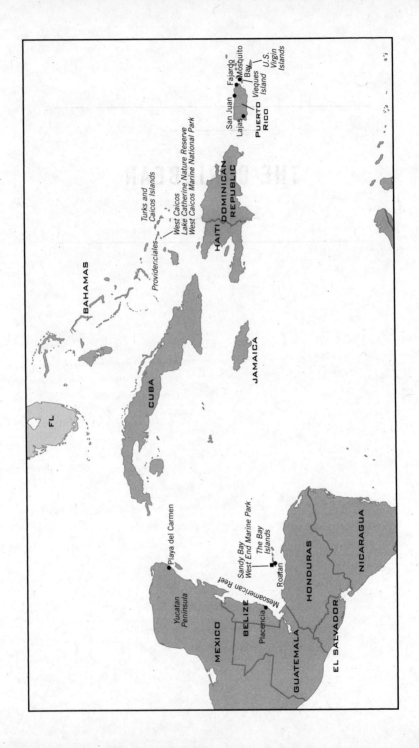

BIOLUMINESCENT BAYS, PUERTO RICO

Vieques, Puerto Rico

ON A NEARLY MOONLESS CARIBBEAN NIGHT, A SILENT
procession of kayakers traces the southern coastline of Puerto
Rico's Vieques Island. As they dip and pull their paddles through
a mangrove-lined inlet, gliding into Mosquito Bay, each stroke
cuts an invisible line through the water until the paddlers register an almost imperceptible change: faint bluish-green sparkles
of light begin to emerge in their wake. As the group moves
deeper into the bay, the glow grows stronger, and every splash
leaves a luminous trail. Fish dart below like tiny rockets streak-
ing across a starry sky, and one by one the kayakers slip out of
their boats to float on their backs in the warm water. They make
glow-angels with their arms and legs, giggling like kids who've
just discovered snow.

Mosquito Bay's remarkable ability to turn swimmers into

human light sticks can be attributed to billions of bioluminescent organisms called dinoflagellates, delicate single-celled creatures that light up when they're agitated into action by a moving object. The concentration of "dinos" in Mosquito Bay is extremely high—a single gallon of bay water contains more of them than San Juan, Puerto Rico, has residents. Paddling a kayak or taking a nighttime swim here is . . . well, enlightening.

Though pockets of bioluminescence occur in oceans all over the world, there are very few biobays where the glow is localized and consistent. Puerto Rico is home to three of them. The brightest are Mosquito Bay and Laguna Grande, on Puerto Rico's east coast. But that wasn't always the case. Fifty years ago, a third bay called La Parguera outshone them both. Its demise is now a cautionary tale.

La Parguera is a quiet bay on the southwest coast of Puerto Rico, just south of Lajas. In a *National Geographic* article published in July 1960, Dr. Paul Zaul documented his visit to the bay, during which his fellow researchers dumped twenty buckets of La Parguera water over his head, then turned out the lights. Photographs show the crown of his head, his shoulders, and his chest glowing in the dark. The scientists were downright giddy.

As word of the so-called Phosphorescent Bay spread, beach homes and houseboats cropped up all along the coast, and entrepreneurs began launching boat tours. The trips were not regulated, and their numbers quickly soared; soon no visit to Lajas was complete without a La Parguera cruise. Hour-long tours remain a nightly event, even though the show isn't nearly what it used to be.

A study conducted in 1997 showed an 80 percent decrease in bioluminescence at La Parguera. Later reports by researchers at the University of Puerto Rico's Mayagüez campus identified the primary culprit: sedimentation, caused in part by traffic from tourist vessels and houseboats. Dinoflagellates, which are considered animals because they have the ability to move around, use chlorophyll to photosynthesize daylight, which means they're part plant. When boats enter the bay, they stir up sediment, reducing the amount of light that reaches the organisms and thereby curbing the photosynthesis the dinos need in order to thrive. "These systems are very fragile," says Michael Latz, a bioluminescence expert at the Scripps Institute of Oceanography, "so if you upset the ecological balance then you could easily change these bays and affect the amount of bioluminescence that is there." The once-brilliant La Parguera could go completely dark within the next few years.

If boat traffic was the only source of sedimentation, protecting the other biobays would be a simple regulatory matter. But coastal development—a force that's not so easily suppressed—is also to blame. Since the mid-1980s, construction has become one of Puerto Rico's fastest-growing industries, with beachfront development leading the way.

That's the main concern for those who worry about the future of Mosquito Bay. Until recently, the island of Vieques, six miles off Puerto Rico's east coast, was all but unknown to Caribbean tourists. The US Navy built a training facility there during World War II and kept two thirds of the twenty-one-mile-long island off-limits to civilians for sixty years. The remaining third—where sugary beaches populated with wild horses fill the space between the two sleepy towns—did not appeal to typical beach vacationers, who were put off by the ubiquitous razor-wire fencing and occasional shelling (including a 1999 bombing run that accidentally killed a local security guard).

That changed on May 1, 2003, when the military, under pressure from an increasingly irate civilian population, packed up its duffels and left. Sure, a few unexploded munitions and a fair amount of martial garbage stayed behind, but most of the razor wire came down, the land was designated a public nature reserve, and a large-scale environmental cleanup began.

Vieques, the poorest of Puerto Rico's seventy-eight municipalities, suddenly became a hot travel destination. The former base comprised about eight thousand acres of waterfront land—now open to the public, though not to developers—and the boot prints of the departing troops had not yet faded when the tourism planners swooped in. The main town of Isabel Segunda demolished its central plaza to update its power and telephone infrastructure in anticipation of the coming boom. W Hotels acquired Vieques's only large resort, on the island's Atlantic side, and gave it a complete overhaul; the resulting luxury retreat and spa opened in December 2006, its swanky villas and bungalows booked far in advance. And plans are afoot to build a fifty-cabin, eighty-nine-campsite Parques Nacionales vacation complex at Sun Bay Beach, the pristine, white-sand launch point for trips to Mosquito Bay.

Amid all the excitement about the burgeoning tourist economy, concerns about its environmental impact have gone largely unacknowledged. "There is so much construction going on in Vieques and no protection," says Elena Humphreys, a longtime resident who leads nature-based tours on the island. "The watershed of the biobay is constantly undergoing bulldozing and deforesting, which causes tremendous runoff of sediment into the bay."

A recent study by a geologist and a marine biologist at the University of Puerto Rico found that Mosquito Bay has about one fifth the boat traffic of La Parguera and significantly less sediment. The researchers established baseline sediment levels in order to measure their progress over time, and they plan to conduct studies that will more precisely detail the link between runoff and the fading bioluminescence. "We are very concerned because of the possible development that could reach Vieques,"

Vieques

says the study's coauthor, Fernando Gilbes, adding that construction is just one of many potential threats to a biobay ecosystem, including agricultural runoff and light pollution. "The simple equation is, more human activity equals less bioluminescence."

Even under the best of circumstances, population growth can take a toll on the biobays. Laguna Grande lies inside the 316-acre Las Cabezas de San Juan Nature Reserve near Fajardo. Lush tropical rain forest surrounds the cove, and raised boardwalks help keep hikers from disturbing the resident flora. Docents lead walks on a closely watched network of trails where staff scientists study the endangered wildlife of the reserve's seven distinct ecosystems. There is a bioluminescence exhibit at the visitor center, half an hour's hike from the real thing, where dinoflagellates are kept in a dark room for daytime visitors to see. Licensed kayak outfitters have access to the bay; motorboats do not. Development within the reserve is strictly prohibited.

Elsewhere on the main island, however, city lights blaze throughout the night, illuminating the sky for miles around. Spotting bioluminescence on a bright night is like watching a movie with the lights on. But light pollution is more than an aesthetic inconvenience; it can actually disable the mechanism that makes dinoflagellates glow. "Conserving the terrain around these bays is not enough," says Olga Casellas of the Puerto Rico Conservation Trust, the nonprofit group that oversees the reserve. "The light-pollution issue is something we're trying to bring up to the public debate."

On Vieques, light pollution has not yet become a problem. This is one of the few Caribbean isles without high-rise hotels and shopping malls, and street lamps are rare. Since most of the roads are unpaved and often waterlogged, traveling to Vieques's much-lauded beaches requires four-wheel drive and a sense of adventure. Despite the pressure to build the island into a more mainstream (and lucrative) tourism product, for now it remains an unpolished destination for intrepid travelers.

Getting there is easy, a twenty-minute flight from San Juan or a seventy-minute ferry ride from Fajardo to Isabel Segunda. Most accommodations are small and funky, like the Hix Island House, a thirteen-room eco-retreat with solar power, alfresco showers, a yoga pavilion, and Egyptian-cotton nightshirts in lieu of the standard hotel terry robes. After renting the appropriate wheels, you can drive to the island's former Navy beaches, which have retained their uninspired military names: Green Beach, Red Beach, and Blue Beach. The bumpy trip to Green Beach (also known by its Spanish name, Punta Arenas, which translates to "Sandy Point") takes you across the island's tropical middle, past a smattering of roadside homes where dogs seem to be in a perpetual state of napping on porches. The beach itself, a prime snorkeling spot with views of the main island, is also conducive to snoozing. The Red and Blue beaches are easier to access and therefore slightly more populated, but you'd be hard pressed to find anything resembling a crowd at them.

You can reach Mosquito Bay by kayak or electric pontoon boat. Either way, it's best seen on new-moon nights, when there's less competing light from the sky. Without exception, the Mosquito Bay guides are well informed on the unusual conditions that make the water glow. They'll tell you about the local dinos, *Pyrodinium bahamense*, and the protective ring of mangroves that desalinates the seawater and tempers the flushing surges of the sea. The more passionate among them may share their concerns for the future of the biobay and oceans in general.

Elena Humphreys argues that the biobays are threatened not only by local development and agriculture, but by the demise of ocean ecosystems worldwide. In September 2005, the Caribbean suffered a major coral bleaching—an unhealthy whitening of the colonies caused by a prolonged increase in water temperature—that could have a lasting effect on the biological composition of the region. "Recent Canadian studies have shown that over ninety percent of the fish have disappeared from the oceans of the world since the 1950s," she says. "Will this cause the destruction of all the habitats in the ocean? The ecological interactions of all ecosystems in the ocean are so interdependent—how could it not eventually cause the biobay to die, too?"

As more outsiders become aware of Vieques, conservationists hope the increased attention will inspire the public to help preserve Mosquito Bay. The Vieques Conservation and Historical Trust, which runs the island's historical museum, campaigns on the biobay's behalf and initiates outreach programs for residents and visitors. And locals like Humphreys preach the gospel of ocean protection to any traveler who will listen. In the meantime, Mosquito Bay is doing plenty of lobbying on its own, converting every awestruck swimmer into a lifelong devotee.

ROATÁN, HONDURAS

Bear's Den, Roatán

HUNDREDS OF FEET BENEATH THE CARIBBEAN'S AQUA-marine surface, Karl Stanley's yellow submarine beams its spotlight on some psychedelic tube sponges gripping the sea wall. Overhead, sunbeams refracted by the water backlight a school of tropical fish. Down below, blackness extends to the mysterious deep sea floor. Few humans can say they've seen the sea like this before.

For most of his life, Stanley has been an ocean explorer, but his passion runs deeper than most people's—literally. The thirty-two-year-old started building his first submarine in his parents' garage when he was just fifteen. The still-seaworthy *C-BUG* ("Controlled by Buoyancy Underwater Glider") now dangles at the end of a quiet dock alongside his second sub, *Idabel*, a bulbous hunk of plexiglass and high-strength steel he pieced together in an Oklahoma airplane hangar. *Idabel* allows him to explore depths below two thousand feet.

On the crescent-shaped island of Roatán, twenty-two miles off the northern coast of Honduras in the Bay Islands chain, Stanley operates a submarine tourism business that gives visitors a rare perspective on Caribbean marine life. For $600 he'll take two passengers down a thousand feet, where sea lilies and pom-pom anemones emerge from the dimly lit crevices. For $1,000 he'll dive to two thousand feet, a pitch-black depth where some of the resident species predate dinosaurs.

Roatán lies at the southern end of the Mesoamerican Reef, the world's second-largest barrier reef (Australia's Great Barrier Reef is the largest), which runs south from Mexico's Yucatán peninsula for nearly seven hundred miles. Its sixty-plus types of corals and sponges sustain some five hundred species of fish. Amid the reef's calcified wrinkles, rainbow parrot fish nibble on coral polyps and queen conchs release hundreds of thousands of eggs in pearly strands up to seventy-five feet long. Spiny lobsters forage in the sea grass beds, their periscope-like eyes scanning for predators. Towering over them all are enormous whale sharks, lethargic, krill-slurping monsters that can weigh as much as a dump truck and dwarf a scuba diver by a good thirty-five feet in length.

Like much of the Mesoamerican Reef system, Roatán's underwater scenery has undergone some major changes in the decade or so since Stanley's first Honduran plunge. "I've definitely noticed a decrease in the number of hammerhead and bull sharks in the two-hundred- to five-hundred-foot range. I used to see a couple a month and now I see a couple a year." Other marine creature populations seem to be dwindling, too. "People comment all the time about how they thought they'd see more big fish on my trips," he says. "I used to see more."

The declines are not just anecdotal. Between 2002 and 2004, the British nonprofit group Coral Cay Conservation sent volunteer survey teams on six hundred dives along a fourteen-mile stretch of Roatán's shoreline. They explored the reefs between three and ninety feet of depth, counting coral, fish, and shellfish species in order to gauge the ecosystem's overall health. What they found was an alarmingly low number of so-called "indicator species." The Nassau grouper, which once ranked among the Caribbean's most common groupers, was all but gone. The same was true for snapper, lobster, and conch, which have been fished into oblivion. The antler-shaped staghorn and elkhorn corals, which have vanished elsewhere in the Caribbean, still exist here but are threatened by runoff from the island and are "at risk of imminent degradation."

The report's conclusion was daunting: "In the absence of immediate and decisive management action, there is no reason to suspect that the reefs of northwest Roatán will not continue to degrade. Apart from losses to the ecological value of the reefs, the associated economic losses will also be great to the artisanal fishing and fledgling tourism industries of the island. In the space of a few short years, Roatán is in severe danger of progressing rapidly from being an up-and-coming Caribbean tourism destination to becoming catastrophically degraded."

Roatán's reefs have sustained a litany of abuses in recent years. Some are related to fishing and poaching; many are related to tourism. Clear water, colorful corals, and inexpensive diving have made the island a major ocean sports destination. Most visitors stay at West End or Sandy Bay, where palapa bars, cabanas, and restaurants fill in the spaces between dive shops. Somewhat sleepy in comparison to other island destinations, these palm-fringed villages host mostly budget travelers who laze on the white sand beaches in between scuba excursions, wander along the unpaved roads at the edges of the inland jungle, and do their best to avoid the cruise ship passengers who storm parts of the island throughout the week. Cruise ship traffic, which brings thousands of day-trippers to swim and step among the fragile corals, has more than quadrupled since 1999. In the past three decades, the annual number of marine recreation tourists has jumped from fewer than 1,000 to more than 250,000. And Roatán's permanent population has swelled accordingly with job-seekers from the mainland and vacationers who decided to stay.

As new islanders build hotels and residences on the lush tropical isle, they pay little attention to issues such as sedimentation from land clearing and pollution from subpar septic systems. Debris and sewage make their way into the watershed at ever-increasing rates, smothering the reef and adding sulfates and phosphates to the ocean. Those added "nutrients" cause harmful algae blooms, which can work their way through the marine food chain, poisoning plankton, fish, marine mammals, and birds. "You can even tell just walking along the beach, there's a lot of algae growing in the water that wasn't there a couple of years ago," Stanley says.

Stanley is on the board of the Sandy Bay and West End Marine Park, a community-managed reserve that covers eight miles of Roatán's northwest coast from shore to a depth of about sixty feet. The delicate mangrove forests at the waterline, where mollusks and tropical birds thrive amid the intricate roots, buffer the island during storms and protect the coral from terrestrial runoff. Thick green strands of sea grass sway to the rhythms of the ocean as currents ripple through their beds. Filtered sunlight streams through the pale green water, illuminating great mazes of brain coral and schools of brilliant angelfish.

On land, scuba diving businesses, hotels, and private homes clutter the coast—this is the hub of island activity.

The park is an expansion of a smaller government-run reserve established in 1989, which suffered from what comanager Nick Bach calls "a complete lack of management." Illegal fishermen and poachers were depleting the so-called reserve at will, and local dive operators feared for their reef-dependent livelihoods. In February 2005, a group of local business owners decided they'd had enough. They pooled funds to buy two boats and hire four employees, and they took matters into their own hands.

The park now runs daily boat and shore patrols to discourage illegal activity. Rangers and police also monitor dive operators and teach park-going visitors and residents about proper reef etiquette. Park rangers have seen local children snapping off bits of sea fans and reeling in undersize fish, Bach says, but education goes a long way toward reducing those behaviors. In one case, a

Sea lilies, Roatán

ranger told a young fisherman with an illegal catch that if he kept it up, Roatán would become like Guanaja, a nearby island whose fishing economy was decimated by overzealous anglers. "The kid almost cried," Bach says.

In the months after the community patrols began, conch and lobster populations started to recover. Then a new problem emerged. "Now all the poachers basically work around our hours," Bach says. "They've become nocturnal." The park hopes to find funding for some nighttime patrols soon.

"We certainly are living in a tough time, and there's a lot of work that needs to be done to reverse a lot of the trends we've seen," says Rich Wilson, manager of Caribbean programs at the Coral Reef Alliance, a nonprofit conservation group that promotes reef health in the Indo-Pacific and the Caribbean. "But there's a lot of work being done. It's not all a bleak, dark picture." As fragile as reefs may be, they are also surprisingly resilient, he says. Given some time to heal and a healthier environment, "the ecosystem as a whole can bounce back."

Wilson's organization is part of an International Coral Reef Action Network task force that launched a Mesoamerican Reef protection project in 2004. The group—which also includes the Nature Conservancy, the World Wildlife Fund, and three divisions of the United Nations Environment Programme, among others—aims to improve watershed management and reef health, in part by developing voluntary environmental standards for local marine recreation businesses in Playa del Carmen, Mexico; Placencia, Belize; and Roatán, Honduras. "It's a very grassroots project," Wilson says. "We've got a lot of industry support, and that's really crucial. They're the ones who are on the front lines, who are out there every day."

The group has led a series of workshops in which seventy-plus participants learned about coral reef ecology and sustainable tourism, then worked to develop a set of voluntary standards for dive operators and resort owners. Once business owners become aware of the impact their practices can have on the island, compliance is an easy sell. "They are dependent on healthy reefs, so they are often very interested in participating," Wilson says.

For Roatán residents Ian Drysdale and Jenny Myton, protecting the reef has become a business in itself. Environmental engineers by training, the Honduran couple owns an environmental consulting firm that contracts with government and nongovernment organizations to assess problems and propose conservation strategies. "Basically I'm like a doctor," Drysdale says. "I see the patient, I see what's wrong, and I tell you, this is the medicine you should take." What happens next can be frustrating—Drysdale's "prescriptions" are often ignored. "The government is really keen on gathering information and issuing environmental licenses, but they have virtually no follow-up on the projects." Even when policies are put in place, enforcement is rare, and fines are often so low that many violators would rather pay the fee than change their behavior. "In that sense we're still a third-world country."

Drysdale hopes to make a more direct impact by tackling what he says is the reef's primary local enemy: sewage. His company, Planeta Azul, developed an aerobic treatment for septic tanks that removes 90 percent of harmful substances that might otherwise seep into the sea. His vision is to use flexible loans and other creative funding measures to provide every Roatán household with some sort of septic treatment, whether or not it is his. "We all go to the bathroom every day. It's all impacting on the reef," he says. "It should be everybody."

But the gravest threat to the region's reefs is something that locals have no power to control: coral bleaching caused by global warming. When ocean temperatures rise as little as a degree or two Celsius above the average annual maximum, corals become stressed and expel the food-producing zooxanthellae algae that give reefs their colors and offer some protection against disease. The result is a coral ghost town populated by the naked white skeletons of a once-vibrant colony. Bleached coral is vulnerable to ailments like white band disease and black band disease, which eat away at the tissues and eventually kill the coral.

The Mesoamerican Reef sustained three major bleachings in the 1990s, one of which, in 1998, destroyed as much as 18 percent of the region's coral. In 2005, the eastern Caribbean logged its highest temperatures in a century, wiping out up to 90 percent of the live coral in the worst-hit parts of Puerto Rico and the US Virgin Islands. It was the worst die-off ocean scientists had ever seen. Damage to the reefs near Roatán was much less extensive, but as ocean temperatures continue to rise, the likelihood of a catastrophic bleaching event grows.

"Global warming might be the overarching biggest concern that we have in relation to coral reefs these days," says Wilson, the Coral Reef Alliance program manager. Global surface temperatures since the 1970s have increased at a rate of 3.2 degrees per century, according to the US Department of Commerce's National Climatic Data Center. That's up from the pre-1970s rate of 1.1 degrees per century, and scientists expect the pace to keep increasing as greenhouse gases rise, trapping heat in the earth's atmosphere. Widespread bleaching was almost unheard of until the 1980s. "But now it's starting to occur almost every other year," says Dr. Robert Halley, a marine geologist with the US Geological Survey in St. Petersburg, Florida. "It's really bad."

Rising temperatures also cause more frequent storms and hurricanes, which batter the reefs and cause structural damage. Shortly after the 1998 bleaching, Hurricane Mitch, a category 5 hurricane, blew through the Mesoamerican corridor, carrying large quantities of coral-choking sediment from mainland rivers to the reefs. "It seems like coral reef ecosystems are weakened so that they can't really survive hurricanes as well as they did before

1980," Halley says. The USGS estimates that without mitigation, most of the world's coral will die within twenty years.

With the increased attention on the impacts of fishing, poaching, tourism, and pollution, Roatán's reef watchers hope to evade scientists' more ominous predictions. But the fate of the Mesoamerican Reef still depends largely on factors beyond their control. As long as the global thermometer continues to register new highs, all reefs will remain at risk.

Karl Stanley continues to monitor the situation from his unusual underwater vantage point. On his daily descents to the deepest accessible depths, he has watched the live coral cover shrink by half, taking with it some of the biological diversity that, for now, draws divers and snorkelers to the Bay Islands in droves. He thinks the island's economy might be able to weather the destruction of its reefs—after all, he says, the live coral cover off Key West, Florida, is down to 6 or 7 percent, and the tourists still come for the beaches. But he hopes it won't come to that. "I'd much rather live in a place that has a healthy reef than a dead reef," he says. The local sharks, lobsters, conchs, snappers, and groupers would certainly agree.

TURKS AND CAICOS ISLANDS

Sea oats on West Caicos

IN JULY 2006, FIVE VISITORS TO WEST CAICOS ISLAND pitched their tents behind a swaying cluster of sea oats on a quiet, white sand beach. They spent the afternoon wading in calm, turquoise ocean water and wandering among the sun-baked silver thatch palms. At midnight, they snorkeled amid tiny, ghost-like fish under a velvet sky splattered with stars. These visitors—a construction foreman, a real estate sales director, a landscape architect/environmental planner, and two travel writers—were the only overnight residents on the eleven-square-mile island. Willing castaways, they were there to witness and oversee a momentous change: new construction on an island that had been uninhabited for one hundred years.

The group had come by boat that morning from Providenciales, an island just six miles to the east but in another world.

On Provo, as it is known locally, high-end hotels and luxury condos clutter the coastline, native plants and freshwater are increasingly hard to find, and on many parts of the island, the ocean waves lap too softly to be heard above the grinding earth movers and beeping construction trucks. Since the 1990s, Provo has experienced a building boom that has rendered much of it unrecognizable to longtime islanders. Its population has soared, and its resources have become strained.

It is precisely the scenario the developers of West Caicos are hoping to avoid. West Caicos is the westernmost link in the Turks and Caicos chain, a British crown colony of Caribbean isles just north of Haiti, east of Cuba, and southeast of the Bahamas. It was a hub of salt and sisal (a plant used to make rope) production in the late nineteenth century, but refrigeration and synthetic fibers made those industries all but obsolete. The island was abandoned in 1906 and had been uninhabited ever since, until construction began on a 125-room Ritz-Carlton hotel and a handful of eighteenth-century Caribbean-style villas. The buildings are the first phase in a carefully crafted development project that will add tourist and resident housing to almost a tenth of the island by 2013, leaving the rest untouched. As the developers see it, it's a minor sacrifice of 296 acres that will ensure the preservation of a few thousand more.

"West Caicos is a classic example of how sustainable development should be done," says Hitesh Mehta, the landscape architect and environmental planner who drew up the ten-year West Caicos development plan in 2003. He ought to know. Mehta has designed award-winning ecotourism projects all over the world. One of the foremost experts on ecotourism, he presented the West Caicos plan at the prestigious International Union for Conservation of Nature World Parks Congress, and his case study for protecting small islands was endorsed by UNESCO.

The plan calls for boardwalks in areas where walking on the dunes would damage fragile flora; battery-powered carts for getting around the island; the preservation and restoration of archaeological sites such as historic Yankee Town, where relics from the salt-production era still stand; the use of a landfill instead of garbage incinerators; downward-facing lighting to minimize light pollution; an on-island naturalist to run a nature and culture center; and the reintroduction of the rock iguana, a prehistoric-looking reptile that once thrived throughout the Turks and Caicos Islands. It also proposes an expansion of the five-hundred-acre Lake Catherine Nature Reserve, one of two protected areas on West Caicos (the other is West Caicos Marine National Park, off the northwest shore). "I know of only one other case in the whole Caribbean where a [protected area] was actually increased in size," Mehta says. Lake Catherine is a mangrove-rimmed saltwater lagoon where lanky pink roseate flamingos gather at the shore to dip their curved beaks in the cloudy water. Situated in the center of the island, it connects to the ocean through a series of "blue holes" that divers are just beginning to explore.

One of those divers is Mark Parrish, co-owner of eco-adventure company Big Blue Unlimited. A Brit who moved to Turks and Caicos in 1997, Parrish has been promoting environmental stewardship ever since. In his spare time, he and a friend are using their scuba diving skills to try to map the narrow holes that push and pull ocean water into and out of the lake. The falling tide makes little whirlpools in the surface as it suctions from below, and the underwater tunnels are barely wide enough to accommodate a diver—the two must carry their tanks over their heads instead of on their backs, and they can explore only one small section at a time. They believe the blue holes, which are teeming with newly identified species, empty into the ocean at about three hundred feet below sea level. That's more than twice the depth accessible to recreational divers with standard gear.

When he isn't indulging in underwater exploration, Parrish takes travelers kayaking, biking, hiking, snorkeling, and diving all over the forty-one islands and cays, which are rimmed with sugary beaches, mangroves, and limestone caves. A robust barrier reef keeps the immaculate water so calm and clear that kayakers can watch tropical fish scurry beneath their paddles. Divers can expect to see eagle rays with geometrically spotted backs, soft white bellies, and five-foot wingspans soar above the gardens of sponges and corals. They can also see hammerheads and whale sharks. On West Caicos, Parrish shows visitors the railroad ties that once carried salt carts from Lake Catherine to the sea, where merchant ships would load the cargo for transport to the New World. And he takes them kayaking on the surface of the lake, whose underwater offerings are becoming more familiar to him all the time. "I love coming to West Caicos," Parrish says. "I wish they didn't touch anything, but it was inevitable. But they're making all the right noises. I think they've got the potential to do an okay job."

The West Caicos development plan dictates that 90 percent of the island will remain untouched until 2013, at which point the developers say they intend to extend the protection clause for another twelve to fifteen years (though they are under no legal obligation to do so). By then, however, what was once a saltwater salina will have become a nine-and-a-half acre, 146-slip harbor and full-service marina that will accommodate sailboats, sport fishing boats, and luxury yachts up to 200 feet. The Harbour Village will feature boutique shops, storefront offices, cottages, apartments, townhouses, and a restaurant and pub. And that is in addition to the villas and the Ritz-Carlton Molasses Reef hotel, which is scheduled to open in November 2008 and which, despite some features that green it up a bit, is a far cry from a genuine ecolodge.

Despite the careful planning for the protected 90 percent, an observer can't help wondering why anyone who claims to be environmentally driven could justify developing West Caicos at all. "If we didn't do it, someone else would do it, and I don't think they'd do it half as well as we are," says David Hartshorn, director of the development company, which, it's worth noting, is made up mostly of Turks and Caicos natives, or "Belongers."

Considering the frenzied pace of development on the surrounding islands, Hartshorn's statement is probably true. High-end tourism is central to the Turks and Caicos economy, and the government is working hard to encourage its growth. Construction began in 2007 on a $1.5 billion hotel and multi-million-dollar residences on the 560-acre Dellis Cay, a previously uninhabited isle northeast of Providenciales. The project is billing itself as "the largest development in the hemisphere." Major developments on North Caicos, South Caicos, and Grand Turk are also in the works. None is being held to a strict environmental standard. "West Caicos is probably the only island right now that has got backing and serious thinking about sustainability, and every other island is slowly just being taken over," Mehta says.

However, the government official charged with overseeing the environment says changes are afoot. "The environment is the cornerstone of our tourism industry, so we treasure it very much," says Wesley Clerveaux, director of the Department of Environment and Coastal Resources. Plans include beefing up the review process to meet international standards in areas like water quality (in the past, developers were simply required to report their water quality impact, not to meet any standards). "We are making [developers] more accountable, more respecting of the environment."

A "Draft National Development Vision" prepared by a foreign consulting firm and published by the government in December 2006 includes promising outlines for improvements in tourism, sustainable land use, and the environment. It acknowledges that "tourism is, by far, the dominant sector of the economy, and its growth drives two other dynamic sectors—construction and real estate," but it sets intentions to strive for ecological balance and increase the involvement of Belongers in business ventures. It identifies the problem of "spontaneous and haphazard development on Providenciales in particular" but aims to increase the protection of sensitive environments and "exercise sensitivity to environmental sustainability in the allocation and use of land." The report also places a dollar value of $47.3 million on its coral reefs, recognizing that their continued health is important for the long-term success of the tourism and fishing industries—an important realization considering the effects a population boom (and its pollution potential) can have on a fragile ocean ecosystem.

How much change can come from such a document is debatable, especially in the face of development pressure and traditionally poor collaboration between government agencies when it comes to environmental planning and regulation. But Clerveaux says all sectors of the Turks and Caicos government are beginning to take sustainability into consideration. His own department declared 2007 the Year of the Environment and launched a yearlong awareness campaign meant to motivate islanders to bring green issues into the spotlight. "This is not just lip service to the environment," he says. "Quite a bit has gone into it." The agenda included an education program for high school students; the Beautiful Bush Extravaganza, an event that highlighted the importance of native plants; an Adopt-a-Beach anti-litter initiative; and sermons from local ministers who highlighted the Bible's environmental messages. The premise is that promoting ecological integrity in a destination whose slogan is "Beautiful by Nature" will encourage economic growth.

The islands' environmental stewards acknowledge that the Year of the Environment was an encouraging step, but its long-term effects have yet to be seen. "It's all well and good to have programs and activities," says Ethlyn Gibbs, executive director of the Turks and Caicos National Trust, a nonprofit organization that aims to protect the natural, historical, and cultural heritage of the islands, "but is it going to be for one year or is it going to be a long-term exercise?" The fact remains that few developers prioritize sustainability, and the prevailing mentality is that increased luxury tourism construction means increased revenue. "The premier says he wants to modernize the country," Gibbs says, "so that means developers coming in to have such developments as condominiums and hotels or resorts."

Turks and Caicos premier Michael Misick, who is also the minister of tourism, started his second term in 2007 by fighting against a new US passport law that had the potential to reduce tourist numbers and pushing legislation that would lighten restrictions on gambling. In general, his governing decisions tend toward the removal of regulations that might hamper economic gain. While the influx of tourism dollars has increased under his leadership, so too have concerns about the long-term effects of largely unchecked growth. More disconcerting to those who value the islands' national parks and reserves is the fact that there have been sell-offs of so-called protected land to developers in recent years. "Unfortunately there are no [international] nongovernment organizations, and that is why the government has free rein on whatever they want to do with the land," Mehta says. "There's no Greenpeace, there's no World Wildlife Fund, there's just nobody."

Even so, there is hope that the success of projects such as Molasses Reef—where hotel rooms that start at $695 per night and villas that list for up to $5.3 million are sure to yield enviable profits—will inspire other developers to consider the value of protecting their surroundings as part of an overall development plan. Certainly Ryan Jones, the real estate sales director who was part of the fivesome that camped on West Caicos, understands that proximity to a vibrant natural landscape is a critical part of his pitch. Every villa on his roster boasts an unobstructed view of the pristine ocean, where eagle rays glide just below the surface and ospreys nest on limestone outcroppings that emerge from the sparkling sea. One of the island chain's most popular scuba diving spots lies about fifty yards offshore, where an underwater precipice whose colorful crevices house a healthy abundance of marine critters plunges to depths so great they don't register on his boat's sonar. "This is a project that everyone involved has become obsessed and in love with," Jones says. To watch Paul Roberts, the burly, tattooed construction foreman, use enormous binoculars to scan Lake Catherine for roaming flamingos is proof enough.

On their way back to Provo, the campers stopped at Delvin's Cove for one last swim in a crystalline bay. They dived off the boat and floated on their backs in the warm, clear water that sloshed at the edges of limestone cliffs. They ran their fingers over centuries-old carvings that mark the landings of pirates who once used this nook as a base for robbing wealthy salt merchants. The cove now holds treasure of another sort: the tropical-fantasy-come-true island experience that's become far more precious than any rogue's loot and will be much harder to recover if it's lost.

SOUTH
AMERICA

AMAZON BASIN

Yasuní National Park in the morning, Ecuador

ON A MAP OF NORTHERN ECUADOR, SQUIGGLY LINES
define the sinuous borders of Yasuní National Park, an unruly
wilderness where tropical rivers carve paths through the dense
forests; tall ceibas, dripping with vines and moss, tower over
giant ferns and waxy heliconias; and the squawks and chirps and
howls of a dizzying abundance of wildlife penetrate the thick,
wet air.

On the same map, eight rigid boxes with precise linear borders look as out-of-place as what they represent: oil concessions
in the world's most diverse and threatened ecosystem. The
boxes, which overlap the north half of the park and the neighboring Huaorani Ethnic Reserve, delineate the blocks allotted to
international oil companies that are devastating the area's biological riches and indigenous communities in pursuit of black
gold.

Like much of the Amazon Basin, this part of northeast Ecuador has been parceled out by a government struggling with poverty at a time when the world's economic superpowers value an untapped fuel source over an ecologically rich forest. The planet's rain forests are disappearing at a rate of 149 acres per minute—that's a landmass larger than New York City each week—primarily due to deforestation and resource extraction. Yasuní, whose southern half remains concession-free, is a flash point in the battle to preserve what's left. "The long-term picture for Yasuní . . . it's scary," says Matthew Finer, a biologist with Washington, DC–based conservation group Save America's Forests, which works to protect forests throughout the Americas. "Ten years from now, it's pretty much impossible to predict what it's going to be like."

More than three times the size of Yosemite National Park, the horseshoe-shaped Yasuní wraps around the Huaorani reserve near the Peruvian border, right on top of the equator. Its unusually biodiverse Napo-fed moist forests sustain some of Ecuador's last viable populations of giant otter, Amazonian manatee, and wattled curassow, a critically endangered large black bird with a distinctive, high-pitched whistle and a telltale orange wattle. Scientists from the Association for Tropical Biology and Conservation have ranked the park "among the world's most biologically important areas," in part because its weather patterns are expected to be only minimally affected by global warming, making it an important refuge for its native plants and animals.

Until recently, this remote place where the Amazon bumps into the Andes was the unmolested home of the fierce, spear-toting Huaorani people, hunter-gatherers who were able to extract everything they needed from the forest and who fought off would-be invaders for centuries. "They'd been living in isolation for so long that linguists can't trace the origins of their language," says Christopher Kraus, a researcher with Save America's Forests. When the missionaries and the oil companies arrived in the 1950s and 1960s, some of the initial confrontations were extremely violent—most notoriously, five young missionaries were speared to death in 1956. But as in many cases, industry eventually prevailed. Today's Huaorani struggle to retain their traditional lifestyle in a land of dwindling resources. Some have launched anti-oil campaigns, even traveling to the United States, their venerable spears in tow, to lobby Congress for support. Others have taken jobs as naturalist guides for tourists who come to explore the jungle. More than a few have gone to work for the very oil companies whose access roads and faulty pipelines have caused widespread hunger and disease. The rest have retreated into the depths of the forest, where outsiders have not dared to venture—yet.

Texaco and PetroEcuador started drilling in the Oriente, as the Ecuadorian Amazon is known, in 1967. Throughout the 1970s, oil companies cut hundreds of miles of roads that gave easy access to illegal loggers and settlers, who brought diseases that the Huaorani had never known. The roads also disrupted animal migration, which affected hunting. Two of the roads— one built by Texaco in the 1980s, the other by Maxus in the 1990s—cut straight through the region that was designated Yasuní National Park in 1979. The park's protected status did not guard it against the allure of oil income, just as its 1989 designation as a UNESCO Biosphere Reserve has failed to shield it from a recent wave of extractions brought on by rising tensions in the Middle East.

In his 1995 book, *Savages*, author Joe Kane wrote about the Huaoranis' earlier efforts to battle "the Company," as Moi Enomenga, now the vice president of the Organization of the Huaorani Nation of the Ecuadorian Amazon, called the oil industry. "The Company planned to extract more than two hundred million barrels of raw crude from Huaorani territory,"

Kane wrote, "and in its quest to exploit that oil, it had revealed itself to be an enemy far more powerful than any the Huaorani had known: an enemy that, as Moi saw it, killed by destroying the source of all life, the forest itself."

More than a decade later, Enomenga is still fighting to protect the Oriente, both through lobbying (not only has he visited countless government officials and oil executives throughout Ecuador, but he has made multiple trips to Washington, DC, to meet with members of the US Congress) and through tourism. When he is available, he leads travelers on tours of a Huaorani community just outside the park with the Quito-based ecotourism outfitter Tropic.

"The Ecuadorian Amazon forest is filled with ecolodges and programs that promote the jungle, the Amazon, the rain forest," says Tropic general manager Jascivan Carvalho. "What we try to do is to promote that, but with a different sense of how these amazing people can live in such good synchrony with the rain forest." The six-day Tropic trip starts with a small-plane flight over the dense forest canopy to a clearing just big enough to contain a landing strip. In the nearby Huaorani village of Quehueri'ono, Enomenga and other guides lead walks into the jungle to identify medicinal plants and look for jaguar tracks. Sleeping quarters are housed at a nearby campsite where tents sit atop raised wooden platforms and meals are prepared in the camp kitchen. On the final day, a dugout canoe trip down the Shiripuno River, amid the animal-chatter soundtrack of Amazonia, ends at the Via Auca, an oil pipeline whose construction wiped out several thousand square miles of rain forest. It's an industrial invasion that stands in sharp contrast to the neighboring jungle.

Most visitors to Yasuní access the park from the town of Coca, 190 miles east of Quito at the confluence of the Napo and Coca rivers. It takes half a day in a canoe on the Napo to reach the mouth of the Tiputini and the entrance to the park. Wilderness lodges are abundant, though their degree of sustainability varies. ("Massive tourism can be as destructive as oil exploration," Carvalho says.) When you venture into the wilds here, having a guide is essential. The Amazon is often referred to as a "green wall," and this section of forest is particularly dense. Attempting to find your own way through it is not a good idea.

The allure of the Amazon extends far beyond Ecuador's borders. Kane was among the first kayakers to run the entire Amazon River from source to sea. In 1985, he joined nine other adventurers in an ambitious first descent, "to see with our own eyes every foot of the four-thousand-mile chain of water that rises in southern Peru and spills north through the Andes and east to the Atlantic." The mere immensity of it was reason enough for that journey. Others have been drawn here by the wildness of a place where so many of nature's oddest creations

Hypsiboas fasciatus, *Yasuní National Park, Ecuador*

exist amid so few human observers. The river carries a greater volume of water than any river in the world, originating in the Peruvian Andes and cutting clear across Brazil before dumping one fifth of the world's freshwater into the Atlantic. Its drainage basin covers almost the entire northern half of the continent—northern Bolivia and Brazil, eastern Peru and Ecuador, southern Colombia and Venezuela, and nearly all of Guyana, Suriname, and French Guiana. The combination of all that water and the equatorial heat has bred extraordinary diversity. The basin holds more plant species than any region on Earth, more than forty thousand of them. The trees that make up its canopy layer can top 250 feet, blanketing the vines, ferns, and palms that grow beneath. A fifth of the world's birds and more than two million types of insects live here. Mammal, amphibian, and reptile communities each have several hundred local species, including the pink river dolphin, the anaconda, and the poison dart frog. In the waterways, piranhas and electric eels swim among a few thousand other types of fish.

But ranching, logging, mining, agriculture, and oil and gas extraction are placing all of that life at risk. According to the World Wildlife Fund, as much as 12 percent of the Amazon's tropical rain forest has already been destroyed. In Brazil, which contains nearly two thirds of the continent's tropical forest, the deforestation level is more than 17 percent. Cattle grazing and mahogany harvesting are well-known culprits, but some of the others are surprising. The slash-and-burn practices of soybean farmers, for instance, have charred hundreds of thousands of acres of savanna and rain forest. And the sugarcane that has allowed Brazil to become a world leader in the use of ethanol-powered automobiles has come at the expense of large swaths of forest.

One such forest is Murici in northeast Brazil. Aerial photographs show barren brown hillsides crisscrossed with roads and fringed with isolated patches of green. Much of the region was cleared for sugar production after the government started offering incentives in the 1970s, but the 7,400 or so acres of forest that remain are home to two endemic bird species and twelve bird species that are globally threatened. Birders flock here to catch a glimpse of the seven-colored tanager, a songbird whose bright plumage would blend seamlessly with the greens and blues of a Caribbean bay. The American Bird Conservancy calls Murici "probably the most important place for bird conservation in the Western Hemisphere." Efforts to preserve what is left include an international endeavor to reforest the area and some of the surrounding farmland.

In Peru, a key battleground is the Tahuamanú forest, where illegal logging is a multi-million-dollar industry fueled by America's unending demand for mahogany. In this place where spider monkeys and macaws thrive beneath the supposedly protected 120-foot-tall trees, government officials look the other way as large sections of the valuable canopy disappear. The Natural Resources Defense Council and two Peruvian indigenous rights organizations—Native Federation of Madre de Dios and Racimos de Ungurahui—are suing the US Department of the Interior, border control agencies, and American mahogany importers in an attempt to slow the transport of illegal wood.

The drive to protect what remains of the Amazon's rain forests is about much more than the birds and the trees. As the world increases its output of carbon dioxide, the canopy's role as a filter becomes more critical. When the number of trees performing that function decreases, pollutants build up in the atmosphere, increasing the rate of global warming. The water that trees and plants release influences climate as well. Scientists have projected that by 2050, the Amazon's temperatures will increase by two or three degrees Celsius. There's only one way to slow that process: stopping the destruction of the trees.

In Ecuador's Yasuní National Park, conservationists are hoping to protect what remains by seeking a ten-year, region-wide moratorium on oil extraction. Their immediate actions are focused on the two southernmost blocks, Block 31, which is operated by the Brazilian oil company Petrobras, and the ITT Block, named for the Ishpingo-Tambococha-Tiputini oil fields, which contain about a quarter of the country's oil reserves, roughly nine hundred million barrels. In 2005, Petrobras started paving a road on its designated plot to just outside the park boundary. Huaorani leaders and international conservationists mounted a successful campaign to halt the construction, but the company now plans to access the oil by helicopter. "[Roadless extraction] makes it easier to prevent settlers from coming in," says Brian Keane, director of indigenous rights organization Land Is Life, "but it doesn't stop oil spills and pipeline ruptures and all these things that affect the lives of the people in that area."

Next door in the ITT Block, Ecuador's national oil company is expected to partner with Petrobras or China's Sinopec in order to start extracting. Needless to say, the financial incentive to remove that oil is immense—not only at the national level, but also among individuals within the Huaorani community who have received bribes in exchange for signatures. The park's guardians worry that tapping those two concessions will put the rest of the park at greater risk. "Slowly but surely, that new incursion into pristine areas has been happening and moving south," says Kevin Koenig of Amazon Watch, a nonprofit that works with indigenous and environmental groups in the Amazon Basin to protect communities from industrial exploitation.

In June 2007, leftist president Rafael Correa tossed his pro-environment supporters a nugget of hope by announcing a deal: if someone would pay the Ecuadorian government $350 million per year (about half of the expected revenue from oil extraction), he would leave the remaining oil fields untouched. Where that money will come from, however, is anyone's guess. An article in the *Economist* said that Correa himself seems to doubt the plan's viability. "But he may earn some credit with environmentalists for trying. And if it does not work, he can always blame the outside world for being so stingy." Less-skeptical observers have launched a letter-writing campaign at www.liveyasuni.org. "Your government's proposal rightly recognizes natural resource conservation and investment in alternative energy, instead of oil extraction, as the sustainable source of Ecuador's national wealth," says the form letter to President Correa, adding that "efforts are under way" to raise the funds to save the forest.

If the plan fails, the ITT Block will fall, another domino in the steady southward tumble into the Huaorani homeland. "If oil happens there, it is the gateway to the country's last real roadless, intact, pristine area," Koenig says. As speculators eye the resources in vulnerable rain forests all over the Americas, it's a warning cry that echoes throughout the Amazon.

AYSÉN, PATAGONIA, CHILE

Río Baker Valley, Aysén

"¡DERECHA ADELANTE, IZQUIERDA ATRÁS!" SHOUTS river rafting guide Yoany Arratia. In the split second it takes his English-speaking charges to translate the command, paddles fly every which way and the raft hits the Class III rapid at an awkward angle, buckling against a wall of water. An icy wave crashes down on the unsuspecting paddlers, and the Río Baker, whose glacial green-blue they had admired only from afar, tastes delicious.

Safely beyond the white water, the raft floats quietly along a shore lined with bushy lenga trees and bright orange calafate flowers. Arratia, who grew up a few hours south of here in the coastal village of Caleta Tortel, leans backward from his captain's perch, fills his water bottle with river water, and takes a good long swig. "*No hay más puro,*" he says. It doesn't get any purer than this.

He's probably right. The Baker is one of five rivers in the Aysén region of Patagonia that flow uninterrupted from source to sea. Its water trickles from the Northern Ice Field glaciers into the crystalline Lago Bertrand, which forms the river's headwaters near the sleepy village of Puerto Bertrand. From there it meanders for 125 miles through temperate rain forests and wetlands, past farming and ranchland where the population density is fewer than three per square mile. Then it empties into the Pacific amid the fjords and canals of Caleta Tortel, which sits at the edge of the 6,500-square-mile Southern Ice Field and its frozen seas of jagged, bluish peaks.

Fly-fishermen travel to the Baker from North America and Europe to wade below the riffles and cast for trout—rainbows and browns up to three feet long. It's a tedious journey from the northern hemisphere, but as one angler from New Jersey said on a recent spring day, "You take one look at this river and you forget how long it took you to get here."

Downstream from Puerto Bertrand, not far past the stretch of raftable white water, the landscape shifts as the river flows through a narrow, rocky canyon where the Baker slams into the Río Chacabuco. The confluence is dramatic, powerful, and full of potential—680 megawatts of hydroelectric potential, that is, enough to power more than half a million homes.

In 2004, Spanish power company Endesa announced plans to build two dams along the Río Baker and two on the Río Pascua, in southern Aysén. Together they will produce 2,430 megawatts. The project will provide some short-term construction jobs and a temporary boost to the local economy. It will also inundate up to thirty-six square miles of land, permanently alter the ecology, and turn the upper Baker stagnant.

The environmental community is up in arms, as is the burgeoning tourism industry. But opposition is far from universal. On the front of a small white house along the brick-inlayed frontage road in Puerto Bertrand, a hand-painted sign reads "*Sí a Endesa, progreso para la region*"—yes to Endesa, progress for the region. It's a common sentiment in a place that, until recently, was almost entirely cut off from the rest of the world. With the towering Andes to the east, a splintered coastline to the west, and colossal ice fields to the north and south, Aysén could not be crossed by car until 2000. The Carretera Austral, a highway project started by dictator General Augusto Pinochet in the 1970s, now runs 770 miles from Puerto Montt in the lakes region to Villa O'Higgins in southern Aysén, with the help of a few ferries. Most of this "highway" is a rutted stretch of gravel barely wide enough for two pickups to pass each other comfortably, but it has succeeded in ushering Aysén into the automobile era and has introduced hope for economic growth. *Desarrollo*, or development, is an enticing concept in one of the poorest parts of Chile, where subsistence farming has long been the norm.

The Aysén hydroelectric project "*producirá mayor dinamismo a la economía*" (will bring dynamism to the economy), says a glossy Endesa brochure that was given to an American reporter in lieu of an interview. The document promises improved tourism, transportation, health care, and education, and minimal damage to the environment. Chile's energy needs are increasing at a rate of 6.8 percent per year and could triple in the next twenty years, the brochure says, adding that hydropower is the key to accommodating this growth.

"Endesa does a good job of selling the project as necessary," says Ian Farmer, co-owner of Patagonia Adventure Expeditions, an outfitter based in Coyhaique, Aysén's largest city. "Their arguments are pretty good if you're talking about somebody who has lived in total isolation all their life and suddenly sees an opportunity to make some fast cash." But the long-term effects of a major hydropower project can be disastrous, as evidenced by Endesa's last Chilean hydropower project, the Pangue Dam on the Río Bíobío in 1996. Once a world-renowned white-water rafting and kayaking destination and home to remote Pehuenche communities, the Bíobío was devastated by the dam, which flooded a narrow valley at the foot of the Antuco volcano. What was once a pristine ecosystem is now an "anti-ecological and anti-aesthetic hydraulic artifact," wrote ecologist Juan Pablo Ortega, president of the Grupo de Acción por el Bíobío, in a letter to the online newspaper *El Mostrador.* "The argument with the Bíobío was that it will improve the economy," Farmer says. Now, however, that region is "the most industrialized and has the highest poverty" in all of Chile, he says.

Farmer, not surprisingly, endorses tourism as an alternative to hydropower for boosting Aysén's economy. It requires less investment capital; ensures long-term, better-paid employment opportunities for local residents; keeps profits from leaving the region; and protects local communities and the environment, he says. In 2005, tourism brought $14 million to Aysén. "This region has been so relatively untouched—that's where its value is," Farmer says. "If you just cut through these hundred-mile swaths of clear-cut to put the [transmission] cables in, then you change that."

Thirty bumpy miles south of the fly-fishing lodges and expedition put-ins of Puerto Bertrand, the town of Cochrane is an up-and-coming outdoor tourism destination at the edge of Tamango National Reserve. Tamango is the twenty-seven-square-mile home of the endangered huemul deer, where visitors can hike or mountain bike the well-marked trails, camp in rustic cabins tucked into *coigue* and *ñirre* groves, or hire the resident guide for a boat ride up the Rio Cochrane to fly-fish in virgin streams.

Cochrane is the epicenter of the Río Baker hydropower debate—if built, the two Endesa dams will lie immediately to its north and its south. Baker 1, the dam at the Chacabuco confluence, is slated for completion in 2012 and would help supply the power needed to build the other three. Baker 2, just downriver

Aysén, Patagonia, Chile

from Cochrane at El Saltón, could be finished by 2018. Together they would produce 1,040 megawatts and inundate up to thirty square miles of land. The project's two southern Aysén dams, Pascua 1 and Pascua 2, would produce more power, 1,390 megawatts, with much less of an impact—they would flood fewer than six square miles.

The local environmental group Agrupación Defensores del Espíritu de la Patagonia is prominently headquartered alongside the tree-filled plaza at the center of town. Flyers taped to its street-front window warn passersby to be wary of Endesa's promises. They compare the hydropower project to a nuclear bomb, warning that it will destroy the region's flora and fauna as well as its tourism economy. They urge community members to fight for a *"Patagonia Sin Represas,"* a Patagonia without dams.

The Endesa office sits just around the corner in an elegant wood-paneled building. In shops and restaurants all over town, radios are tuned to a local radio station that runs an ad at regular intervals: "Endesa: *energía natural por Chile*." But that doesn't necessarily indicate support. At one local restaurant where the radio plays throughout the day, the owner keeps a guest book where visitors can record their impressions of Cochrane and their opinions about the dams. Almost every comment is about the beauty of the region and the importance of resisting detrimental change.

The book's most famous and controversial contributor is Doug Tompkins, the American businessman who founded the North Face and Esprit brands. Along with his wife, former Patagonia CEO Kristine McDivitt Tompkins, he has purchased more than two thousand square miles of Chilean land for conservation. In 2004, the Tompkinses acquired the 270-square-mile Valle Chacabuco ranch near Cochrane for $10 million, with hopes of turning it into a national park. In 2005, they donated Parque Pumalín, a 1,115-square-mile swath of northern Patagonia rain forest, to a national foundation that designated it a nature reserve. Because the Tompkinses are foreigners using their personal wealth to buy Chilean land, they are the subjects of widespread distrust among Chileans. But their message never wavers: Patagonia must be protected from environmental destruction in the name of progress. Regarding Endesa and the Río Baker dams, Doug Tompkins wrote in the restaurant guest book, "*Nosotros estamos aborado un nave sin timón, rumbo al abismo*"—we're all aboard a ship without a rudder, directed to the abyss.

Chileans are skeptical because they have a strong tradition of laissez-faire economics that developed in reaction to the brutal Pinochet era, when the secret police and a murderous military taught them to distrust state control. Even the current president, Michelle Bachelet, a pro-environment socialist, is unlikely to come between a private company and its development plans.

Endesa was a state-owned utility under Pinochet, but it was privatized in 1988, and the majority shareholder is Spanish. Now the company owns the water rights to 85 percent of Patagonia's river flow, including that of the Baker and the Pascua. Furthermore, a new federal law requires private holders to use their water rights by 2012 or else pay royalties to the government.

Despite the petitions filed by activists throughout Patagonia and the nation, Endesa expects the feasibility studies, environmental reviews, and other bureaucratic matters to be behind them by 2008. Then construction will begin. "The people of Aysén don't have anything to say about the water rights because they're not the owners of them," says Fabian Bourlon, vice president of CODESA, the Corporation for the Development of Aysén, a Coyhaique-based nonprofit that promotes the local, sustainable development of the region. Nor do the people have much say in how the hydropower makes its way to Santiago, he says. Energy infrastructure company Transelec, whose ex-president is Chile's minister of the economy, will easily gain the necessary government approvals to build transmission lines. "It's not a fair deal," Bourlon says. "It's not a transparent process. It's a political process."

Bourlon fears that damming the rivers and crisscrossing the hillsides with transmission cables will spoil the unadulterated beauty that inspired him to move here from his native France (and brought Ian Farmer from England and the Tompkinses from the United States, in addition to attracting tens of thousands of tourists each year from all over the world). "You're damaging what made us come here," he says. "Transmission lines will slow down tourism. They'll change the impression of the place. It's a question of vision. Economic survival is number one." If the region moves toward hydropower, he says, "no one will hear about Aysén other than providing energy for the rest of Chile."

That's why CODESA and CODEFF, the National Committee for the Defense of Fauna and Flora, are pushing the government to recognize Aysén as a "*Reserva de Vida*," a life reserve. While the title carries with it no legal protections like "national park" or "national reserve," it could have economic implications. By creating a regional identity that centers on preserving Aysén's resources instead of exploiting them, the nonprofits hope to give business owners and community leaders a financial incentive to choose sustainable development.

As for meeting Chile's growing energy needs, dam opponents have outlined alternatives that include geothermal and wind power. They have also advocated a solution that has been used successfully elsewhere in the world, run-of-river hydropower plants, which direct flowing water through pipes to harness a river's energy without the use of reservoirs. And federal officials have estimated that energy efficiency measures could reduce the future demand for power by as much as 15 percent. The fact remains, however, that Chile's economy is largely dependent on megawatt-gobbling mining operations—copper extraction alone accounts for one fourth of the country's current energy consumption. There is also concern about the reliability of Argentinean natural gas, which Chile depends on for more than a third of its electricity. In 2004, Argentina reduced its next-door neighbor's allotment by 14 percent, a move that added fuel to Chile's pro-hydropower fire.

In Aysén, where life is simple and electricity consumption is minimal, such matters as the national energy supply seem to have little relevance. That's certainly so in Caleta Tortel, where many of the 550 residents make a living by harvesting the local cypress trees and turning them into the sturdy, weather-resistant fence posts that are favored by sheep and cattle ranchers throughout the region. This quaint village, at the mouth of the Río Baker and not far from the Río Pascua, sits at the edge of a peninsula where cypress walkways connect the colorful buildings. Until the gravel highway arrived in 2000, Tortel was entirely car-free. Yoany Arratia, the river rafting guide, was a teenager here when everyone in the village shared a single phone line—barely a decade ago. Amid all of the buzz about progress and whether the population will swell with workers who will need housing when construction begins, Arratia worries about the future of his home. It's not just Tortel that will change, he says. It's the whole region—the immaculate rivers that will no longer flow freely, the lenga-dotted hillside views that will be marred by power lines. *"No comprendo cuando la gente dice que será una buena cosa,"* he says. I don't understand when people say this will be a good thing.

CHACALTAYA, BOLIVIA

Until recently, the Chacaltaya glacier outside La Paz, Bolivia, was known as the world's highest ski slope. Twenty-five years ago someone gazing white-knuckled over the precipice of the Andean peak would have witnessed a vast yawn of ice and snow, dotted with thrill-seekers pointing their skis toward sea level. An antiquated rope-tow powered by an old Ford engine pulled the adventurers—many from a century-old ski club in La Paz—to the 17,785-foot apex. What remains of Chacaltaya, meaning "cold bones" in native Aymara, now clings forlorn to the mountainside. A horizontal rock swath now bisects the glacier, making skiing perilous at best. But cachet and curiosity still propel gawkers, hikers, mountain bikers, and—for a short time more—sledders and skiers to Chacaltaya's cap.

A ramshackle, unheated "resort," the hare-brained scheme of a German immigrant in the 1930s, still teeters at the rocky top of the Cold Road. The Club Andino Boliviano—a one-hundred-year-old ski group—is currently giving the hut a face-lift, but before they finish, the club itself may dissolve, along with Chacaltaya's slopes. "This has been a serious problem for the club; the ski slope was the only real source of livelihood and it has practically disappeared," says Eduardo Mamani Quispe, a club guide and an expert mountaineer. "There was a plan to move the slope to a neighboring mountain, but it is suffering the same fate and may only be around for a few years more than Chacaltaya," he says. That shared warm future is the result of a dreaded and inexorable change in climate throughout the Andes that is transforming the landscape beneath his crampons.

Chacaltaya has shed at least 90 percent of its heft since 1940; 40 percent was lost between 1992 and 1996 alone. Scientists predict that since less than 2 percent of it remains, it could soon completely evaporate. Bernard Francou, with the Institut de Recherche pour le Développement in La Paz, has carefully watched the spectacular and emblematic retreat of Chacaltaya and other South American glaciers. His files are thick with aerial photos of Chacaltaya from 1940 to today, and given its dramatic retreat over time, Francou predicts that the peak could be free of ice as early as 2010.

From the summit of Chacaltaya, looking north across the Altiplano—a rugged, desolate high plateau—the surreal view of the Cordillera Real, a one-hundred-mile stretch that includes twenty-two peaks over nineteen thousand feet, still lives up to the nickname given it by early climbers, the "Himalayas of the New World." They are called *achachilas*, or "givers of life," by the Aymara. The Quechua believe that each mountain has an *apu*, a spirit or deity. To this day they are worshipped by native Bolivians as spirit beings that impact the human world greatly by controlling the weather. From here nearby Huayna Potosí is a visible mass of rock and ice—19,996 celestial feet of it. The mountain is a good example of the fine line between the formidable and the accessible that characterizes Bolivia's rough topography. With enough experience or a good guide, reaching the top of Huayna Potosí is a moderate two-day hike into one of the world's most breathtaking mountain ranges. Climbers here seldom forget to carry a rock from the base of the mountain to add to the *apachetas*, or stone cairns, that mark high passes, as an offering for safe travel (crosses, coca leaves, and alcohol are also often left). More moderate walks include the Camino del Inca—the Choro, Takesi, and Yunga Cruz trails, which link the Cordillera Real to the Yungas Valley. Time unwinds along these historic paths through ancient villages, above which condors still circle.

But before attempting to climb even a flight of stairs, acclimatization to mountainous Bolivia is critical. It's best to pad the front end of a visit to the country with a few days in La Paz, at an elevation of about twelve thousand feet, in order to adjust to the altitude. This de facto capital (the official capital is Sucre) is a great base from which to explore the country's diversity. Bolivia is generally and fairly characterized as a poor but safe, less-visited, landlocked South American country. It's the size of Spain and France combined but has only nine million citizens, most of whom live on the Altiplano. Thirty indigenous languages are spoken in the busy streets of La Paz and across the mountains, jungles, pampas, and salt flats of the country. Spanish is now the official language though traditional customs and beliefs endure among the populace, many of whom still have Amerindian blood flowing through their veins. Bolivia is dominated by the Andes and has a higher average elevation than any other South American nation, making it one of the continent's most isolated countries. But that sense of remoteness dissolves in the heart of the country while trading smiles with women in brightly colored shawls in downtown La Paz and snacking on *salteñas*, the omnipresent pastry pockets filled with meat and vegetables.

Mamani Quispe, who was born and raised outside of La Paz, in Chacapampa, at the base of Huayna Potosí, has a long history with its crags and crevasses. "My relationship with the Cordillera Real started from an early age. I used to play on the mountains as a kid," he says. When he was eight years old, Mamani Quispe made his first attempt to reach the top of Huayna Potosí, making it within 2,200 feet of the summit before turning around. "From there me and my dog, Boby, decided that was enough for this time. Since then, I haven't looked back," he says. He now makes between 130 and 160 summit attempts a year throughout the Cordillera Real, with outfitter Bolivian Mountains Climbing and Trekking. He's also a member of the Bolivian mountain rescue service and assisted the nation's Military Geographical Institute in drafting the only official map of the range. If anyone knows the passes and peaks of the Cordillera Real, it's Mamani Quispe.

In the past few years he has noticed some alarming alterations afoot. "There are many areas which are suffering from quite dramatic glacial melting," he says. According to government estimates, Bolivian glaciers have shrunk by 60 percent since 1978. These new conditions present growing risks for climbers. "Mountaineers generally prefer to walk or climb in soft or hard snow, but this meltwater is leaving smooth ice on many of the popular routes, making things much more complicated," Mamani Quispe says. "If a climber loses his footing on an icy patch it is much harder to stop yourself from falling." Not to mention the avalanches and multiplying crevasses.

These changes are not exclusive to Mamani Quispe's beloved Bolivian behemoths. The future of Huayna Potosí, and of wild and weird Chacaltaya, is shared by every Andean peak, from Venezuela to Patagonia. While each of the thousands of glaciers along the bulging spine of South America has been in retreat since the eighteenth century, the actual rate of thaw has accelerated. Since the 1980s, melting has been three times faster than it was just thirty years earlier, and in those three decades Andean glaciers have lost one quarter of their load.

Andean climbers can expect conditions there to continue to slip and slide toward chaos as climate change advances along the continent. While rising temperatures throughout the region are certainly to blame, warming is but one underlying factor. As the Pacific Ocean warms, the weather phenomenon El Niño becomes more frequent and more intense, depriving the Andes of precipitation. When insufficient snow fails to replenish summer melt-off, glaciers recede, exposing more rock to rising temperatures. (The southern hemisphere has experienced a greater rise in temperature than the global average.) When the surface temperature of rock near the glacier rises, melting accelerates.

For nearly three decades the world-renowned glaciologist Lonnie Thompson, of Ohio State University's Byrd Polar Research Center, has been monitoring tropical glaciers. He's paying consistent attention to them for several key reasons. First, he feels that they are a strong indicator of what's in store for the rest of the globe. "I believe that glaciers in the tropics are the 'canaries in the coal mine' for the Earth's climate system," he says. "To me it's a warning sign we should be paying attention to. They're not going to have a big impact on the sea level because they're too small, but they are vital in telling us what the real condition of the planet is."

Thompson frequents some of the world's highest peaks to collect climate data locked deep within glacial safes. Here the climate's clues are available for excavation, offering a glimpse into what weather was like before humans started impacting it. So important are these vanishing records that he and a dedicated crew have endured weeks at high altitudes (they once spent fifty-three days on Peru's Nevado Huascarán, elevation 22,205 feet)—breathing half of the oxygen available at sea level—in order to drill ice cores. After these thin cylinders of glacier are removed from the drill they're sealed in plastic sleeves, packed in tubes, secured in insulated boxes, sledded to the glacier's edge, hauled down the mountain, and shipped back to Ohio. Once back at the lab, air bubbles, dust, and isotopes captured in the cores are analyzed to create a history of climate.

Not far from Huayna Potosí and Chacaltaya is Sajama, elevation 21,420 feet, Bolivia's highest peak. Before being allowed to drill on the mountain, Thompson had to meet with the entire hamlet of Sajama, seventy-two residents in all, including the village leader and one highly skeptical medicine woman. "In the Aymara culture the gods live on the mountaintops and in the glaciers, so they were really concerned about angering the gods and what that might do to the climate," he says. "So we had to do a four-hour presentation on what we planned to do on these ice fields, why we were going, and why it was important." As Thompson fielded questions and concerns, his crew and six tons of equipment sat idle outside. "The last question that they asked me was, if they decided not to give me the permission, would I take my people and my stuff and go away? I told them yes, we would, because if every mountain had a village that protected it, then we wouldn't have all of the environmental issues that we have in today's world."

After debating for three hours, the village agreed to allow the expedition, on three conditions: donate $500 to the local library, hire villagers to support the project logistics, and participate in an ancient ceremonial sacrifice. "I said, okay, what are we sacrificing?" Thompson says, laughing. "It turned out to be a white alpaca." The entire village and drilling team gathered around the sacrificial rock and watched the alpaca's throat be cut and its blood be collected and sprinkled. "You're actually asking forgiveness for what you're about to do," says Thompson. "In the end this is the fate of the alpaca." Later, at the top of Sajama, with more than half the earth's atmosphere below them, the team drove the solar-powered drill deep into the ice in search of history.

Much of Thompson's field work was done across the border from Sajama, in neighboring Peru, where 70 percent of tropical glaciers are located. It was 1974 when he first ascended Quelccaya (18,602 feet), the largest tropical ice cap on earth, which stretches impressively across the country. The behavior of the Qori Kalis glacier, which makes up the western side of Quelccaya, is indicative of conditions on the cap. "In 1978, we decided as an afterthought that it might be good to document how a tropical glacier behaves," says Thompson. "Back then few people were worried about global warming. Qori Kalis is now the best-documented tropical retreat story." Thompson and his team have kept a close watch on Qori Kalis ever since, returning at least every two to three years to photograph its attrition. It retreated over five hundred feet a year between 1998 and 2000 alone, about three times faster than in the three years before. The entire ice cap could be gone in twenty years. "If you've worked as long as we have on glaciers like Quelccaya, it's kind of sad to see the current state of affairs there and to consider the diversity that's being lost," he says.

For Thompson, glaciers are like curators in a frozen museum indifferently encasing history until the day certain items are exhibited. Beyond stark photographic evidence, other material is beginning to emerge from beneath Quelccaya. During an expedition in 2005, Thompson's twenty-fourth trip to the ice cap, he collected twenty plants from the glacier's fringe, vegetation that had not absorbed sun rays in at least six millennia. All of the samples are wetland plants with no woody tissue, evidence that they've been frozen for a very long time. "The fact that they are being exposed now tells us that the ice cap has not been as small as it is today for at least sixty-five-hundred years."

That means that at no time in recent history have the Andes been as warm and, in some cases, as dry as they are now. And that's alarming in a region that's always been defined by its temperature uniformity. "In the zone that's known for very little temperature variation, every glacier is disappearing, and where we have time-lapse data, the rate of loss is actually accelerating," Thompson says. "The documentation of the loss of ice in the tropics I find particularly disturbing," he says, because 70 percent of the 6.5 billion people on Earth live there.

And people need water. Which is why many scientists are sounding the alarm about what happens when glaciers go extinct. "Mountain glaciers, which can be seen as 'nature's water towers,' store the snowfall in the wet season and release it in the dry season," says Thompson. "Of course, that water goes downstream and is used for hydroelectric power. It's used for irrigation. It's used for municipal water supplies, and as these glaciers get smaller, there's going to be less and less discharge in the dry season to support these types of activities."

Bernard Francou, the glaciologist in two-mile-high La Paz, agrees, and recognizes how such a crisis could be felt in cities all along South America's west coast. Of La Paz, Bolivia (population over 2.5 million); Lima, Peru (population over 7 million); and Quito, Ecuador (population over 1.5 million), he says, "The glacier recession, and possibly the extinction of many of them, could have important consequences in terms of freshwater." On the Pacific side of Peru, for instance, 80 percent of the water resources originate in snow- and icemelt, according to a report by Francou's institute.

Francou also voices concern over the buildup of that rapid glacial melt into roaring rivers and precarious lakes that bulge and sometimes burst, laying waste to towns beneath them. Parts of Peru's Cordillera Blanca are in danger of an outburst from glacial-moraine-dammed lakes. Over a thousand lakes have been formed by recent glacial retreat there.

Despite his changing environs, Eduardo Mamani Quispe continues to brave the technical climb up Pequeño Alpamayo and Illampu, which he calls the "Bolivian K2." "If you manage to reach the summit, there is no greater challenge," he says. But he may already be facing one. "What I am seeing, doing, and enjoying nowadays will not be able to be repeated by my kids or their kids," he says. "They will only see it in photos." The dissolving of Andean peaks similarly affects a stalwart scientist like Thompson, although he insists he climbs only for work, never for pleasure. "When I look at these ice fields, in the Cordillera Blanca and other places, they're kind of like the crown jewels of the earth," he says. "To think that the next generation may look at bare mountains—that these glaciers will only be in textbooks—is sad. We're losing something that's hard to put a value on."

Most South American communities, and even national governments, are not prepared for such a rapid loss of the area's resources, character, and mysticism. But for now, around Sajama, herds of alpaca continue to graze the lush Altiplano, fragrant with jasmine and magnolia, and residents still sip maté as the lights of burgeoning La Paz glimmer.

GALÁPAGOS, ECUADOR

Bartolomé Island, Galápagos

UNLIKE HIS NORTH AMERICAN GUESTS, SQUEEZED snugly into wet suits, Rafael Pesantes slides over the side of the rubber Zodiac dinghy and into the water in only swim trunks. These choppy Pacific waters, cool despite being at the equator, have been his backyard for over forty years. They are as familiar to him as the sands on his home island of Santa Cruz. The native Galapagueño and naturalist for Lindblad Expeditions dives down fifteen or so feet rapidly, surveying the area just off the shore of rocky Champion Islet. Moments later he bolts back to the surface, gesturing like an excited child for his two companions to follow him. A small, black-tipped reef shark circles below, followed by graceful spotted eagle rays and a thick school of deep-blue-and-yellow-striped sergeant majors that zigzag around indifferently. Few seem to take notice of the snorkelers until they meet a cadre of sleek brown sea lions, intent on goofing around. They dart toward, around, and beneath their human visitors, often mimicking human acrobatics. Finally they haul their massive hides awkwardly onto the beach, and some plop down almost atop one another. Pups snuggle up to their mothers to nurse in the warm autumn sun.

There are nineteen islands in the Galápagos archipelago, all of which are strung along a 174-mile stretch of the equator, 600 miles west of mainland Ecuador. Each of its nine main islands has an enduring personality, presenting a lifetime's worth of exploration possibilities. A few are dominated by people, like Isla Baltra, which acted as a US Air Force base during World War II and now houses the archipelago's only airport. And Santa Cruz Island is home to both the largest human settlement, Puerto Ayora, and the headquarters of the national park and Charles Darwin Research Station. El Chato reserve, in the humid highlands of Santa Cruz, is one of the best places to see giant tortoises in the wild. And just off its northwest coast, Cerro Dragon, on the nearby Venecia Islet, is full of towering cacti and a myriad of cherry-colored crabs.

Others clearly display the islands' volcanic nature. Tiny Seymour Island is scattered with black lava boulders against which massive frigate birds with inflated red throat pouches lumber through the air conspicuously. On Santiago Island, agile marine iguanas ride the waves onto black volcanic sand, and whimbrels, plovers, lava herons, and oystercatchers frequent the shore. Española, one of the most paradise-like islands in all of Galápagos, boasts wide expanses of blinding white sand and aqua-blue water, which is occasionally interrupted by huge hardened chunks of tar-colored lava where marine lizards warm themselves. Bartolomé Islet is barren and dominated by volcanic ash. The milky-white tuff cones and rusty-looking spatter cones rising from its landscape are leftovers from past eruptions. Bartolomé's muted colors are enlivened by many female lava lizards with scarlet-striped necks, striking a pose for would-be suitors. Pinnacle Rock, just off its shore, is a great snorkeling spot frequented by Galápagos penguins, white-tip reef sharks, and endless schools of fish.

By contrast, Isabela Island, the largest of the Galápagos, and Fernandina, the farthest west, are influenced by the cold water currents that swirl around them. Mist often rolls over the tops of the islands and creeps down their clifflike walls, earning the Galápagos the nickname "Las Encantadas," or Enchanted Isles, because to mariners, they would seem to simply disappear into the fog. The cool air and water draw diverse marine life here, including dolphins and whales. Fernandina, the youngest of the islands, has the added notoriety of being the most active volcano in the Galápagos chain. It erupted in 1995 and again in May 2005.

Floreana is one of the oldest islands, and unlike the others, it has gently rolling hills with blooming prickly pear cacti and tons of rare birds. Off the coast of Floreana is Corona del Diablo, or Devil's Crown, said to be the best diving spot in all of the islands because it's a partially submerged volcanic cone with rocky underwater ledges where a wide variety of marine life seeks food and shelter. Punta Cormoránt offers another superlative on the island—dozens of bubblegum-colored flamingoes feeding on brine shrimp in a salty lagoon.

The islands are entirely volcanic in origin; each island violently fought its way to the surface of the sea three to five million years ago. The area remains a geological hotspot of seismic and volcanic dynamism, beneath which a maze of underwater fissures still regularly expels magma. In geological terms, volcanic eruptions are commonplace in Galápagos—in the past hundred years, there have been fourteen events, the latest an eruption of Sierra Negra on Isabela in October 2005. In part owing to their geology, the islands have a raw, primal feel and wildlife is still unprecedentedly fearless and accessible. Humans don't seem to belong.

Galápagos remains, in many ways, as pure and dramatic as it was when Charles Darwin saw the place in the mid nineteenth century and scribbled excitedly in his journal about how unique and powerful he found the islands. "One is astonished at the amount of creative force, if such an expression may be used, displayed on these small, barren, and rocky islands," he said. On Galápagos, time is still measured by the rhythms of nature and the place continues to be defined by the extremes of life and death, wet and dry, dormant and explosive, and native and alien. The islands retain a staggering 95 percent of their endemic species, a feat unparalleled on any other archipelago in the world. Traveling there is like wandering into a parallel universe. Certain phenomena, such as heat, wind, and gravity, are familiar, but many aspects are otherworldly. Sea lions approach unperturbed, even inquisitive; iguanas dive headfirst into the surf; birds with powder-blue feet prance around during courtship; and century-old tortoises with shells the size of beach umbrellas roam through one century to the next.

But the Galápagos are islands in reluctant transition. In 2007, nearly three decades after it was designated as the first World Heritage site, UNESCO put the Galápagos on its "in danger" list, citing the perils posed by the introduction of alien species, illegal fishing, unsustainable tourism, and illegal immigration and population growth.

As evidenced on the northern coast of Floreana Island, in a smooth, sea-carved niche called Post Office Bay, it was long ago that people first intruded on this place. This sheltered cove lined with thick tangles of mangrove was favored by the British, who began aggressively harvesting whales in the late eighteenth century. In 1793, a wooden post barrel was erected there as a makeshift post office for the islands. Since whalers were often away for two or more years, this became the only means of communication between them and those waiting expectantly at home. When arriving at the barrel, the mission of passing sailors was twofold: to address and deposit correspondence in the barrel, without postage, and to take any letters from the bin that they might be able to personally hand-deliver. The barrel was the first human mark upon the area, but large-scale whaling practices would eventually drive those sea behemoths to near extinction and also severely deplete the populations of sea lions, birds, iguanas, and the namesake and prototypical symbol of Galápagos—the giant tortoise.

Nowadays at Post Office Bay, a short walk over coarse, caramel-colored sand reveals not only the barrel but a virtual shrine erected by visitors: a crudely painted portrait of a blue-footed boobie on a bit of plywood, plastic license plate covers that frame visitors' names, and a host of flashy bumper stickers.

Rafael Pesantes brings travelers to the spot, opens the barrel's sturdily hinged door, and pulls out stacks of postcards jammed into protective Ziplocs. He calls out addresses on the correspondence. "Can anyone deliver to Australia, Israel, England, Germany, the US, Singapore, or Bahrain?" A dozen or so postcards are taken with the promise that they will be delivered, according to tradition, by hand.

Post Office Bay is now one of the only places on the islands that acknowledges its rich and destructive human history in the natural bastion of Galápagos. But Floreana's dark history and colorful present could portend a changing reality for the islands. Darwin visited Floreana (he referred to it as Charles Island, named not for him but the king) during his five-week trip to the islands in 1835. By the time he trod on Floreana, pirates, whalers, and explorers knew it well. They frequented it to fill their ship hulls with hundreds of giant tortoises, considered a great source of fresh meat because they could be kept alive for a year without food or water. The permanent settlers who Darwin met on Floreana cultivated bananas and sweet potatoes and hunted giant tortoises (despite their being well on their way to extinction). In *The Voyage of the Beagle*, named for his sailing vessel, he wrote: "In the woods there are many wild pigs and goats; but the staple article of animal food is supplied by tortoises. Their numbers have of course been greatly reduced in this island, but the people yet count on two days' hunting giving them food for the rest of the week." Hundreds of thousands of giant tortoises—which can grow to five hundred pounds and outlive generations of humans—are thought to have been harvested during the nineteenth century alone. Darwin's observations on the difference between races, or subspecies, of tortoises—fourteen in all (of which eleven now remain)—on different Galápagos islands contributed greatly to his revolutionary theories of evolution and natural selection.

In 1959, a hundred years after *The Origin of Species* was published, Ecuador (which has had possession of the Galápagos since 1832) declared 97 percent of the islands' landmass a national park, excluding the existing areas of human habitation. The islands were declared a World Heritage Site in 1978. The marine reserve was established in 2001, protecting over 53,000 square miles of Pacific Ocean and all that lies within it. But it was too late to save the giant tortoises on Floreana and on neighboring Fernandina and Santa Fe islands, where they are now extinct. What remained of the endemic species on Floreana—the delicate, cotton candy–colored flamingoes and indifferent sea lions lying hide to hide—was taken off the marauders' market. Three of the fifteen national park "Rules for Preservation," which are still in place, seemed to apply a healing salve to some of Galápagos's wounds:

- Animals may not be touched or handled
- Do not startle or chase any animal from its resting or nesting place

- All groups that visit the national park must be accompanied by a qualified guide approved by the park

The fearlessness that had made the animals such easy human prey (like shooting fish in the proverbial barrel) again seemed appropriate.

But in the frenzy of globalization, the conditions that the islands' biota demand for survival (the ones toward which these species specifically evolved) are becoming difficult to sustain. Keeping Galápagos biologically pristine has been, and continues to be, a constant and hard-waged battle.

While not a new threat, the introduction of foreign species to the isolated islands remains the single greatest danger to biodiversity in the Galápagos. Over the years, people have brought into this harsh though balanced environment a score of biological intruders. When prisoners, cocky entrepreneurs, political exiles, and eccentric Europeans took up residence on Floreana centuries ago, they both inadvertently released alien species and intentionally planted their own non-native gardens. Introduced plants compete for vital soil and water resources and put delicate ecosystems in peril. The new flora on Floreana resulted in the crowding out of native species. Now in their place are highlands where lush foreign plants blanket the terrain. Today, throughout the islands, the most treacherous plant intruders include three species of blackberries, the quinine tree, and the lantana shrub, known as the "curse of India" for its voracious appetite.

These aliens in the Galápagos—there are now several hundred spread over 120 islands and islets—have the strength to overpower highly vulnerable island natives, which are quite unaccustomed to such aggressive competition. In 2001, the World Conservation Union, which provides UNESCO's World Heritage Committee with site evaluations, sounded the alarm about plant life on the Galápagos. It put the entire endemic flora of the archipelago on its Red List of Threatened Species. In 2006, the Charles Darwin Research Station, the research arm of the Charles Darwin Foundation (now Galápagos Conservancy), which has supported the Galápagos National Park for fifty years, determined that the number of known introduced plant species rose to 748, outnumbering the 500 native species for the first time in history.

One of the most obvious examples of animal invasives in the Galápagos is the case of goats on Isabela, a sea-horse–shape island made up of a string of six giant shield volcanoes. Isabela still has the best concentration of endemic species on the islands, as well as 50 percent of the archipelago's giant tortoises. This is despite having a small town—Puerto Villamil, population 1,600 (which was founded in 1897 as a fishing village)—and a big problem with goats.

Domestic goats were first introduced to Galápagos centuries ago by fleets of whalers and fishermen and allowed to multiply as a ready food supply. And proliferate they did. Left to their own devices, the tough, ruddy beasts eventually turned feral. The goats decimated the delicate vegetation and jeopardized native species. By 1998, estimates put the population of goats as high as 125,000 on the 1,771-square-mile hunk of basalt. The goats' merciless grazing flattened tree fern forests and even threatened to alter the climate on the island, where a lack of vegetation means the highlands cannot capture or retain moisture. Without a freshwater reserve, lean days followed for the giant tortoises.

In 2003, after several years of exhaustive planning and training, the Charles Darwin Research Station waged a multi-million-dollar war on the goats, which had devastated not only Isabela but also Santiago and Pinta islands. With the use of high-tech tracking devices, satellites, helicopters, guns, sterile female goats, and trained dogs, progress has been made. To date, most goats have been killed, and it's estimated that only 2 percent remain. In 2006, total eradication of feral goats (and feral pigs) was achieved on Santiago and northern Isabela.

However, human overpopulation still represents a major stress on native species. The once modest population on the islands has exploded over the past several years, from about ten thousand in 1990 to an estimated twenty-four thousand legal residents in 2006. Illegal immigration accounts for at least six thousand additional residents who come for higher salaries than can be found in mainland Ecuador. Humans are now settling, like the persistent mist that often dangerously shrouds these jagged shores. Prevention and enforcement are known locally as a farce. "Population growth is a major constraint for good conservation practice in the Galápagos Islands," says Veronica Toral, a marine biologist for the Charles Darwin Research Station who has lived on the islands for a decade. "Migration is illegal but they do not have the human and technical capacity to enforce it, and they don't have the money to pay your ticket back, so they just say, 'Please, please go back.'"

With people inevitably comes demand for basics such as clean water, housing, education, health care, and employment. "The higher the number of people," says Toral, "the greater the demands. And there's going to be a time when they demand land. And where is that land going to come from? The national park. And the resources to live on? The marine reserve and the park area."

Many argue that these human necessities are at least as important as conservation itself. Felipe Cruz, a Charles Darwin Research Station scientist, is in favor of a strategic plan for Galápagos that cares for its people, because decent living conditions would make them less vulnerable to illegal profitable activity. "The world thinks of Galápagos as this place with strange creatures that are found nowhere else in the world, as well as a whole bunch of crazy scientists, like Darwin, that are going around with white [lab] coats, long beards, and microscopes. They do not think of a population who lives here on a day-to-day basis," he says. "That is the problem that is not being contemplated. The main efforts have been put into the protected area. But the world needs to understand that if you want us to protect Galápagos, well, for God's sake, we need basic things here."

The ballooning population, which is uncomfortably pressing up against the physical, legal, and philosophical boundaries of the national park, is largely a response to a recent boom in tourism. In 1980, when the first commercial flight from mainland Ecuador landed on tiny Baltra Island, 17,445 visitors landed on Galápagos. That number rose to 41,192 in 1990 and then to more than 120,000 in 2006. While each foreign visitor now pays a $100 national park fee, the cost is not deterring the current wave of mass tourism that seems poised to saturate the Galápagos. Each time a flight arrives on Baltra, the line to pass through customs is so long that it snakes through the open-air terminal and spills over onto the tarmac.

Every theoretical cap that has been put on the number of visitors over the past three decades has been exceeded. Such was the case in May 2006, when history was again made as the MV *Discovery*, a five-hundred-passenger ship operated by Discovery World Cruises, dropped anchor off the coast of the easternmost island, San Cristóbal. The island administration hopes that its faltering economy, and the lives of its six thousand inhabitants, will be steadied by cruise ship revenue. Experts predict that the island could earn from twenty to thirty million dollars annually in fees, tours, and T-shirts from the ship's monthly visits. While the *Discovery* must anchor off San Cristobal's Puerto Baquerizo Moreno and passengers can only visit that island, those in the know are concerned about the slippery slope that these visits create. With so much money flowing into San Cristóbal, increased illegal immigration seems a given. And worse yet, says Cruz, is the possibility that this inroad will become an economic highway along which other islanders will want to travel. "My fear is that it might get successful. And then Isabela will want a five-hundred-passenger boat. And then they might also be successful. And then Santa Cruz also wants five hundred passengers," he says. "The worst-case scenario for us is that the people in San Cristóbal might get so much money that they'll want a boat every week."

For some the ship heralds the decline of the Galápagos from biological tour de force—a must-have notch in the naturalist's belt—to Caribbeanesque chaos, as the nature of its visitors shifts from conservation-minded travelers on strictly regimented itineraries to uninvested tourists just stopping by for a day or two during a fifty-three-day megacruise.

Veronica Toral voices another concern about the risks of several hundred people arriving in the Galápagos from far-flung ports of call—the microbes they bring in tow. Scientists have a major advantage in the fight against Galápagos invasives like goats, cats, rats, dogs, pigs, pigeons, frogs, and even those red ants that target papery tortoise eggs: they can see them. More daunting, and potentially more destructive, are the introduced species that Toral can only view under a microscope. Infectious disease could cause widespread mortality—even extinction—of native species, which may be highly susceptible to viral, bacterial, and parasitic agents because they have evolved in the absence of these pathogens. "We are still free of many, many diseases that could not only affect biodiversity but people," says Toral. "But imagine if West Nile virus or bird flu comes over here. And we have the chance that it might come in the *Discovery*."

While disease surveillance and monitoring are a priority, the attentions of national park and research station officials are already spread as thin as the wings of a Galápagos locust. In recent years the political and financial support of the mainland

Ecuadorian government has seriously lapsed, resulting in several episodes of park management paralysis. As it is, the vast waters of the marine reserve are difficult to adequately patrol, and chronic underfunding makes keeping rangers with institutional knowledge nearly impossible.

The drama and difficulties of fishing versus conservation have cast a wide net over the Galápagos. The latest heated rows have revolved around various bans: long-line fishing (which has a high rate of "bycatch," meaning unintended prey are captured), shark finning (upwards of three hundred thousand sharks are taken illegally every year to satisfy the Asian shark-fin soup market), and the harvesting of sea cucumbers. The federal government is sensitive to pressure from the powerful Galápagos fishing lobby, referred to locally as a "mafia," which consists mainly of a thousand fishermen who migrated from the mainland. It seems that whenever a restriction on unsustainable fishing practices is imposed, it is boisterously, and sometimes violently, opposed by the fishing community and is eventually weakened or dropped entirely. Take the case of a government limit set on catching sea cucumbers—pricey urchinlike creatures that are considered an aphrodisiac in Asia. In mid-2004, a group of fishermen went to court demanding that the new rule, which capped their catch at four million sea cucumbers within the two-month harvesting season, denied them their constitutional right to reap the Galápagos's bounty. A month earlier, roughly thirty fishermen occupied a national park office on San Cristóbal for two days in protest of the restriction. Three months before that, nearly fifty fishermen took over the park offices on Isabela and the Darwin Research Station on Santa Cruz. At the latter, which is home to a giant-tortoise breeding project, young tortoises were held hostage. In a courtroom in Quito, the judge sided with the fishermen and the ban was lifted.

The ruling was horrifying, if not surprising, to island scientists. Sea cucumbers, or *pepinos del mar* as they are called locally, are a species in crisis. "We have a really bad trend in the population," says Toral. "It used to be common to see these animals everywhere but now it is very seldom that you see them." She says that the number of adults has dropped dramatically and there are no young. A lack of juveniles in the population will prevent the pepinos from recovering. For the first time in the Galápagos, says Toral, "We are facing the first overexploitation of a marine resource by commercial fishing."

Pepinos are desirable to fishermen because they're easy money. While no technical equipment or know-how is needed to scoop up the defenseless creatures, the work is well paid. Fishermen make $17 per pound (ten to twelve dried animals per pound). On Galápagos $150 can support a family for a month.

For all of its challenges, the national park remains cognizant of the intrinsic and inimitable beauty of the islands. It asks visitors a sincere, lingering question upon their arrival to the archipelago: "Galápagos is yours to enjoy. Will your grandchildren have the chance to see it as you do?" For now, the strength and fragility of this place, where species stand alone in history, is balanced but teetering. This is evident on Floreana, at a beach where toes sink into sand the consistency of powdered sugar. Not far off that shore, sea turtles mate, and when the female feels the time is right, she leaves the water. She struggles steadfastly up the sandy embankment, leaving a trail in the sand with her tail. With her powerful flippers she digs a depression and laboriously lays her eggs. She does not stay to protect the delicate eggs or to help her offspring navigate to the sea but instead makes a U-turn, back into the hostile surf.

MACHU PICCHU, PERU

Urubamba River and Machu Picchu

THE BEST VIEW OF MACHU PICCHU IS FROM ABOVE, after traveling on the Inca Trail, the way travelers have first seen it for generations. From here, the whole of the so-called "lost city" comes into view. The peaks of Uña Picchu and Huayna Picchu tower behind the citadel, and 1,500 feet below, the Urubamba River snakes around it on three sides. From the trail's end, the walk down into the city—past the thatch-roofed guardhouse and the steep agricultural terraces, and through the double-jambed main gate—is a journey back in time, to when this was a bustling summer retreat that welcomed Inca ruler Pachacuti and his *panaca*, or royal entourage.

Machu Picchu's highly structured architecture, flawless crafts-manship, and brilliant engineering seem almost superhuman when put in the context of its location. The city was built on a precipitous wedge of land that dropped down between the Machu Picchu and Huayna Picchu peaks along two major geological fault lines. To imagine the landscape before the Incas arrived is to think it impossible to build on. Before they could even begin to erect any of the two hundred houses, temples, and courtyards on the 8,040-foot-high ridge, they had to level much of the area. It is estimated that more than half the labor of constructing Machu Picchu was expended before a single visible stone was laid. Such a remote and unlikely site made the enigmatic citadel intentionally difficult to get to and thus accessible by invitation only.

Although there are countless other Inca ruins in the warm, lush Vilcanota Valley, where Machu Picchu is located, many worthy of respect and awe, and although there are several other Inca trails, Machu Picchu earned its hype. It is a singularly enchanting and goose bump–raising experience. Not only does its precipitous placement conjure the specter of workers moving and placing fifty-ton blocks of granite on a rocky ledge, without using a single wheel, but the refined craftsmanship is almost unbelievable. With only the use of silver, stone, and bronze tools, and sand to smooth rough edges, the Incas built the round, two-story-high Temple of the Sun and a wall so perfect—hardly a blade of grass could be coaxed between its blocks—that Hiram Bingham called it "the most beautiful wall in America." All of the architecture in Machu Picchu was painstakingly designed to complement the natural elements around it—rock, river, vegetation, creatures, and sky. Steep rooflines mimic the slope of backdrop peaks, and shrines were carved to imitate the river and valley below, and to symbolize the sacred serpent, puma, and condor. The Incas worked so hard to build in harmony with their landscape because they believed that these earthly items each had their own supernatural powers. Their mission was successful, as Machu Picchu seems as though it grew organically from that plateau. It is a vast and impressive layout, though also welcoming and comfortable; it's easy to imagine that it was once a place for celebration, reflection, worship, and refuge.

Even today, roughly 475 years after Machu Picchu was abandoned (presumably to conceal it from the Spanish, who had conquered the nearby Inca capital of Cusco forty-five miles away), getting to Machu Picchu is a challenge. There's no airport nearby, no freeway. In fact, the nearest paved road is many miles away. One way to get there is on foot, twenty-seven miles via the most popular four-day Inca Trail trek, which crosses three mountain passes. The other is a four-hour, switchback-filled train ride from Cusco to Aguas Calientes (more affectionately called Machu Picchu Pueblo by locals), followed by a thirty-minute bus crawl up Hiram Bingham Road. The nosebleed-inducing stretch of dirt road is an homage to the Yale-based scholar, who reportedly spent much time intentionally avoiding his family and searching for the fabled city. Up until that point he had heard only rumors of Machu Picchu's existence and its importance as a focal point of religious and political life for the Incas. When Bingham was led to Machu Picchu by the twelve-year-old son of a local farmer in 1911, four hundred years' worth of tropical rain forest had concealed it. But through the mess of vines Bingham could still see clearly that he had found the city to which he had devoted so much of his life.

The United Nations Educational, Scientific, and Cultural Organization (UNESCO) confirmed Bingham's notion of the prominence of Machu Picchu in Incan history when it put the sanctuary on its World Heritage list in 1983, recognizing it as one of the planet's most important cultural sites. It wasn't until almost a decade later that the ruins began to receive a steady, though still modest, stream of travelers. In 1992, nine thousand tourists visited the citadel. After the ouster of corrupt president

Alberto Fujimori in 2000, tourism in Machu Picchu shot up to one hundred fifty thousand visitors by 2002. In 2005, an estimated seven hundred thousand visitors trod on Machu Picchu's mystical terrain. Peruvian tourism officials estimate that the number of travelers to the site will continue to increase by 15 to 20 percent per year.

Today Machu Picchu's remoteness is no impediment to the madding crowds, and many worry about the city's structural ability to handle an estimated 2,500 visitors daily. In 2003, the UNESCO heritage director, Francesco Bandarin, remarked that the relentless march of tourists threatened to irrevocably damage the stone houses, farm terraces, temples, and plazas. The organization warned that if conditions weren't improved and the number of visitors slashed, Machu Picchu would land itself on the World Heritage in Danger list, which would be a profound embarrassment to the country.

The UNESCO warning came on the heels of another call for control in the Machu Picchu region. In 2000, the World Monuments Fund, a forty-year-old conservation group based in New York, added the location to its watch list of the one hundred most endangered sites. The fund's director, Bonnie Burnham, says that what landed Machu Picchu on the list was the Peruvian government's awarding of a contract to Peru Hotels SA to build a cable-car funicular to shuttle even more tourists up the mountainside to the citadel. Peru Hotels is a subsidiary of Orient-Express, which owns both the pricey Hiram Bingham train from Cusco to Aguas Calientes and the Machu Picchu Sanctuary Lodge, the only hotel on the monument grounds. UNESCO later removed the ancient city from its list when the Peruvian government scrapped plans to build the cable car.

But six years after the World Monuments Fund shone a light on the mismanagement of tourism in the area, little progress has been made toward sustainability. "The fact is that the tourism delivery system that they have is not adequate. The buses aren't safe, the roads aren't safe, and nobody knows what the capacity of the site really is," says Burnham. The reason, which comes as no surprise to observers of corrupt South American leadership, is politics.

In Peru, there are as many layers of politics as there are ancient Inca farming terraces. Burnham says that such a complex and often self-serving bureaucracy is Machu Picchu's major challenge. "It's a combined political and economic shortsightedness that doesn't augur well for the future," she says. "It doesn't support the highest level of respect, which you would expect in such a circumstance." One popular example of that shortsightedness involves a beer commercial, approved by the powers that be, that was filmed inside the citadel in 2000. Not long after the crew positioned a half-ton crane, it tipped over, chipping off a chunk of the *intiwatana*, or "hitching post of the sun," one of the most sacred spots in the city. (The area is suspected to have been instrumental during the Incas' *intiraymi*, or summer solstice celebration, when vessels of beer are thought to have been raised to toast the sun, which the Incas considered a deity.)

From Peruvian government officials to regional stakeholders, including the mayor of Aguas Calientes and local business investors and entrepreneurs, there are simply too many hands in Machu Picchu's honeypot. "Local business interests and the wealthy in Peru have invested a lot of money in developing Machu Picchu, in developing the tourism and managing access to the site," says Burnham. "They have inevitably a vested interest in continuing to develop tourism and to underscore those investments." As for the federal government, Machu Picchu generates at least $40 million for the Peruvian economy each year.

If you visit Machu Picchu during the rainy season, from October to May, you may wonder what the fuss is about. The vegetation has had some time to recover, fewer buses are chugging up the Bingham switchbacks, and maintenance crews are putting on its best face for the throngs that are presently deciding in which shoes they will stride across Machu Picchu's granite greatness. During that season there are still two times a day, before the day-trippers arrive on the train from Cusco and after they leave, that the sanctuary is a place worthy of quiet contemplation.

But most visitors flock to the sanctuary in the dry season, from June through September, creating a different vibe and leaving more obvious marks. Many come into Aguas Calientes

Machu Picchu, Peru

on the morning train, bus it right up to Machu Picchu, then head back to Cusco in late afternoon. In khakis, athletic shoes, and wide-brimmed hats, slick with sunblock and bug repellant, many seem unaware of the delicate nature of a place that was built to accommodate only an estimated seven hundred to one thousand people at a time. An oily hand leans against a temple wall to support a weary traveler; a bottom is planted on a centuries-old wall to give the legs a rest; hundreds of thousands of feet pound up and down intricate carved staircases. And though the regulations plainly make some specific demands, such as "Walking sticks are only permitted for elderly and handicapped," it seems most avid walkers, regardless of age, tote and poke a set of trekking poles. The same goes for picnics and horseplay. During this time, it's no revelation that Machu Picchu is the most heavily visited site in South America.

Unless you're arriving at Machu Picchu via the Inca Trail—and only a small percentage of travelers do—you must pass through Aguas Calientes. After the dizzying, jerking train chug from Cusco, a herd of travelers is prodded through an outdoor flea market labyrinth. Once you've successfully cleared the maze, on the bridge over the spectacular and ferocious Urubamba River you'll catch your first glimpse of downtown Aguas Calientes. Crammed in between the creases of several steep, slick, and lushly green peaks, the pueblo is bursting at the seams. Given their inclination toward worshipping nature and carefully integrating their structures into their environment, the Incas would surely be baffled by what's going on here, almost within view of their sacred city. Extensive construction is under way, pushing up the hillsides and into the sky as one building story gets stacked uneasily on another. A fleet of buses lines the Urubamba, pointing up the road to Machu Picchu. Steep cobbled streets are lined with shops and restaurants, with a visual sea of colorful placards meant to entice tourists in for a crisp Cusqueña beer, a bubblegum-flavor Inca Kola, rotisserie-cooked guinea pig (a Peruvian delicacy), or the ubiquitous pizza pie.

The current state of Aguas Calientes is another major concern for conservationists. Because it is the gateway to Machu Picchu, UNESCO is particularly concerned with its runaway development. More and bigger accommodations and other infrastructure would likely encourage an even greater number of visitors. And with the exception of the Machu Picchu Sanctuary Lodge, at the entrance of the citadel, and the Rupa Wasi Cóndor House Ecolodge in Aguas Calientes, very few other establishments seem concerned with the ecological impression they're making.

Fearing the worst, many large donors have gotten together to try to reach a compromise with the local government and to pull the plug on architecture that's absconded with authenticity and taste. Roberto Chávez is an urban specialist with the World Bank who is overseeing the administration of an $8.8 million loan to Peru that will benefit six communities in the Vilcanota Valley, including Aguas Calientes. The money will be used for a variety of needs, including sustainable tourism development. In Aguas Calientes, important talks have taken place with the local government in hopes of getting the town off UNESCO's list of undesirables. "We're negotiating with the mayor that there'll be a building code so that there'll only be X number of floors, so we don't start getting high-rises in there," says Chávez. "And we're trying to put a ring around the town because one of UNESCO's concerns is that it doesn't continue to grow and grow and grow. We've agreed with the mayor that there will be a boundary beyond which there will be no further growth. It will be in a form of a walkway, cut into the mountain, so that it's a very clear divider."

Whether or not the efforts will appease UNESCO is still

unclear. "If they had their way they would like to have Aguas Calientes removed entirely, but that's politically totally unfeasible," says Chávez. "There's no way to resettle a town like that outside the sanctuary." Once a hamlet of a few hundred natives, the town now brims with three thousand industrious people from all over Peru, drawn by the lure of tourism dollars. "They are determined to keep going and don't want to give up under any circumstances," says the World Monuments Fund's Burnham. "And it's not right for the local people to have to cede their interests and for just wealthy businessmen to profit." But she says so many grabbing hands will not likely grasp the urgency of putting the brakes on development. "Because there's no will to resolve this, to suit everybody's interests, it seems like a relatively hopeless situation," says Burnham. "It's probably too late."

Navigating all the levels of Peruvian politics is more difficult than steering a raft down the Urubamba's Class V rapids. This means that the recent $130 million so-called "master plan" for protecting Machu Picchu will likely go the way of the Incas. "A lot of it is pie-in-the-sky, as master plans so often are," says Chávez. "I thought of it as window dressing to keep UNESCO from declaring them on the endangered sites list."

In the meantime, the World Bank is continuing to help some Aguas Calientes residents move their homes, which had been built without regulation in hazardous landslide areas. The process calls attention to another instability that is often overshadowed, perhaps rightly, by the Machu Picchu tourism shuffle. While not much has been said publicly about them in recent years, landslides are considered the greatest threat to the ancient city. While Machu Picchu was skillfully built upon its seismic perch to withstand earthquakes, it's doubtful that the Incas knew the royal retreat they worked so hard on could possibly take a catastrophic trip into the roaring Urubamba River below. In late 2005 Kyoji Sassa, the president of the International Consortium on Landslides, led a meeting on the risk of slides at Machu Picchu. The scientist was the first to say that the monument was in danger several years ago when he and a team of researchers from the Disaster Prevention Research Institute at Kyoto University measured land slippage at ten different places around Machu Picchu. They found that the steep slope behind Machu Picchu was sliding downward 0.4 inches per month. The movement, Sassa told UNESCO, was the precursor to a significant landslide, though the time frame for such a disaster remains unknown. The Kyoto scientists are urging stabilization of the area, where landslides already occasionally strike Hiram Bingham Road, rendering it impassable.

Regardless of what the quintessential threat to Machu Picchu really is, the site cannot withstand the love and appreciation that hundreds of thousands of visitors lavish upon it every year. "There is such a thing as a tipping point," says the World Monument Fund's Burnham. "It may be that when these situations reach this point, people will pull themselves back and realize that they are about to lose something irreplaceable." In order to save it, perhaps one day we too will abandon Machu Picchu, where llamas still munch grass in the main plaza, ethereal mist rises from the Urubamba, and a rainbow from a passing shower lingers.

EUROPE AND
THE MIDDLE EAST

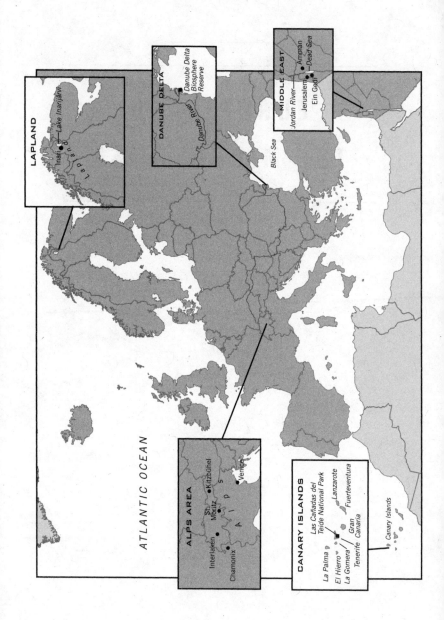

LAPLAND

Inari ● — Lake Inarijärvi

L a p l a n d

DANUBE DELTA

Danube Delta
Biosphere
Reserve

Danube River

MIDDLE EAST

Jordan River — Amman
Jerusalem ● — Dead Sea
Ein Gedi

Black Sea

ATLANTIC OCEAN

ALPS AREA

St. ● Kitzbühel
Moritz
A l p s
Interlaken ● Venice ●
Chamonix ●

CANARY ISLANDS

Las Cañadas del
Teide National Park
Lanzarote
La Palma ● Fuerteventura
El Hierro ● Gran
La Gomera Canaria
Tenerife

Canary Islands

THE ALPS

Ski resort near the Matterhorn

THE FILTERED SUMMER SUN PERMEATES A SWATH OF stately Scotch pine and Norway spruce at the base of the Kitzbüheler Horn in the Austrian Alps. It settles in warm pools on a wooly fern blanket and upon massive, fragrant pine cones that crunch underfoot. Before long, the treeline is reached and the tinkle of a cowbell announces a caramel-colored bovine nibbling gorse and heather. Opposite the Horn, through a thin haze, stands Hahnenkamm (elevation 5,616 feet), famous for its annual World Cup ski races. Beyond its steep, tidy slopes, the Wilder Kaiser massif dominates the northwest horizon, its magnificent wall of rock crags cradling glaciers to its bulky breast. More than 6,500 feet below the tip of the Horn, an elongated emerald valley lies, with the Tyrolean village of Kitzbühel at its center.

For over seven hundred years, humans have strolled the cobblestoned streets of Kitzbühel among chocolate-colored church roofs and Easter egg–hued edifices. And while each season reveals its own Alpine characteristic—from the profusion of wildflowers throughout the spring and summer to the blaze of color that streaks through the valley in autumn—winter has always been the main event in Kitzbühel. In 1898, skiers started flocking there from nearby Salzburg and beyond. Before long, its winter *Wunderland* emerged as the après ski town for hordes of wealthy Europeans. Today its narrow lanes are crammed with high-end shops, five-star chalets, and canopy-covered cafes. And when the snow starts to coat the cobblestones, the crowds converge to slalom through fresh powder on the pistes above the village.

It's hard to imagine Kitzbühel stripped of its starring role as ski central. But that's what prominent scientists like Martin Beniston, head of the geosciences department at the University of Fribourg in Switzerland, are predicting. Kitzbühel's cool blue winter glint is expected to fade as temperatures rise and snowfall becomes increasingly erratic. "In the next thirty years, I think we're likely to see some major changes, in terms of snow in the Alps," says Beniston. "The snow line on average will probably be higher than it is today so the lower elevations are going to get worse." That means low-lying resorts like Kitzbühel, at a scant 2,624 feet, are expected to face hard times. In the coming decades climatologists expect the snow line in Austria to rise by 656 to 984 feet, which will leave the village estranged from its runs.

Kitzbühel (where, ironically, a portion of the Beatles' 1965 movie *Help!* was filmed) is not alone. All along the beguiling 650-mile band of Austrian, Swiss, German, French, and Italian Alps, historic playgrounds face ruin. "Basically most of the Alpine chain is living through the same problem," says Beniston. In the past century winter temperatures warmed 3.6 degrees Fahrenheit in the Alpine region, and the weather is getting less predictable. While a few degrees seems barely perceptible, it is as significant as the first domino in a neatly formed row. "You get these very subtle temperature changes but they may lead to some very extreme events," says Beniston. While scientists once hesitated to attribute isolated events—such as the record floods, blizzards, and heat waves on the continent over the past several years that have cost thousands of lives and millions of Euros—to climate change, that's no longer the case. For example, in late 2006, the prominent UK-based Hadley Centre for Climate Change said that if the worldwide level of atmospheric CO_2 increases as predicted, what now seem like isolated periods of warmth will occur much more frequently. Severe heat waves lasting five or more days (as in July 2006 in the UK) now happen roughly every twenty years, but according to new climate models, such heat waves are likely to occur almost every year (sometimes several times per year) by 2100.

Rising temperatures and chaotic weather are already hitting ski resorts hard. The winter of 2005–2006, in particular, was one of the most bizarre on record. Little or no snow fell before the December holidays. Then, that February, temperatures plummeted to −15 degrees Fahrenheit and it snowed for days. Fearing hypothermia, lift operators were forced to close the slopes. That season Kitzbühel's prestigious Hahnenkamm race was canceled for only the fifth time since 1931, because the snow came down so furiously.

But the unusual weather shouldn't be a big surprise. A United Nations Environment Programme report published in 2003 had previously given the region a wake-up call: "It appears clear that many resorts, particularly the traditional, lower-altitude resorts of Europe, will be either unable to operate as a result of lack of snow or will face additional costs, including artificial snowmaking, that may render them uneconomic." Many ski resorts below 4,265 feet already lack snowfall reliability and "ski security," meaning a hundred uninterrupted days with at least one foot of snow cover. Warming in recent years has led to only about seventy days of guaranteed snow cover.

Business owners who have already seen major changes to their terrain and believe that conditions will continue to degrade are fighting vigorously to defend their empires of snow. Despite the high cost, resorts desperate to keep their winter character and clientele are actually trucking snow from neighboring peaks onto their slopes, and many, including Kitzbühel's fifty-four runs, are investing heavily in snowmaking. European resorts had never relied upon artificial snow, but Austrian resorts now make roughly 40 percent of their snow each season and Switzerland seems poised to follow suit.

Laying the infrastructure—water pipes and turbines—for fake flakes can cost as much as $1 million a mile, and maintenance is around $50,000 a year. Even then, making weather is a fussy business. On the world-famous slopes of Verbier, Switzerland, snow cannons are shot at the peaks when there's a shortage of white. But if it's not very dry and cold, slush showers the slopes instead. In addition to being labor intensive (because manufactured snow melts as quickly as natural snow) and financially unsustainable, snowmaking is also under fire for consuming too much water and energy (which advances climate change).

Other Alpine resorts hoping to defy Mother Nature are considering moving their operations uphill from their current location. This has experts concerned about both the fragility of high-Alpine ecology and the aesthetics of having even the highest regions in the Alps developed. In a joint study by the Swiss Federal Institute for Snow and Avalanche Research, the University of Zurich and the University of Potsdam predicted that preparing a peak as a ski run, using grading machines to even out the surface, would seriously damage delicate Alpine vegetation. From about 6,600 feet and up, such plants take at least thirty years to recover (if they do at all). Stripping slopes of plant cover encourages erosion, which, coupled with the exposure caused by glacial recession, causes peak destabilization.

During the 2006–2007 ski season, a report released by the Organisation for Economic Cooperation and Development (OECD), whose members include the five Alpine countries, reflected on the worsening conditions in the region. "The Alps are particulary sensitive to climate change, and recent warming has been roughly three times the global average. The years 1994, 2000, 2002, and particularly 2003 have been the warmest on record in the Alps in the past 500 years," said the OECD. The report warns that record warmth and unpredictable snow will continue unabated. "Climate models project even greater changes in the coming decades, including a reduction in snow cover at low altitudes, receding glaciers and melting permafrost at higher altitudes, and changes in temperature and precipitation extremes." A similar conclusion was reached by Austria's Central Institute for Meteorology and Geodynamics, which announced in December 2006 that the Alps are the warmest they've been in 1,300 years.

The UN report predicts that temperature change will be more violent in the winter in the northern hemisphere, possibly surpassing the expectation of a rise of 5.4 degrees Fahrenheit in global temperatures over the next fifty years. Beniston says the ski season throughout the Alps loses three weeks for every 1.8 degrees of temperature increase. Under the best circumstances, that means that at least two months of a four-month season could dissolve. According to that projection, Switzerland alone—with some of the region's poshest resorts, such as those near Davos and St. Moritz (where World Cup races were cancelled recently due to snowlessness)—could lose over half of its 230 resorts. Fifteen percent of them, like Wildhaus and Unterwasser, already don't get enough snow. Half of Italy's resorts are below 4,300 feet, as are many in Germany and France. The experts from the

The Matterhorn

University of Zurich who led the UN study said that warming in the region will eventually force skiing upslope to between 4,900 and 6,000 feet.

A shortening of, or the total lack of, a ski season would mean economic collapse for a significant number of the Alps' six hundred resorts (that's nearly one resort for every mile of mountains). Billions of tourism dollars, at least 70 percent of those spent in winter, are propping up a service industry that was built almost entirely on the cold. The UN report suggested that Switzerland alone could lose over a billion dollars a year under such a warming scenario.

The potential cultural and aesthetic losses are also staggering. The injury to the Alpine identity of the region, which is closely linked to the 140-year-old ski industry, is foremost in the minds of many. The winter image of the Alps as a place where lithe, fashionable skiers carve serpentine tracks through perfect powder may soon go the way of handsome men in lederhosen clutching steins of beer. While resorts congested with couture-obsessed tourists and valleys sometimes socked-in with smog from the fifty million cars and twelve million trucks that cross the Alps every year may be a more accurate characterization of the seasonal influx, there remains an authentic Alpine spirit that has endured throughout the area's five-thousand-year human history. Its reputation as a place with haughty peaks, bucolic beauty, and stoic multigenerational families was earned and is still deserved.

In Austria, the Pinzgau Saalach Valley is almost too Alpine to be real. Livestock graze on endless knolls and charming window boxes spill color. There are enough hiking options to last a month, through the valley or up onto mountaintops, from which you'll spot jaw-dropping peaks in neighboring countries.

In Germany, the Bavarian Alps are at their best in Berchtesgaden National Park. You can travel back through time on the thirty-minute battery-powered ferry ride across placid Lake Königssee to the red domes of St. Bartholomew's, built in the twelfth century and accessible only by boat. The sheer and stoic Watzmann range (including Watzmann peak, which, at 8,901 feet, is one of Germany's highest) provides the backdrop for the charming town of Berchtesgaden, where the lederhosen aren't donned for show. There are many foot trails from town, and one popular day hike ends in Kärlingerhaus, a huge nineteenth-century ecohostel nestled in its own piece of Alpine heaven, which serves up warm food and, of course, beer.

In Switzerland, the Swiss Glacier Express chugs directly into the awe-inspiring landscape for a look at the Alps' glittering ice, tony villages, and chic chalets. It takes about eight hours to ride from St. Moritz to Zermatt, passing through 91 tunnels and over 291 bridges (which can only be described as engineering magic). The high point of the trip, in terms of elevation, is Oberalp Pass at 6,670 feet, near the town of Andermatt in the breathtaking Urserntal Valley.

In Italy, Alpine peaks and lakes go hand-in-hand. Some of the best lake views can be seen by hiking above them through the dense wilderness (especially in Val Grande National Park near Miazzina) and medieval towns of Italy's foothills. Henry James was mezmerized by Italy's Alpine atmosphere while traveling from Switzerland to Lake Como in 1873. In his book *Italian Hours*, published in 1909, he said that the beauty of the lakes there defied description, that one ought not even to try. Looking upon the mountains, James observed the "shimmering, melting azure of the southern slopes and masses; in the luxurious tangle of nature." He was also taken by the unique, warm glow of the place. "Most of all it's the deep yellow light that enchants you and tells you where you are," he said.

In France, Chamonix is irresistible. Whether you take on some of the French Alps' famously formidable peaks or just stare up at the granite pinnacles while lazing around its historic hub nibbling a croissant at Aux Petits Gourmands, Chamonix is classic Alps. The stark, stunning glaciated topography of this region is often compared to the Himalayas, with good reason. At 15,770 feet, Mont Blanc is western Europe's highest peak, and its pyramidal perfection makes it one of the most recognizable. From the flanks of the Mont Blanc massif, you'll catch views of nearby Mer de Glace, a roughly six-mile-long glacier. The massive, snaking sea of ice was once visible from Chamonix but, like all Alpine glaciers, is quickly recoiling.

Glacier recession in the Alps is nothing new—it's the rate of modern melting that has climatologists concerned. From 1970 to 2000, glaciers receded almost three times faster than they did from 1850 to 1970; most of that melt happened from 1985 to 2000. Roughly two thirds of the volume of all Alpine glaciers has been lost since 1850. A few years of exceptional heat since then have led to further record losses. A heat wave in the summer of 2003 hit northern Italy, France, and Switzerland particularly hard. Scientists blame that surge alone for a nearly ten-foot total loss of Alpine glaciers, which is about five times more than the average annual loss. It accounted for the loss of 10 percent of Italy's mountain ice.

Switzerland also lost an amount that would make the typically stoic Swiss weep. The Swiss Academy of Natural Sciences said that glacial retreat in 2003 in the country exceeded any loss in any year since records began in the nineteenth century: nearly five hundred feet. The situation in the breathtaking Jungfrau-Aletsch-Bietschhorn World Heritage site—150 square miles of ice—near Interlaken is of particular concern. The size of the remarkable Aletsch glacier, Europe's largest at fourteen miles long, is approaching a historic low. It has drawn back two miles since 1860, like a turtle pulling its head back into its shell. At the current recession rate, about half of the total volume of current Alpine glaciers will melt by 2025, and less than 10 percent will be left in 2100.

A growing number of resorts are trying the rudimentary but effective tactic of cloaking their frozen slopes in fleecelike polypropylene fabric in the off season to reflect summer rays. Austria's Pitztal Glacier ski resort covers fifteen acres of its assets, at an elevation of about nine thousand feet, which costs $121,000 per year. Another resort, Gotthard Sportbahnen in Andermatt, Switzerland, pulls a similar white sheet over its Gurschen Glacier, a three-thousand-foot vertical ski run that has been spiking the adrenaline of Europeans for over fifty years.

Initial reports from the Swiss Federal Institute of Technology in Zurich say the experiment, in which the resort spread twenty-seven thousand square feet of white fleece over the upper reaches of the glacier, appeared to work in Andermatt. "The fleece is doing its job and has prevented the [glacier] from disappearing at the same rate as hitherto," they said. Another Swiss resort in Verbier swaddled thirty thousand square feet of the Tortin ice field in a pricey fleece parka from June through September to keep the melt to a minimum.

The Alps, which are explored by upwards of eighty million visitors each year, have even more to lose than than their story-book ski towns and ice-shrouded peaks. In its report, the OECD also warned of the increased risk of natural hazards resulting from climate change that could further threaten habitation and recreation in the region.

Ice in the Alps is like a glue that keeps everything in place. Receding glaciers, melting permafrost, and heavy snow and rain pounding the peaks cause landslides. And the densely populated slopes of the Alps are a recipe for disaster. While there's perma-frost throughout mountainous Europe, none is as tangled up with infrastructure—roads, resorts, rails—as it is along the Alps, where there are fourteen million residents. That's why the Swiss town of Pontresina spent $5 million to erect a four-story earthen dam to hold back the permafrost cliff hanging over the village. Should it liquefy, the town would be destroyed. Even now, resi-dents of Pontresina aren't strangers to the effects of climate change. Morteratsh glacier, which used to terminate at the town, is now a 1.2-mile walk away.

Avalanches are already on the rise at all altitudes as heavier winter snow blankets peaks that can't support it. In the summer of 2003 France's Matterhorn and Mont Blanc were actually closed for a time because of the hazard. Since access to these mountains had never before been restricted, the closures were a milestone for Jonathan Bamber, a professor of physical geography at the University of Bristol. "For the first time in the history of human exploration of the mountains, they actually had a gendarme at the base of Mont Blanc saying, 'You're not going up there. It's too dangerous,' " says Bamber. The absence of snow on the mountains' crowns revealed the true instability of the ice and rock on their slopes. As the peaks warmed, the ice fell in Peugeot-size boulders. Seventy climbers needed to be rescued from the Matterhorn that year. By spring 2006 many areas were at level 4, out of 5 on the European Risk Scale, which indicates a high likelihood of these disasters occuring. Eighty-six tourists were killed that season; fifty-six deaths were in France alone. "An increased avalanche hazard is likely because you'd have quite a heavy snowpack on very steep slopes, which makes these slopes extremely unstable," says Beniston.

Some Alpine areas facing the reality that skiing may not be viable in the long term are beginning to diversify. The call to take summer tourism more seriously is coming from all corners. In Chamonix, Davos, and Zermatt, sports that don't depend on snow—including fishing, sailing, hiking, mountain biking, even zip-lining—are taking center stage. Some are even trying global warming–themed tourism. In the summer of 2006, several hundred people per day hoofed it an hour up a steep slope to an isolated hostel above Grindelwald in hopes of seeing a rock the size of two Empire State Buildings (two million cubic meters) fall from the east face of Switzerland's famous Eiger Peak into the uninhabited valley several hundred feet below. The cliff was previously fastened to the mountain by glacial ice, but geologists began observing fissures in the face that June. The crowd got what they came for when four hundred thousand to seven hundred thousand cubic meters of limestone (up to one third of the cleaving cliff) rumbled down the mountain. Officials, who had been monitoring the rock slab for months, had closed popular hiking and climbing routes as well as the gorge beneath it. No one was injured, but rock dust cloaked the nearby resort town of Grindelwald for hours. And until the spring of 2007, there was a popular exhibition called "Glaciers in the Hothouse" at Bern's Alpine Museum. Giant photographs compared present-day ice-less landscapes to images of years past, when they were covered with glaciers. In the exhibition, creators Sylvia Hamberger and Wolfgang Zängl of Munich's Association of Ecological Research asked, "Do we belong to the last generation that can admire the magnificent giants of ice?"

While attracting visitors year-round seems a sensible survival strategy, it is proving difficult to change the cultural mind-set that skiing and the Alps are inextricable. As a result some re-searchers are suggesting starting small, with the exploitation of oxygen. Advertising "fresh mountain air" (like resort owners did in the nineteenth century to draw tuberculosis sufferers) seems to be making a comeback. Tourism literature now touts the attributes of the Alps' "clean" air. Whether or not this tactic will give the Alps' industries room to breathe remains uncertain. Meanwhile, the span of mighty peaks, out of which the tremen-dous Rhine, Rhône, Po, and Danube rivers flow, still connects cultures and dazzles travelers as the range curves across the land-scape and into the future.

BOREAL FOREST, LAPLAND, FINLAND

FROM THE SIMPLE HIKER'S HUT ON THE TOP OF Otsamotunturi Fell, Finnish Lapland sprawls out in all directions. At this high latitude, above the Arctic Circle, the terrain is sturdy and impressive. The 1,371-foot peak is carpeted with bright bells of alpine azalea, blue heath, and Lapland diapensia. This is a low, rolling landscape where primose-trimmed riverbanks cut through fields of lingonberry and marsh tea and drain into grand lakes. Beneath the meadow are forests of alpine birch and Scotch pine whose trunks are thatched with pale green lichen.

The woods of Lapland are a vital part of the boreal ring, the crown of ancient forest and freshwater ecosystem that encircles the Arctic. This ring, also known as the taiga, consists of forests in Alaska, Canada, and the Fennoscandia region, including northern Norway, Sweden, Finland, and Russia's Kola Peninsula. This band of forests, which lies just beneath the barren polar landscape, was named for Boreas, the Greek god of the cold north wind. The boreal ring accounts for roughly one third of the earth's total forests. These forests are constantly at work regulating the world's climate, air quality, and water cycle. Grizzlies, black bears, wolves, and wolverines roam there, and countless bird species migrate there to hatch their young.

Forests in Fennoscandia are rooted farther north than those in any other region. And thanks to the influence of the warm Gulf Stream, Finnish Lapland boasts green at surprisingly high latitudes. Despite conditions that are somewhat less harsh than most circumpolar areas, growth there is slow. These brawny forests endure winter months in total darkness and withstand constant summer sunlight. While Lapland has always been measured by extremes, it is also marked by its striking subtleties. It's a place where light has varied hues and the sounds of nature are melodic, where you run out of words to describe all the different shades of green, and where plump orange cloudberries taste like the sun.

From the Otsamotunturi Fell cap, Lake Inarijärvi, sheltered by some of Lapland's oldest pines, appears massive and intriguing. Ten fish species manage to survive in the ancient, frigid lake, including arctic char, trout, and pike. Over seventy million years ago, the earth's crust sank here crudely, leaving some rocky, cliff-like shoreline as well as smooth beaches and quiet coves. Inarijärvi is so large that it's often characterized as an inland sea; from its center, no shoreline can be seen. It stretches sixty-two miles from north to south and thirty-seven miles from west to east, and it is deeper than three hundred feet in spots. Lake Inari (for short) has over three thousand islands, including a small but prominent one that's famous locally. Visitors to the area will hear about the bulky, humpbacked island called Ukonsaari, Ukonkivi, or simply Ukko, meaning "old man." It remains a sacred site for the native Sami, whose ancestors made sacrifices there in exchange for successful fishing. Other islands are revered Sami burial sites, chosen to be far away from scavenging wildlife. The lake's many skinny, protected straits, called *nuori*, are perfect for exploring by kayak.

While it seems far-flung and isolated, this area is actually a favorite jumping-off point for exploring Finnish Lapland. Outdoorsy types generally fly into Ivalo, twenty-four miles south of Inari; head north by coach; and hook up with a guide such as Gro Husmo of the UK-based outfitter Explore Worldwide. Husmo takes travelers trekking, mountain biking, canoeing, and kayaking through the wilds. (Those less interested in navigating trail-free wilderness or Arctic rapids can join the sauna set. The origin of saunas in Finland has been traced back two thousand years, when it was believed that sweathouses cured illness. The practice of splashing water on hot rocks and beating oneself with birch branches to instill good health and relaxation is still hugely popular.) While most people head to Lapland in the endless light of summer—the beginning of June to the start of July, when the sun never drops below the horizon—Husmo insists that it's a place for all seasons. "In the spring [come] the flowers and the reindeer calves," she says. In the fall, "the grouse changes color for the winter and hides in the snow, with only its head popping up to scout for predators." Perhaps most spectacular, she says, are the winter skies streaked with the northern lights. "On a cold, clear winter's night the moon and the stars reflect on the snow. And people think it's dark up here."

Husmo says that those who dismiss these northernmost reaches of Europe as a tangle of tongue-twisting names, or as vast expanses of nothingness, are missing Europe's last vestiges of wildness. Finnish Lapland is thick with character, charm, and history. It's sprawling, sparsely populated, untamed, and remote. It's so appealing, says Husmo, because "there are still these huge areas of virtually untouched wilderness in the world where nature is still too extreme for ordinary people to thrive."

Yet some people have lived here for centuries, and though their survival is in question, they're still trying to get by.

Just a few miles southwest of Lake Inarijärvi is Inari, a lively village and the de facto Sami capital of Finland. The Sami homeland, which they call Sapmi, is also known as Samiland or Lapland. It extends across northernmost Norway, Sweden, Finland, and Russia's northwest corner. There are an estimated seventy thousand total Sami in Sapmi, approximately eight thousand of whom live in Finland. The history of the Finnish Sami, well documented in Inari's world-renowned Siida Museum, is a rich and tumultuous one. They are thought to have lived in southern

Scandinavia from sometime after the last ice age ended, and to have migrated north under pressure from incoming foreign cultures. There are at least ten known Sami dialects, though many people were forced to learn Finnish during a period of ethnic cleansing in the mid twentieth century. Their religion was also suppressed as pagan during that time but survives today. To the Sami, for whom the spiritual and natural worlds are one and the same, the North Star is known as the "pillar of the world." Their storytelling tradition, called *joik*, a combination of tales and song, is also still actively practiced.

The Sami in and around Inari survive largely on tourism dollars, selling handicrafts and showing off reindeer. But many others, like Outi Jääskö, subsist solely on the centuries-old practice of reindeer husbandry. Sami have been herding in Lapland for over four hundred years. Jääskö is the head of the Muotkatunturi reindeer herding cooperative, in which the one hundred or so herders maintain 6,800 reindeer and sell mature animals for their meat. Her co-op is one of eight family-run groups in the Inari area. "Basically all the activities are done together, as families, work groups, as a co-op," she says. "That's what makes reindeer herding very special. It ties people together, keeps the knowledge and language and passes it from one generation to the next."

But aggressive logging in Finnish Lapland has been interfering with tradition, causing chaos for reindeer and threatening the culture and livelihood of Sami herders. Logging is certainly not new to Finland's forests. The huge saws and jaws of cranes and tractors have been cutting, piling, and loading logs onto flatbed trucks and freight trains for decades. According to the UN Environment Programme, Finland supplies the world with one quarter of its writing and printing paper and one sixth of its paperboard. Metsähallitus, the state's forestry agency, has routinely harvested tons of trees per year. Since Finland is the most forested of the European nations—roughly 86 percent of the country is covered with trees, or about sixty-four million acres—

it accommodated the intensive cutting for decades. But now that Metsähallitus has begun targeting ancient trees, herders have sought help from the international community. They turned to Greenpeace in 2002, because after centuries of moving farther north, their survival was at stake, says the organization's forest expert, Oliver Salge. "They always ran to the north of the country but there is no more north," he says. "They are totally nonviolent people. They have never fought against anybody, never raised a weapon against anybody, and never had war among themselves. This is the main reason why they are on the verge of extinction." If they don't fight now, says Salge, "they know that they will die."

At the root of the conflict between Metsähallitus and the Sami is the fact that the groves of old-growth pine that are especially lucrative for logging happen to closely overlap with critical reindeer grazing areas. "These tree lichen areas are exactly the pine forests that are the most valuable for forestry as well," says Jääskö. The damage is threefold: tree lichen, which can take centuries to grow, ends up on a flatbed truck; branches and other cutting waste smother ground lichen, causing it to rot; and the loss of productive grazing areas increases pressure in other regions, leading the government to limit the number of reindeer that can graze in any one place. Jääskö says that herders then have to supplement reindeer feeding with costly hay. "The ministry suggests we allow logging and get money as compensation to buy hay for the reindeer," she says. "But that changes the natural cycle, we lose the knowledge and language of natural grazing, and the collective social connection within the co-op, i.e., the Sami culture." And when it becomes impossible for them to subsist on herding, a phenomenon that's already begun, says Jääskö, "people lose their living and have to find other jobs, which means they have to move from the reindeer herding villages and leave their culture and language."

Ninety percent of the forests in Samiland are government

owned, which accounts for pretty much every tree that can be seen from the top of Otsamotunturi Fell and west to the Norwegian border, east to the Russian border, north to the Arctic Ocean, and south to Helsinki. Because ownership is so skewed, any so-called negotiations regarding logging around Inari are equally imbalanced. "It says right in the constitution that the logging operations in the Sami homeland must be done in a way that the culture and livelihood of the Sami people is not threatened," says Salge. "But when the Sami say, 'This is threatening our livelihood,' the state says, 'No, it's not.'" And when herders complain, says Jääskö, Metsähallitus and the Finnish Parliament each say that the other is responsible for deciding which areas are for logging. This makes the process of seeking relief from logging extremely complicated, and the hope of negotiations becomes laughable. "They just announce the amount they need to cut. There are no negotiations about how much logging each reindeer herding cooperative can tolerate without suffering harm," says Jääskö. After a brief moratorium, during which herders were hopeful that their protests had been recognized, Metsähallitus resumed logging in Inari grazing forests in mid-2007.

It's not just the taking of trees but the busting up of grazing land that's problematic. In 2005, the UNEP reported, "Finland's forests—including its remaining old-growth fragments—are being exploited by clearcutting, forest thinning, road construction, and ditching of soils. The result is the severe and extensive fragmentation of natural habitat." Reindeer are not adjusting well to the changes, says Sini Haarki, a forest specialist with the Finnish Association for Nature Conservation. "Fragmentation has destroyed the pasture routes, and the reindeer get lost now when looking for the forests that used to be there," she says. The forests around Inari are some of the most critically endangered, where logging is planned in several intact forests. "These forests are very rare remnants of wild European nature," says Haarki.

Finland retains less than 5 percent of its old-growth forest. "The trees in these forests are hundreds of years old. Many started growing in medieval times," she says.

Greenpeace's Salge says that the loss of scores of endangered and threatened species in these woods is already happening. The flying squirrel, the golden eagle, the three-toed woodpecker, and many lesser-known species may disappear if logging doesn't stop in the most ecologically sensitive regions. "They argue that those species are protected in national parks and the rest is for logging," he says. Other often overlooked pitfalls of logging old growth are the more global and long-term ones. "The worry is that the politicians will never really see that the protection of that area is more economically beneficial than clear-cutting it, from an ecological point of view and in terms of climate and social welfare," he says. "Short-term profit objectives are hindering the long-term economic and environmental welfare."

For as long as possible Jääskö, the Inari herder, will continue to round up and mark her reindeer calves on cool July evenings on the fell, where, she says, "The nights are as light as the days." She'll look them over carefully to assess how successful their summer eating has been. Come autumn, when her reindeer are most plump, some will be hunted. In winter and spring, she'll drive her herd from one area to another based on weather, predators, and grazing resources. If the snowpack is too deep or icy, the reindeer will search for lichen dangling, soft and green, from tree branches. It's a difficult but fulfilling life, says Jääskö—that is, when nature follows its course.

CANARY ISLANDS, SPAIN

Pico Viejo, Teide National Park, Tenerife

FROM THE WINDOW OF AN AIRBUS PREPARING TO LAND on Tenerife, the Canary Islands look like hunks of a jagged volcanic puzzle tossed haphazardly into the Atlantic. The landmasses themselves—there are seven large islands—are a precipitous and active cluster of shield volcanoes offering some of the most diverse and stunning terrain on Earth. While the islands have been provinces of Spain since 1495, they lie just sixty-seven miles west of the Moroccan coast.

Because of the warm Sahara winds that blow across the islands, the Canaries have year-round appeal. Each of the islands has a distinct character that may influence which one travelers choose as a base, but all are linked by flights and an efficient ferry system. Most holiday-goers head for the bustling hub island of Tenerife, where the resorts and high-rises on the south side cater to the suntanning-and-shopping stratum. But Tenerife also still has some of the islands' most charming and historic towns, including Puerto de Mogán, Garachico, and La Orotava, resplendent with colonial mansions and sprawling, flower-filled plazas. Like Tenerife, Gran Canaria, to its east, is fertile and subtropical in the north and arid and sunny in the south. Some of the most pristine strips of sand are found on the easternmost islands of Fuerteventura and Lanzarote. The westernmost islands of La Gomera, La Palma, and El Hierro are much less developed. Ancient trails still link villages there, where nature, culture, and craft are the main events. Dry, rocky El Hierro has lava pools, scenic coastal stretches, cliffs, and crisp white architecture gleaming most spectacularly in Sabinosa. La Palma is often called the most beautiful of the Canaries, given its extreme landscape of steep volcanoes, deep craters, and abundant green in between. La Gomera is still home to the ancient Silbo language, composed of lyrical whistling that can be transmitted up to two miles away. Many types of traditional crafts are still toiled over here, including the well-known red clay pots of El Cercado. Palm tree honey and home-brewed *mistela* spirits are highlights of the local cuisine.

The primo peak in the Canaries is Mount Teide; at 12,188 feet, it's the highest point in the Atlantic and the third-largest volcano in the world. Teide, which lies smack in the middle of triangular Tenerife, has erupted spectacularly several times since the island was settled in 1402. Most recently it blasted off its northwest flank in 1909. The Cañadas caldera, in which sit Teide and two other peaks, Montaña Blanca and Pico Viejo, is thirty miles around. From the edge of the Cañadas crater, other islands, including Gran Canaria, La Palma, La Gomera, and El Hierro can be seen. The best way to escape the summer heat and desolation in the crater is to ride the Teleférico cable car to the summit.

On most days, northeast trade winds conjure Los Vientos Alisios, Tenerife's famously mystical cloud seas, layers that look dense enough to walk on. In the caldera below them, which lies entirely within the borders of Las Cañadas del Teide National Park, there is abundant evidence of the intense forces that sculpted the landscape. Afternoon sun spotlights serrated lava escarpments, and the flaxen-hued pumice, pitch-black obsidian puffs, and deep red *picónes* (ash cones) evoke the occasions on which sulfur puffed to the surface and lava bled from this earth.

A walk down through the national park—crunching over lava bits like you're trekking over burnt toast—reveals subtle aspects of Tenerife's chaotic character. The *malpais*, or badland, looks like a dark chocolate cake freshly frosted, the result of thick rivers of magma that cooled into enormous charcoal slabs. Other areas were showered with liquid magma that, when cooled, left the Huevos de Teide. Some of these "egg" rocks were spat from Teide's mouth two millennia ago. By contrast, Los Roques de García are a giant's geological sculpture garden, where whimsically named rock formations like the Queen's Shoe and imposing lava towers such as the 6,719-foot Cathedral dwarf their surroundings.

Deep within the park, trees are scarce, though stately Canary pines and sturdy Canary cedars offer sporadic shelter. Through the rocks appear gutsy retama plants, bowl-shaped bushes with fragrant white or pinkish buds that cling to the rough red volcanic soil. The ash-green leaves and bold red blooms of the *tajinaste* explode from the rocky soil like bits of magma frozen in time, and lightly scented broom and juniper hold fast. The rare Teide violet and Guanche rose will reward the careful observer. Tenerife lizards, called "charred" lizards because of their black-and-orange coloring, scurry around, and many species of birds keep watch, including the great spotted woodpecker and the island canary (the bird was named after the islands; the islands were named for the wild dogs, *canis* in Latin, that early travelers encountered here).

Exploring the crater's slopes has been popular since German scientist Alexander von Humboldt first climbed it in 1799. Despite his miserable hike in the gale-force winter winds that blast snow and ice deep into Cañada's hardened lava fissures, and his inadequate footwear for the hot lava beds, many blazed a similar trail over the centuries, including Spain's King Juan Carlos and Neil Armstrong, who was no doubt drawn to Teide's lunar landscape.

But long before the king, the astronaut, or the scientists laid heavy footsteps around the smoldering caldera and across the verdant plains, the Guanches worshiped Teide and led their cattle along these trails. "Guanche" is the name given by the Europeans to the estimated eighty thousand tall, blond, blue-eyed indigenous people they found in the archipelago in the fifteenth century. By the time the Spanish conquered the Canaries in the 1490s, they had killed many Guanches; over time they assimilated the rest into their gene pool. But the Guanches' pre-Hispanic history is something of a mystery. While most anthropologists now believe that they descended from the Berbers, who sailed from North Africa around 500 B.C. or earlier, some still believe that they are the remnant residents of Atlantis, which people speculate sank into the deep trenches between the islands.

Whether or not they believe the Canaries are what's left of Atlantis, many residents and travelers feel that they are still fantasy islands. But their treasured terrain now faces many threats to its environment and culture, including unchecked development, tourism, and infrastructure weakness, as well as the occasional swarm of locusts, the increasing number of dust storms, and a crush of illegal immigrants.

One major concern for the Canary Islands' two main environmental watchdogs, the Asociación Tinerfeña de Amigos de la Naturaleza (ATAN) and Ecologistas en Acción de Canarias, is the huge port project planned for the southern Tenerife town of Granadilla. The project threatens the wide expanses of fine golden sand on the area's pristine beaches, including El Médano, La Tejita, and La Jaquita–Windsurf. The picturesque and agriculturally rich town of Granadilla (population nineteen thousand) is also in jeopardy from potential port traffic—some estimates say two thousand trucks a day may grind up and down its winding byways. ATAN fears that fuel spills and pollution at the site are inevitable and will be deadly to the fishing industry, which relies on the marine biodiversity there, and to the unique *sebadales*, or marine meadows, where five varieties of endangered sea turtles can be seen. Despite an intense and widespread campaign against the port, mainland Spain is determined to carry out the plan, insisting that no viable alternative locations for it exist.

Local government officials, including regional environment vice minister Milagros Luis Brito, insist that the new port will actually help reverse another growing environmental issue on the islands: pollution. They argue that by allowing an influx of liquid natural gas into the port (which is part of the plan to wean the region's power supply off oil), air quality will eventually improve. A recent article in the *Tenerife News* said, "The sub-tropical, bucolic image of the archipelago that the Canary authorities are so fond of promoting was in tatters . . . when news broke of how greenhouse gas emissions from these Fortunate Isles have escalated by a staggering 81% since 1990." Increased traffic and tourism are blamed for the spike in carbon emissions into the air above the islands.

The number of tourists in the Canaries has skyrocketed in the past fifteen years. According to Carmelo Leon at the University of Las Palmas de Gran Canaria, from 1990 through 2003, the number of tourists grew from 3.5 million to 12.4 million. The islands were addicted to tourism, but when the market got saturated (too many tourists, not enough accommodation), visitation dropped off. But a recent boom in building, mostly the construction of hotels and restaurants to meet tourist demands, has been encouraged by massive tax breaks from the Spanish government. In 2005 the islands had 9.3 million visitors (the majority of whom visit between mid-November and mid-March), dwarfing the permanent population of 1.9 million. A report released by Greenpeace in mid-2007 said that in the past several years, developed areas increased by 194 percent on Tenerife alone.

When Delioma Dorta, a Tenerife native who is currently attending a university in Britain, returns twice a year to visit her family, she is flabbergasted at the ceaseless crush of construction. "It's quite amazing how Tenerife is getting totally encroached upon," she says. "The infrastructure development and the construction of roads—for transportation and of course tourism—it's too much. It's too, too much." At the end of the flight from the UK, when she lands on Tenerife after dark, the drastic changes of the past fifteen years really strike her. "In the night you can very well realize how much it's been invaded by the buildings and all because everything's lit up," she says. "It's something that I'm really concerned about because it seems like it just won't stop." Any laws in place to regulate construction remain exclusively theoretical, says Dorta, because of the bond between business and politics. "The companies that build there, they are very powerful," she says.

While the archipelago has a land area of 2,876 square miles, population density statistics do not take into account the four national parks, more than a hundred and forty protected natural areas, and four biosphere reserves, where the population is near nil. There are also fifteen golf courses on the islands; nine new courses are under construction and ten others are being planned. Take away the uninhabited tracts of land, which account for some 40 percent of the Canaries' surface area, and the islands emerge as one of the most population-dense archipelagoes in the world. Some coastal areas of the islands, such as Playa de las Americas on the west coast of Tenerife, now look more like Vegas than nirvana. Veronica's Strip, in Playa de las Americas, throbs with clubs and discos filled with scarlet Europeans who have spent the day indulging in sun and cervezas out on the white sand. That sand, incidentally, was brought by barge from the Sahara desert.

If hauling sand from the Sahara seems absurd, that's the price the tourism industry, which accounts for 22 percent of the islands' GDP, is willing to pay to feed its habit. The World Wildlife Fund cites unregulated tourism-related construction as the top menace to Canary Islands critters: "First, tourist resorts and illegal building destroys habitats. . . . Many local and foreign enterprises have overdeveloped different areas of the islands, causing enormous habitat destruction. The illegal construction of houses inside protected areas is also a large threat." This encroachment of humanity on the natural surroundings has crammed the islands' original ecosystems into the meager 20 percent that remains undeveloped. Of the 2,000 species of flora on the Canaries—of which 520 are considered endemic—at least 593 are on extinction watch lists. Many are found nowhere else in the world.

But some islands, specifically El Hierro and La Gomera, are shrugging off their party-hard image by embracing and promoting their rural past and present and the staggering biodiversity that makes the Canaries unique. La Gomera is the anti-Tenerife, with no large-scale commercial or tourism infrastructure to speak of, though there is a good variety of quaint *casitas* to choose from. While it's only twenty miles from Los Cristianos on Tenerife to San Sebastián on La Gomera—less than a two-hour ferry ride (or forty-five minutes on the hydrofoil)—the island is a world away. The Valle Gran Rey, or Valley of the Great King, on La Gomera's west side is still an active farming corridor where dates, papayas, mangoes, and avocados sprout from the dizzying terraces that flank the steep valley walls. Nestled within the valley is a cluster of small villages, including La Puntilla, La Playa, Vueltas, and La Calera. La Calera is a quiet town tucked into a cache of banana plantations with cozy shops and eateries that many visitors to La Gomera, most of whom spend only a day here, often miss.

You can also amble through La Gomera's Garajonay National Park in the island's highlands without seeing many other people. Its 154 square miles of intact woodland are protected by UNESCO as Europe's largest laurisilva, or ancient laurel grove. Most of the park is cool and shady, thanks to a canopy formed by sixty-five-foot evergreen laurels with lichen dangling from their branches. Hikers who can withstand some steep, exposed sections of trail will be rewarded at Alto de Garajonay, the park's 4,879-foot peak. From there, past rock outcroppings that rise sharply from the pale green laurel and rings of clouds that envelop all but the peaks of neighboring islands, Tenerife, La Palma, El Hierro, and Gran Canaria can be seen. But there are walks for every level in the park; the easy, mist-shrouded path to Laguna Grande, in particular, is a pleasure. And from the Mirador de Bailadero lookout, the densely wooded ravines that zigzag through the park are mesmerizing. Rare birds, including the long-toed Canary pigeon, can be scouted here among juniper and tree heather.

Tenerife should not yet be written off. In the hopes of capitalizing on its own brand of ecotourism, "Tenerife Natural" has sprouted as a new branch of the island's tourism department, focusing on rural trekking, mountain biking, and stargazing excursions. In the lush and fertile Anaga Mountains on the extreme northeast tip of the island, there are still some remote villages where herbs and ferns continue to outnumber visitors.

An intriguing, storied human history and terrain sculpted by geology and microclimates are still the best of what the Islas Afortunadas, or Fortunate Islands, have to offer. Staring through blackness as distant galaxies come into view in the heavens above Teide, it's not difficult to imagine the Guanches raising their faces skyward here millennia ago. The absence of light pollution on the mountain still makes it a stellar place to gawk at the constellations. But the glare of greed and progress are just over that hillside.

DANUBE RIVER AND DELTA

Fisherman, Danube Delta

THE DANUBE DELTA, ALONG THE WESTERN FRINGE OF
the Black Sea, is one of the world's best intact wetlands. Eastern
Europe's Eden, as it has been called, is thick with reed swamps
and tree-jammed forests that appear to float on the marsh.
Minks and otters scamper here, and rare protected species like
the pygmy cormorant, great egret, and crested pelican hunt
relentlessly for endangered sturgeon and paddlefish. The Delta
is home to dozens of varieties of freshwater fish, and the fish
have drawn generations of canoe-paddling fishermen. Millions
of migratory birds—312 species in all—from Asia, Africa,
Europe, and the Mediterranean also frequent the Delta. The
prodigious floodplain forests of oak, marsh poplar, and drowned
willows there, along with dune islands and open pastures, are the
last remaining safe haven for rare waterfowl including the white
pelican and the black stork.

The Delta is an oasis of wilderness suspended between the
bustling Danube River and the high-rises of the Black Sea's

megaresorts. It's also equidistant from the North Pole and the equator, giving it brief, mild winters; flood-prone springs; hot, enduring summers; and cool, calm falls. For decades it was all but forgotten by outsiders (and most locals). These wetlands were generally inaccessible to the masses, with the exception of a few travelers who followed the Danube River across the Wallachian Plain to the broad, shallow marsh. Others found their way to the region from Bucharest, 186 miles southwest of the Delta's historic but industrial gateway city of Tulcea (pronounced "tool-cha"). Since the fall of communism did little for Romanian tourism, the only options for travelers were Tulcea's Iron Curtain–era hostels, which come in various shades of gray. And the only way to enter the lazy, labyrinthine Delta narrows was to rent a rowboat, or better yet, to hire a local fisherman to navigate the maze (which you can still do today). But the buzz around the Delta in the past few years has some calling it Europe's next must-see eco-destination, its last real frontier.

While still in its youth, traveler infrastructure with an eco-bent is burgeoning. (The Association of Ecotourism in Romania is a good place to start to assess legitimate outfitters.) The Danube Nature Resort, which opened in 2005, is Romania's great green hope in the Delta. The five-star, thirty-two-acre complex has thirty wood-and-stone bungalows with wide, lazy porches overlooking Lake Samova. It's located twelve miles from Tulcea and is easily reached from there. Since the resort is as much about the local ecology as it is about Romanian culture, it offers tons of ways to get out into the Delta, including kayaks, canoes, and naturalist-led boat tours, as well as land-based trips. Cultural destinations that give a taste of the country's traditions, architecture, and cuisine are also plentiful. There are local vineyards, out-of-the-way fishing villages, convents, and monasteries to visit.

The Delta, 2,419 square miles of which is a UNESCO Biosphere Reserve, is split mainly between Ukraine and Romania

(Moldova also controls a small sliver). The Danube River forms the border between Romania and Bulgaria, stretching for some three hundred miles. On the southern (Bulgarian) side, tabletop plateaus and steep, rocky bluffs give way to vineyards and sprawling fields of corn and sunflowers. To the north, on the opposite bank, the Romanian Delta is a far different setting; marshy lowlands are dotted with over three hundred *baltras*, or shallow lakes; labyrinthine *ghiols* (canals); and stands of centuries-old white willow, oak, and poplar dripping with silk vine. Although most of the area has been protected as the Danube Delta Biosphere Reserve since 1990 (which sought to end many practices that were trashing the wetlands), the future of this globally significant region is still precarious. The potential for recovery and the possibility for irreversible harm are tangled together here like the chaotic roots of the Delta's abundant reeds.

The first sign of trouble for the Danube Delta came in 2001, when plans surfaced to redredge a deep-water canal through the Bystroye Estuary of the Ukrainian Delta. The Ukrainian government was seeking an alternative route from the Danube River to the Black Sea that wouldn't go through Romania. (Before reaching the Black Sea, the Danube splits into three branches—the Chilia, the Saint George, and the Sulina. The shortest and most navigable of the three, straightened by humans over a century ago, is the central Sulina channel, which, after parting from the river's main artery, stretches forty-seven tame, silty miles through Romania to the sea.) The Ukraine also hopes the new $40 million Bystroye Canal will revitalize the old Ukrainian port of Ust Danaysk, whose heyday ended when the old canal filled with silt and became unnavigable nearly five decades ago. As the deepest (at 27 feet) and widest (at 328 feet) egress to the Black Sea, the Bystroye would be Ukraine's new "Gateway to Europe."

Despite the area's protection under international agreements, construction on the first phase of the two-mile-long canal was nearly complete in 2004 but ceased during the so-called Orange Revolution, when millions of Ukrainians protested daily in Kiev against corruption and election fraud. For two years the international community fought Ukraine over the construction while the relentless Danube refilled the canal with silt, and in 2005, Ukraine's own Ministry of the Environment rejected the planned redredging after it reviewed the environmental impact assessment. But when the deputy minister who had sunk the canal plan was removed from her position, an expedited environmental review was rubber-stamped, and dredging resumed in 2006. The canal officially opened to small vessels (fifteen feet or less in length) in May 2007. There are new plans to dig even deeper into the Delta floor to permit the passage of larger boats.

For Andreas Beckmann of the World Wildlife Fund's Danube-Carpathian Programme, which has chosen the Delta as one of the world's two hundred most important regions for biodiversity conservation, the desire of the international community to protect the Delta is no match for Ukraine's will. At the last major meeting of the area's stakeholders in Odessa, Ukraine, in early 2006, Beckmann says there were some positive developments, including many countries' agreeing to sustainable development of the Danube Delta. "But the whole Bystroye issue hung over the conference," he says. "That's one of the many contradictions that exist. At the final press conference when they said, 'We'll all work together and everything will be wonderful,' one of the journalists asked the Ukraine's deputy transport minister point-blank whether this would have any impact on the decision to continue construction on the Bystroye Canal, and he answered, 'Nope, none whatsoever.' "

The countries of the European Union, the International Commission for the Protection of the Danube River, and a host of NGOs are pleading with Ukraine to abandon phase two of the canal construction. They fear the dredging machines, which gutted nesting sites and fragmented wildlife habitats, will destroy the Bystroye and send shockwaves through the remainder of the Delta. The WWF's Beckmann explains that destruction in the Bystroye would not be confined to that area. "It has larger impacts in terms of the water regime especially," he says. "And also in terms of the biodiversity. If you have a breeding area for birds, for example—and the construction in Bystroye did go through some breeding areas of rare birds—that then affects the whole population, so you're not just impacting the birds that are relevant to that specific area but those that are much further reaching."

Because Ukraine is not an EU member, the consortium cannot make it comply. "It helps a lot if the countries are in the EU or going to get into it, because the EU has a very strong law—the Water Framework Directive—possibly the strongest water-protection legislation in the world," says Paul Csagoly of the United Nations Development Programme's GEF Danube Regional Project. "But countries not in the EU, or ones not likely to be soon, like Ukraine, have voluntarily agreed to WFD but are not legally bound to it."

The attempt to protect the Ukrainian portion of the Delta has had many champions within the country, such as the employees of the Ukrainian Biosphere Reserve, but the government is heavy-handed, says Beckmann. "They've been doing a heroic job of trying to stand up to some of these pressures. One of the rangers even had his house burned down," he says. "But there's been more powerful people in other places that have decided to push this canal through." Hope for Delta-friendly construction grows concurrently with democratic reform in Ukraine. "Hopefully, unlike before, decisions will be made more transparently and environmental concerns will be included," says Beckmann. "But it's still not clear if it will be enough to stop the actual project."

A second project that worries Beckmann is Moldova's $38 million oil port in the reserve. After the Moldovan government announced the project in 2004, it stalled for lack of funding until 2005, when an Azerbaijani company, Azpetrol, bought the old, unfinished Giurgiulesti terminal and reconstructed it. The new Free Port Dzhurdzhulesht, which opened in late 2006, is linked to Ukraine's Brody-Odessa pipeline, which transports 180,000 barrels of oil per day. "Besides the actual impact of building this thing and having tankers coming up there is the problem of potential spills," says Beckmann.

Just as any missteps in the Ukraine or Moldova may carry over to the remainder of the Delta, much of the region's destiny is thrust downriver by the Danube itself. And the river—which has become the EU's best hope to alleviate highway congestion—has reached a fork en route to its future. One course leads to increased shipping on the Danube with boats designed to appease its finicky nature, which is marked by shallow depths and hairpin turns. The other fork leads to shaping the river to fit the boats, dredging where necessary, and smoothing out its fussy meanders.

To better understand the current conflict on the Danube it helps to look at its origin and complexity, and the way it has united and divided people throughout history. The massive, lengthy river actually has a modest start, surging springlike from the foothills of the Black Forest in southern Germany. It flows south at first, then jerks east, widening along its journey through or past nine other countries. The river of Karl Isidor Beck's imagination—"On the Danube, on the beautiful blue Danube," he wrote, inspiring Johann Strauss's famous 1867 waltz—has a tradition of fueling creativity but also of progress and conflict. For many miles, through the capital cities of Vienna, Bratislava, Budapest, and Belgrade as well as countless small villages, the riverbanks are studded like a silver chain with the charms of centuries of burgeoning civilization, tile-roofed cathedrals, ornate arch bridges, and arresting palaces. Historically, the river was also a freeway of conquest; the Romans, Franks, and Bavarians followed it east, while the Huns, Goths, Avars, Slavs, and Turks followed it west. Two millennia of often brutal human history have played out along the Danube's banks. The past two hundred years have also emphasized growth along the river. To accommodate new towns and encourage agriculture, 80 percent of the Danube basin and wetlands was drained during that time, and the river and some of its three hundred tributaries have been dammed, diverted, and straightened to suit human settlement and navigation needs.

Making the Danube more hospitable to industrial shipping than it's ever been before has now become a priority to the nations along its course that share its shores. "The whole reason that they want to expand navigation on the Danube is because there is a serious transportation problem in Europe," says the UNDP's Csagoly. Most cargo now moves along the continent's jammed highways, and the European Commission is seeking solutions. "It has already identified the Danube—they call it Transport Corridor Number Seven—as the main answer to the problems of the future. They've already said that it's a good idea that the Danube becomes a kind of highway for the future," says Csagoly.

While the Danube seems a reasonable alternative, as it's always been used for transportation, it's never been a major route for transporting industrial products. "Nevertheless a lot of these navigation interests, for example, construction companies that would like to straighten the river or build ports or build harbors, are increasing," says Csagoly. One major navigation lobby is the Austrian agency Via Donau in Vienna. "Austria is the country which is pushing most for expanding navigation on the Danube. They are promoting heavily making the Danube into this superhighway."

Improving navigability—known to some as manipulating the river—is a big part of that plan. That worries environmentalists, who fear that existing environmental law, while rigorous, will not be enough to protect the river, its shrinking basin, and its delicate delta from the stress of its new role. "It's clear that shipping will increase—that's inevitable," says Beckmann. "They're supposed to remove some 'bottlenecks' along the Danube, which are those areas where the waters are especially shallow, where the river spreads out over a wider area and creates wetlands. From the nature point of view, these are especially interesting and valuable." And that's why the WWF is pushing innovative approaches to shipping using shallow boats and less harmful propellers that would preclude the need to scoop out the riverbed. "It's business as usual, basically, fitting the river to boats rather than the boats to river, which has been the traditional approach so far," says Beckmann. "That basically could mean turning the Danube into a shipping canal—turning a living river into a transportation corridor."

The harm of dredging and diking Europe's second-longest river—altering the basic flow of water—impacts far more than the riverbed. "It changes the whole hydrological regime," says Beckmann. "They basically put a corset on the river, and as a result, there's less space for the water to go. And with dredging, the water table goes down. The water then travels much faster." The immediate impact of that can already be seen in the increase and severity of flooding all along the Danube. Floods causing the loss of human lives and property in 2002 and again two years later were one-upped in April 2006, when the Danube reached its highest level in Romania in 111 years. Villages were abandoned, farmland was inundated, and ports were submerged.

Without the floodplains that once lined the long, lanky Danube, the river has all but lost its ability to regulate the quality and amount of water that it carries. Instead of absorbing sediment and pollutants, a river basin devoid of its vast filtration network will jettison those substances downstream, thereby destroying water quality and wildlife habitats. The resulting eutrophication, or overload of nutrients like nitrogen and phosphorus that fuel an algae that deprives fish of oxygen, is already one of the Delta's demons. It would be greatly exacerbated by dredging and narrowing the river. "That then of course has knock-on effects for wildlife of all sorts, from fishes to the three hundred different kinds of bird species that are in the area," says Beckmann.

Would the EU really flout its own environmental protections in one area to alleviate environmental pressures elsewhere? "The EU, like the US government, is a bundle of contradictions," says Beckmann. "They have on the one hand some pretty progressive environmental legislation, and according to it, they shouldn't be doing a lot of things. But, at the same time, you have other factions—the transportation interests. In the end these two different kinds of interests can't coexist. At some point it's brought to a head. It becomes a political conflict and the stronger one wins."

In the meantime the Delta's lifeline still ends its 1,776-mile journey in grandeur. The true terminus of the river lies in Romania, where the residents' ancestors, the Dacians, traditionally drank the Danube before going into battle, so convinced were they that the water instilled luck and courage. The fishermen there, cutting through marshes marked by bright yellow water lilies, still rely on the Delta to live. But through the channels, past tamarisk and plovers, progress pulses toward them.

DEAD SEA, ISRAEL, PALESTINE, AND JORDAN

The Dead Sea, Israel

WHEN THE DOR KAYAK CLUB IN BINYAMINA, ISRAEL, held its inaugural Dead Sea paddling excursion in the spring of 2003, the group's packing list contained some unusual items: goggles (to protect their eyes from the salty spray), eye rinsing water (in case of accidental splashing), and weights (to help the kayaks sit lower in the buoyant sea).

It also made one notable omission: personal flotation devices. In the world's saltiest body of water, where swimmers bob at the surface like human corks, using a PFD makes about as much sense as wearing a bike helmet on a nature hike.

The kayakers parked their trailer at an off-road access point in Ein Gedi, on the sea's west shore, and pulled their boats into the water. Paddling was awkward at first. "It feels like you have salt on your hands when you hold your paddle. And you float a little bit higher," says club manager Tomas Herdevall. But soon they were cruising along the salt-rimmed coastline with ease as onlookers gawked from shore. The crusty striations at the edge of the water gave way to pale, sandy hillsides; dwarf shrubs poked out from behind clusters of smooth boulders; crag martins darted in and out of their nests in the seaside cliffs.

The trip was such a success that it now runs two or three times a year. But getting to the water isn't as easy as it used to be. Quicksand-like mud and sinkholes have made parts of the shoreline unstable—the original Ein Gedi access point is now too hazardous for casual off-road entry. Instead, the paddlers unload their boats at an officially designated beach and carry them down a long set of stairs to the sea. "You cannot just enter with a kayak anywhere," Herdevall says. "A few years ago you could just go off-road and stay by the shore. You can't now because it's dangerous."

The problem is that the Dead Sea is shrinking. The water level drops a few feet each year, primarily because of water diversions from its main source, the Jordan River, and mineral extractions from its southern basin. As the sea dries up, it exposes deep pockets of boot-sucking mud. It also leaves underground salt deposits that dissolve in the fresh groundwater, causing the earth above them to cave in. The sinkholes—more than a thousand of them so far—have consumed date palms, paved roads, and entire buildings without warning, not to mention the occasional passerby (though no one has been seriously injured yet).

A briny oasis amid a palm-dotted, calcium-crusted desert at the base of the Jordan River, the Dead Sea straddles the borders of Israel, Palestine, and Jordan. At 1,370 feet below sea level, it is the lowest body of water on the planet. With a salt content as high as 33 percent, it is also the most saline. The Dead Sea makes Utah's Great Salt Lake—at 20 to 27 percent salt—seem downright fresh. It is ten times saltier than the Mediterranean and most other seas, and it's getting saltier all the time. Salt mounds sit like snowbanks at the edges of the water, which laps at the base of sandstone and limestone escarpments that rise up on the eastern and the western shores.

The sea formed a million years ago when a massive earthquake created the Syrian-African Rift. In its infancy, it stretched all the way to the Sea of Galilee, but it has long since sunk into the valley. Throughout most of modern history, the sea held steady at about fifty miles long. Now it barely covers thirty miles.

"There's nothing natural about the demise of the Dead Sea. It's all man-made," says Gidon Bromberg, the Israeli director of Friends of the Earth Middle East, a nonprofit group that addresses transboundary environmental issues in the region. Records dating back to the 1600s show a relatively stable water level until the late 1950s, when Israel built a large pumping station at the Sea of Galilee to accommodate its recent population boom and subsequent demand for freshwater. Syria and Jordan followed suit in the 1960s and 1970s, building dams on a major tributary and constructing the King Abdullah Canal, which spreads water throughout the Jordan Valley. The population of the Dead Sea region has more than tripled since 1960, and the availability of water has had to keep pace. Now 90 percent of the Jordan River is siphoned off for farming and hydroelectric power. When it flowed unhindered, the river was able to compensate for the sea's evaporation rate of about five feet per year. Now it provides less than a tenth of that.

The primary reason for the demise of the Dead Sea is that the surrounding population is using more water than is available, says Pascal Peduzzi, head of the Early Warning Unit at the UN Environment Programme in Geneva, where scientists study the preliminary signs of environmental degradation throughout the world. As more water is pumped out of aquifers than can be renewed, Peduzzi explains, the groundwater level drops. In the Jordan Valley, the water table has fallen fifty-three feet since 1969. In the densely populated and politically jittery Gaza Strip,

Kayaker on the Dead Sea

where the situation is particularly dire, the levels have gotten so low that seawater has infiltrated the shallow aquifers. "The political instability prevents the establishment of otherwise easy solutions," Peduzzi says. "Water is a crucial issue for this region and is—and will be—a source of tensions."

Mineral extraction exacerbates the problem. The Dead Sea is a "terminal" lake, meaning that it has no outlet. The mineral-rich sediment that hitches a ride on seabound waterways eventually settles at its base. Israeli and Jordanian companies harvest those minerals by pumping water from the sea's deeper northern basin to the shallow southern basin, which would otherwise be completely barren. The water is collected in rows of pools that are about three feet deep, then is evaporated at the rate of roughly 180 million gallons a day. Extracted potash is sold as fertilizer; magnesium becomes industrial metal; bromides go into water treatment chemicals, pesticides, and flame retardants.

There is also a market for "therapeutic" Dead Sea salt, used for bathing. About a third of the sea's water loss has been attributed to mineral extraction; the rest comes from water diversion.

The Dead Sea has lost a third of its surface area in the last fifty years. Experts say it could lose another third—or more—before the water hits its maximum salt saturation and evaporation stops. "We're not going to have much of a sea left," Bromberg says. "We're losing a site that is truly unique to this world."

In 2006, the Global Nature Fund, an international environmental foundation headquartered in Germany, named the Dead Sea its Threatened Lake of the Year because of the threat its decline poses to the region's ecology and tourist economy. Though nothing lives in the sea itself, the surrounding ecosystem sustains a vibrant mix of birds, reptiles, amphibians, mammals, and hundreds of plant species. Endangered ibex, leopards, and hyraxes drink from the area's freshwater springs, and millions of migrating birds stop here to breed and to rest before continuing their long journey between Europe and Africa.

Tourists come to the Dead Sea to revel in their own buoyancy and luxuriate in the water that has long been touted for its supposed healing powers. The dry heat and the nutrient-dense water and mud are reputed to reduce stress, relieve aches and pains, and ease the itch of skin ailments like psoriasis and eczema. And the air, which is up to 10 percent richer in oxygen than at sea level, makes ordinary people feel superhuman. Several thousand hotel rooms house seabound travelers, and plans are in the works for tens of thousands more. But so much depends on the availability of water.

At the Ein Gedi Spa, a mineral springs retreat where soothing water bubbles into six large pools at a constant temperature of 100 degrees, visitors alternate between soaking and slathering themselves with black mud, and indulging in massages and spa treatments. At an outdoor picnic area, they nibble on snacks while taking in views of the Mountains of Moab and the Judean Hills. It's an idyllic setting that lends itself to pampering.

But in recent years, the spa has lost one of its main attractions: proximity to the Dead Sea. When it opened in 1986, you could walk from the front door to the western shore in just a few steps. Now the water is a mile away, and a train shuttles visitors back and forth. The journey gets a little longer every year.

Healing and relaxation aren't the only Dead Sea attractions. Visitors also come to explore what Bromberg describes as "an archaeological mother lode," a place that appears in Muslim, Christian, and Jewish texts and has turned up more than a few relics from the distant past. This is, of course, where Bedouin goat herders stumbled upon the Dead Sea Scrolls in a seaside cave in 1947. It is also a stone's throw from Jericho, possibly the world's oldest continuously inhabited settlement. The Masada fortress, where Jewish refugees chose mass suicide over Roman capture nearly two millennia ago, sits on a plateau overlooking the sea. And some believe the sea's confluence with the Jordan River is the site of Jesus' baptism. "We're completely altering a site that every child on this earth has heard about," Bromberg says.

Slowing its destruction would require a major conservation effort and a complete overhaul of the region's water policies, particularly as they relate to food production. "A good part of the water that used to flow down the Jordan River goes to agriculture," Bromberg says. Israel, Jordan, and Syria have a long-standing tradition of supporting unlimited water use for farming. Israeli farmers have received water subsidies for most of the state's history, and the powerful agriculture lobby is fiercely opposed to any reductions. The region's farmers grow water-greedy crops such as wheat and flowers for domestic use and for sale to Europe and the Gulf states. "In fact what we're doing is exporting our water," Bromberg says. "The irony is that we're exporting it at subsidized prices."

A more elaborate solution was first proposed in the 1970s:

digging an enormous canal that would divert water from the Mediterranean Sea. At the time, it seemed impossibly ambitious, but as the Dead Sea's water level dwindles, the concept gains appeal. A more recent proposal to channel water from the Red Sea is also being considered. But building the "Med-Dead" and "Red-Dead" canals, as they are known, would be expensive and, in this tense political climate, logistically tricky. And engineers estimate that a canal built today would take two decades to replenish the sea—too late to save some of the plant and animal species that scientists say are already in decline.

For now, conservationists are focusing their efforts on developing a region-wide water plan that would discourage increased mineral extraction and the construction of new highways and hotels. They're also campaigning for international help—UNESCO offers funding and support to places that it designates Man and Biosphere Reserves. Advocates from Israel and Jordan are seeking that distinction for the entire Dead Sea Basin.

As a traveler, you can access the sea from Jordan or Israel. On the Jordan side, it's a thirty-minute drive from bustling Amman to the serenely silent valley where spagoers congregate at the one-hotel town of Sweimeh. The main Israeli entry points are Ein Gedi and the much more developed Ein Bokek, both within day-tripping distance of Jerusalem. The main attraction is swimming—or, more accurately, bobbing. Step into the sea until your feet pop up from under you, and indulge in the regional pastime of reading *The Jerusalem Post* while balancing on your submerged keister. Or, if you'd rather stay dry and avoid the sting of highly concentrated salt water on your skin, there's always the sit-on-top option. The Dor Kayak Club has no plans to stop its Dead Sea excursions anytime soon. They'll let you join them for about $100 and will even supply the boat (but don't forget to bring your own goggles and eye-washing water). "It will be more and more difficult to put in and put out," Herdevall says, "but we'll do it as long as we can."

VENICE, ITALY

Venice

A GREAT WAY TO GET THE LAY OF THE LAND IN VENICE IS to leave it. Step out of the Santa Lucia train station in the north onto a flat-topped *vaporetto* (number 1 or 82), one of the city's omnipresent waterbuses, and wind your way through the city on the Grand Canal. The *Canalazzo*, as it's known to Venetians, twists and tucks through the city in the shape of a great question mark. While floating down the bustling canal you'll brush by intricate Gothic, Renaissance, and Byzantine palaces that seem to float on the shallow channel. Continue on beneath the bulky, stone-arched Ponte di Rialto, the bridge that has linked the banks here for over four centuries. On the way you'll bump by some of the four hundred or so gondoliers who still offer a pricey paddle and past other *vaporetti*, inside which locals sit reading *Il Gazzettino* while tourists dangle from the railings.

Your two-and-a-half-mile journey ends in the Dorsoduro district, a captivating and less-visited area of the city. The hearty Dorsoduro peninsula is quintessential Venice. It boasts the wooden span of the Ponte dell'Accademia, an Asian-influenced bridge over the Grand Canal; the Campo Santa Margherita, which is crammed with cafes; and the broad-domed Santa Maria Della Salute, built as a tribute to the Virgin Mary by locals who believed that she halted the plague that was killing Venetians in the seventeenth century. A stream of luminaries—artists, actors, writers, royalty, and politicians—has historically flowed through the Dorsoduro, including John Ruskin, the celebrated nineteenth-century British author who lived in the district. He said of Venice, "Thank God I am here; it is the Paradise of cities."

Anna Somers Cocks couldn't agree more. She first saw Venice as a girl, when she was a guest at her grandmother's villa in the Dorsoduro. "I remember going there when I was seven years old and thinking this is the most amazing place I've ever been to," she says. There's a restaurant around the corner from her grandmother's place called Da Montin, to which Cocks has been returning since those early days. It's part of the cozy Locanda Montin hotel, marked simply by a wrought-iron lamp hanging from its façade. Since the time when Peggy Guggenheim used to bring Mark Rothko and Jackson Pollock there, contemporary art has hung from its walls and patrons have feasted under a long, lush arbor on *granseola* (fried moulting crabs) and antipasto Montin. "That restaurant has never changed. It feels exactly the same as when I went there fifty years ago," says Cocks.

But as Cocks knows well, that aura of timelessness, as well as Venice's physical beauty and practicality as a residential city, is threatened more every year by the rising sea level brought on by climate change. She heads the UK-based nonprofit Venice in Peril, which is working to bring to the international stage the threats to the iconic city's existence. "Flood protection is the fundamental thing that has to be looked at," she says. The *aque alte* ("high waters," in the Venetian dialect), which have sloshed into nearly all of Venice's shops, residences, and plazas seasonally for centuries, is now much higher and much more frequent. "Venetians will tell you in a rather defiant way, 'Venice has always flooded, we don't mind.' But actually they do mind," says Cocks. "It's hard to conduct a business if your shop is on the ground floor and the water comes in. And it's hard to get around when the water comes swimming up to your ankles during unpredictable moments in the winter months."

In 1897, a tidal gauge was installed near the Dorsoduro's Santa Maria della Salute church. The zero on the gauge denotes what the mean sea level was then. During *aque alte*, which generally happened half a dozen times a year then, brackish surges entered the Venice Lagoon from the northern Adriatic and rose one foot above the gauge's baseline. At low tide, the watermark dropped roughly the same distance below that line. Nowadays, zero is seldom seen. Across St. Mark's Basin from Santa Maria, in the low-lying Piazza San Marco, traditional high tides, once confined to spring and fall, now occur year-round. In 1900 there were seven high tides recorded. During a particularly bad year, 1996, there were ninety-nine. Today locals lay down *passarelle*, or raised wooden "duckboards," and tourists pull on pastel-colored rubber galoshes an average of sixty times a year.

Venice has always been an unlikely city, built with resolve but without the benefit of any real land. The city, its murky lagoon, and its lanky barrier islands are tucked into a dimple in northern Italy's coast. The historic city hugs the shore within a thirty-two-mile-long, eight-mile-wide crescent. Best estimates say that the Venice Lagoon was formed three to six thousand years ago when the Adriatic Sea spread northward, flooding terra firma. Then during the following centuries silt carried down rivers on the mainland emptied into the lagoon, creating a bunch of small landmasses—little more than glorified mud flats, really—covered with delicate grasses.

While it looked more like a place to boat in rather than to build on, the area was chosen sometime in the fifth century as a home safe from marauders. Soon after that, in order to make the region more liveable, humans began altering the lagoon's complex ecology and halted the process of new land being formed by nature. At the behest of the then-republic's leaders, called doges, early Venetians tirelessly dredged canals and diverted most of the rivers that dumped material into the lagoon so that they flowed directly into the Adriatic.

Keeping open Venice's waterways was essential to navigation, commerce, and security. "While they didn't write down the science of it, they had a very good practical knowledge of how to look after the lagoon," says Cocks. "They knew that they had to divert the rivers to keep the lagoon from filling with silt." She points out that in the days when Venice was a republic, the doge would be rowed out from the lagoon into the Adriatic in a golden boat, where he would toss a blessed ring into the sea with the words *"Desponsamuste, mare,"* or "We wed thee, O sea."

The weight of Venice's grandeur actually rests on 118 islands, some provided by nature and others achieved by hand-boring hundreds of thousands of skinny alder trunks through several feet of mud into the lagoon's sand and clay bottom. Upon those piles and planks, builders laid a firm foundation of white Istrian marble. Above the layer of impervious rock, which was designed to lie beneath the level of the lagoon, came bricks and stucco, which were designed to be strictly above water. Little by little, broad squares, narrow alleys, striking basilicas, and extraordinary bridges (378 in all) gradually took shape. Out of muck and brine had risen the maritime trade titan of the eastern Mediterranean, a title the so-called *La Serenissima*, or "most serene," republic held for roughly four hundred years from the thirteenth century onward.

Throughout the past several centuries Venetians have continuously manipulated their watery wedge of the world. In addition to diverting river runoff from the mainland so that it flowed into the Adriatic instead of the lagoon, early engineers also closed most of the channels that had led from the sea to the lagoon. Today only three remaining slots (there were once nine) divide the slender, sandy barrier islands of Cavallino, Lido, and Pellestrina and offer access from the sea into the lagoon. In the twentieth century major alterations continued in support of the Porto Marghera industrial zone, on the mainland opposite the city. Beginning around 1925, freshwater was extracted on a large scale from the long, deep aquifer underlying the lagoon. Three decades later, the rise of chemical plants, steelworks, and an oil refinery necessitated access to Porto Marghera by much bigger vessels than the shallow lagoon could accommodate. "In order to bring these deep-hulled ships through the narrow lagoon, they dug two massively deep trenches," says Cocks.

The molding of the lagoon, while a remarkable feat of relentless engineering, left the city a legacy of woes. In their haste to keep the lagoon navigable and their economy viable, irreparable damage was done to the lagoon ecosystem. The earliest diversions that prevented new silt from being deposited in the lagoon harmed the salt marshes that mitigate the tides. And Venice drew freshwater from beneath the lagoon from the 1920s until the early 1970s, which actually sank the city. That compression, along with the natural compaction that Venice experiences because it rests atop river sediment, accounts for lowering the city six inches since the end of the nineteenth century. The new channels driven through in the mid twentieth century strengthened the current flowing in and out of the lagoon, making it deeper and saltier with each passing tide. Chemical dumping also killed off much of the remaining eelgrass, which had absorbed water and pollution and controlled erosion. "The lagoon has become deeper, more like open sea, and it behaves much more rudely," says Cocks. "It has far more waves and it floods much more frequently."

The worst flood in Venice's history, known as the *Aqua Grande*, overtook the city in 1966. Looking from the Dorso-duro's Salute basilica across St. Mark's Basin and into the Piazza San Marco, it appeared that Venice had drowned. From one end of the serpentine Grand Canal to the other, squares, shops, and homes were inundated, docks were submerged, and gondolas were swamped under a record-high 6.3 feet of water that lin-gered for twenty-two hours—almost four times longer than a typical high tide. An estimated $6 billion in art was ruined. The images of Venice's soggy and suffering façades and interiors gal-vanized international support. Through organizations like the fledgling Venice in Peril and World Monuments Fund (then the International Fund for Monuments), donors leapt to Venice's aid and many successful renovations were undertaken.

In the years following the Great Flood it became clear that while that event may have been an anomaly, the marriage between Venice and the sea would certainly be a lifelong union. The alternating winds that have always visited Venice—the sirocco, a hot wind that blows in from North Africa, and the bora, the cold gusts that come from the north—drive water into the lagoon with frequent furor. Global warming has also accounted for a three-inch rise in the Adriatic (on top of the six inches Venice has sunk due to aquifer draining and natural com-pression). While ancient Venetians had allowed a wide margin between the water level and vulnerable building materials, the lagoon is now often rising above the impermeable marble and soaking into the porous brick and stucco. This *risalta salina*, or "salt rise," is a much-feared phenomenon. What Cocks calls a "green slime line" is visible evidence that brackish water is over-taking brick, with dire consequences. "As the water dries out, then the salt in it expands and crumbles the brickwork," says

Cocks. "There is a constant process of attrition to the housing stock of the city, as ongoing maintenance is immensely costly."

Understanding why little has been done on a municipal level to secure Venice from continued decay is about as easy as navigating the city's 150 canals blindfolded. "Italy is famous for being a most artistically rich country, and Venice is one of its great assets," says Cocks. "Therefore you'd expect it to be rather high up the government's list of priorities to protect its cities of art." In the momentum of concern that continued after the 1966 flood, government meetings were held on the subject of saving Venice and declarations were made, but forty years on, inaction reigns.

Bonnie Burnham, director of the World Monuments Fund, says that because of a lack of consensus and will, Venice presents one of the world's greatest conservation challenges. "It's a really dire situation," she says. What makes Venice's peril so palpable is not only the inexorable rise in sea level (which, by all accounts, promises to worsen) but also the apparent paralysis of Italian officials trying to decide on a course of action to protect one of the country's rare beauties. "In order to address the challenge there really needs to be a sense of resolve that's just not there," says Burnham.

That dearth of determination certainly hasn't come from a lack of discussion about the problem. In 1970, the central government first proposed putting in place a system of mobile gates that could be raised to shield the city from high water. Five years later, the Italian Public Works Ministry put out a call for the best plans to build the gates. In 1981, the *Progettone*, or "big project," was unveiled, and with some trepidation, the Venice City Council agreed to it, as long as an ecological and hydrological balance was also restored to the lagoon. The Consorzio Venezia Nuova, or "New Venice Consortium," was then tasked with drawing up the plans to build the barriers. In 1988, soon after its Modulo

Sperimentale Elettromeccanico (dubbed Moses after the biblical figure who parted the Red Sea) was introduced to the world, the Venice City Council protested against the construction. It insisted that Consorzio was an unwieldy monopoly that was more interested in making money than crafting the best solution for Venice. The council feared that the funds allocated by the federal government to protect Venice would all be used on the barriers and none would be left over for other flood mitigation measures. "Instead of it being simply a question of science, and possibly finance, it became a question of ideology," says Venice in Peril's Cocks. "This held up the decision to build the barrier from the early 1990s to 2003, and the question is being raised again now." During that holdup, in 1996, high water nearly matched the catastrophic 1966 level, and in 2000, the Venice lagoon rose five feet, flooding 93 percent of the city. In the wake of this disaster Italian prime minister Silvio Berlusconi decreed that despite Venetian opposition, Moses' construction should continue. Romano Prodi, Italy's current prime minister, has also publicly approved of the project. He announced in late 2006 that despite the discord, construction would continue.

The roughly $6 billion barrier project consists of seventy-nine steel dams placed at each of the three inlets. Most often, the gates, which are ninety-eight feet high and sixty-six feet wide, will lie flat on the floor of the Adriatic (about ninety-one feet below sea level). At times when the water level threatens to be forty inches or more above average, the mobile dams will be raised vertically to hold back the sea. Moses is approximately one-quarter complete and could be done in 2011, barring delays.

But local opposition to the project reignited recently when a new mayor of Venice, Massimo Cacciari, was elected. "The mayor of Venice has launched an appeal to the new government to say, hang on, hold it all up, let's think again," says Cocks. "But one knows damn well that if they think again there'll be absolutely nothing done for the next twenty to thirty years." The bottom line, according to a Cambridge University study commissioned by Venice in Peril, is that a barrier system like Moses must be built. The scientists who produced the study agree that while the mobile dams can't completely protect Venice in the long term from the rising sea level, it will buy the city some time to sort out other measures that can be undertaken to prevent flooding. "It's not possible to go back and start planning again," says Cocks. "Too much has already been invested, in terms of thought and the actual building." To date, an estimated $1.2 billion has already been spent on Moses.

The political vacillation and relentless flooding is beginning to depress, and in some cases drive away, Venetians. "There's a desperate feeling of hopelessness. None of them know what we ought to be doing," says Cocks. Couple that with a deep skepticism of large municipal projects, and opposition to Moses is mounting among the general Venetian populace. "It's almost as if the will has gone out of people to take a strong stand, to say that we'll definitely do this," says Cocks. "They would rather take no decision than the wrong decision." The way that increasing numbers of residents are dealing with the floods, during which tourists take to kayaking across St. Mark's Square, is by abandoning their homes. "People have made that decision, with these circumstances, often with very heavy hearts," says the World Monument Fund's Burnham. "It's not cynical; it's just sort of an irrevocable process that no one seems to be able to influence. Almost no one lives there anymore, in terms of a traditional population. It's very sad." While local government claims it's higher, most statistics on Venice put the population at about 60,000 (it was double that in 1951), with an influx of as many as 125,000 students while school is in session.

The exodus of residents is facilitated by the tourism ogre, which has cast a stocky shadow across much of the city in recent years. As locals flee the inconveniences of flooding, permanent homes are being replaced by higher-revenue-producing hotels, and a crush of kiosks awash in tourist trinkets caters to fifteen million annual visitors. Tourism supplies 70 percent of the city's income and accounts for 50 percent of its employment. "The law of the market is that the quickest return on your investment is by tourism," says Cocks. This conversion is driving property prices so high that no regular Venetian can afford their city. "People can't get a decent space to live in if they're living on an ordinary income," says Cocks. Grocery shops, cinemas, and mom-and-pop bakeries are all succumbing to tourist tender. St. Mark's Square is now flooded year-round with foreigners filling brightly colored cafe chairs and feeding the copious pigeons. And during the times when the piazza is inundated by the lagoon, everyone in the square appears to be on one long line, as travelers pack the duckboards to keep their feet dry while the occasional local wades knee-deep wearing an Armani suit.

Anna Somers Cocks insists that despite the chaos that's brewing there, a sense of community endures in Venice, though she's not sure how long it will last. She's also cautiously optimistic that the central government will prevail over Venetian opposition to the barriers, though she's not positive if it will be in time to save the city. For now, Da Montin in the Dorsoduro continues to serve up delicacies from the sea that is too close to its front door, and there are still alleys where row upon row of clean laundry is strung above ancient cobblestones. Fire-in-the-sky sunsets can still be seen from a bridge across the Grand Canal, which winds inexorably through Venice in the shape of a backward S. From above, the *Canalazzo* looks like a giant question mark ironically punctuating the city's uncertain future as it weaves its way toward the open sea.

AFRICA

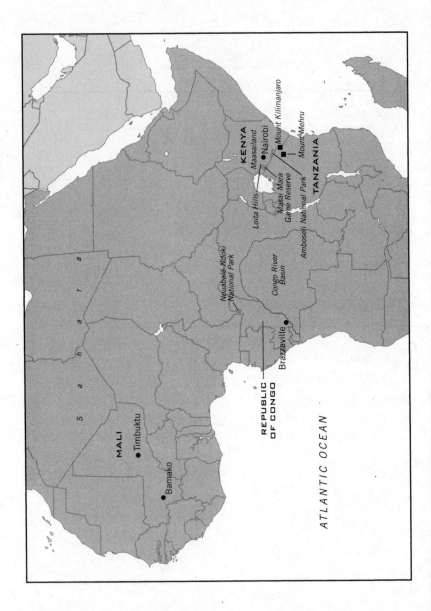

CONGO BASIN, CENTRAL AFRICA

Navigating the Congo Basin

FOR YEARS, EMMA STOKES HAS BEEN WATCHING GORILLAS come and go from Mbeli Bai, a natural swampy clearing in the remote north of the Republic of Congo. As the research coordinator for the Wildlife Conservation Society's Nouabalé-Ndoki National Park project, Stokes has carefully observed western lowland gorillas emerge from the impenetrable-looking thicket of rain forest into the open bai. The bai, a roughly thirty-two-acre area in the southwest of Nouabalé-Ndoki, is crisscrossed by streams and dotted with murky pools covered with floating mats of luscious vegetation frequented by elephants. There the massive, agile gorillas forage for leafy, nutritious *Hydrocharis chevalieri*, a favorite food, which grows plentifully along the boggy bottom. For hours on end, Stokes has seen gorillas wade and search, sometimes through three feet of viscous mud, tearing up green wads and painstakingly rinsing away the muck before closing their fierce teeth around the shoots.

Stokes has spent so much time in the verdant, steamy recesses of this jungle, at times within pulse-pounding proximity of four-hundred-pound gorillas because it's one of the last places on the African continent where some of humankind's closest relatives can still be observed in an intact sanctuary. Everywhere in Africa where "great apes," including gorillas, chimpanzees, and bonobos (endemic pygmy chimps known to be genetically nearest to humans) make their home, humanity is closing in. To the north, south, and east of Nouabalé-Ndoki's pristine one million acres, and across equatorial Africa's Congo Basin, once-thick forests are being transformed, with tragic consequences for their residents.

The Congo Basin is the world's second-largest rain forest (after the Amazon) and accounts for one quarter of the remaining rain forest on earth. "Trees, trees, millions of trees, massive, immense, running up high," wrote Joseph Conrad of the Congo in *Heart of Darkness* in 1899. The Congo stretches like a loose green belt across Africa's belly, from the Gulf of Guinea on the Atlantic coast east to the Rwenzori Mountains (formerly called the Ruwenzori Range) in Uganda and the Democratic Republic of Congo. It accounts for seven hundred thousand square miles of tropical terrain in six countries and is a biodiversity powerhouse. At home in the Congo are four hundred species of mammals, including forest elephants that steamroll trails through walls of growth, African forest buffalo, red river hogs, leopards, duikers, and aardvarks, to name a few. Also in residence are ten thousand kinds of plants, including moabi trees, whose massive umbrella-like canopies shade the forest floor. They can take a century to reach their full potential, and when they do, they are the tallest trees in the rain forest. Nesting in the moabi might be any of the Congo's one thousand bird species, like the Congo weaver, which builds large nests with vaulted ceilings out of branches and strips of leaves.

There's no getting around the fact that the Congo's tropical climate, which makes the rain forest so fertile, is less appealing to humans. While its temperature stays around eighty degrees Fahrenheit year-round, the constant humidity hovers around 93 percent. But the weather is a small price to pay for seeing the world's remaining great apes in their backyard. The rains come from October through May (though December is usually fairly dry) and are especially heavy in the north, and the official dry season runs from June through October.

While the political situation is improving (it was destabilized by widespread civil conflict as recently as 1999), the Republic of Congo—not to be confused with its war-scarred neighbor to the east, the Democratic Republic of Congo, formerly Zaire—is visited by few westerners. The capital, Brazzaville, does have some luxury hotels, but tourism infrastructure in the rest of the country is still limited. Getting to the rain forests of the north is challenging and sometimes unpredictable. Taxis, minibuses, and trains are cheap and link most main cities, and travel by steamer, barge, or, for the most adventurous, motorized dugout canoe up the Congo and Ubangi rivers can be invigorating. For those short on time or nerve, flights run regularly from Brazzaville to Loubomo, Ouesso, and Pointe-Noire, all jumping-off points for exploring the Republic's rain forests, one of the most critical forest ecosystems on earth. This area in the north of the country, and the popular Odzala National Park on the Gabon border in particular, is usually accessed through neighboring Gabon. The Republic's increasing political stability is also leading to a growing number of organized tours, almost all of which are run by groups outside the country, from the United Kingdom or United States, but with local guides.

One part–outfitter, part–nonprofit organization, the Programme for Conservation and Rational Utilization of Forest Ecosystems in Central Africa, or ECOFAC, is based in Brazzaville and is focused on sustainable development in the Congo.

With the help of ECOFAC, ecotourism is making significant inroads in the Republic's northern rain forests, specifically Odzala. Since 1992 it has been making the park visitor-friendly, when the political climate permits. Since Odzala encompasses both forest and savanna vegetation, it supports a mind-boggling concentration of large mammals. Gorillas, bongo antelopes, monkeys, and chimpanzees traverse the thick underbrush. The forest/savanna mix also attracts forest buffalo, elephants, giant forest hogs, and lions. ECOFAC is working with villagers in Lossi, about twelve miles southwest of Odzala National Park, to establish permanent, reliable gorilla-viewing areas and a guiding base for travelers.

At a time when few areas of the globe remain mysterious, the forests deep within the Congo Basin are still largely a tangle of virgin lowland wilderness waiting to be explored. But twenty-four million people live on the fringes of the rain forest, and they're increasingly dependent on the forest's plenty for water, food, medicine, and timber.

Commercial logging is by far the greatest current killer of Congo's vast canopies. Infrared satellite photos taken of the Congo rain forest by NASA and the National Oceanic and Atmospheric Administration show intact forest in green and clear-cut areas in red. Over the past decade the red specks and clusters have spread like a rash. Sickly yellow veins show logging roads, along which trucks flow relentlessly. The World Wildlife Federation estimates that at least 11 percent of the total forest cover in the Congo rain forest has been degraded. At the current loss rate of two million acres a year, that amount is expected to rise to 30 percent by 2030. From 1990 to 2000, the greatest loss of forest was in the Democratic Republic of Congo, which lost 1.3 million acres per year. The Republic of Congo lost 420,000 acres during that same decade.

The Republic of Congo's northern tip is a tale of two forests.

Along with critical populations of great apes, Nouabalé-Ndoki National Park is the stomping ground of forest elephants and bongo antelopes, which skillfully navigate the rain forest. More than three hundred species of birds nest and flutter in a canopy so thick with endangered old-growth mahogany that day and night are indistinct. The preserve was set aside in 1993 thanks to the aggressive conservation action of one of Emma Stokes's Wildlife Conservation Society colleagues, J. Michael Fay. Fay shone a light into the "heart of darkness" in 2000 when he completed his two-thousand-mile "megatransect" walk across the rain forest, from northeast Democratic Republic of Congo to the Gabon coast. In 2003, before US funding for Nouabalé-Ndoki and neighboring parks was secure, he told Congress, "We have a historic opportunity in the Congo Basin today to create what will be one of the world's most important national park systems . . . in one of the richest areas in terms of biodiversity."

In taking the Congo off the chopping block, the hope was also that locals could make a more sustainable living by preserving the forest. When trees like the big-ticket sapelli mahogany are clear-cut, it is a boon for loggers but a blow to locals. At times indigenous Ba'aka pygmies subsist on the caterpillars that favor those trees, and they also sell bags of smoked caterpillars at a premium. The seed oil, called *karité*, from the huge moabi tree is used for cooking, and the tree's bark is used for healing (particularly to ease back and tooth pain). It's also extremely valuable when traded to the Ba'akas' neighbors and when sold internationally (the oil has recently attracted attention from the French cosmetics industry). "We have an opportunity to shift how entire landscapes are developed to assure that future generations can sustain and enhance their lives," said Fay.

As a result of Fay's efforts, and those of a cadre of other dedicated conservationists, money streamed in through the new Congo Basin Forest Partnership, and dozens of national parks and other protected areas were established. It was an enormous victory—logging had been cut short in those zones and a virtual army of guards was trained to chase out poachers. The great apes of Nouabalé-Ndoki continued to roam unmolested by industry, allowing researchers to continue to observe the previously mysterious western lowland gorillas. In the past few years, as great male silverbacks with chestnut-red heads, silver flanks, and ink-black arms, and their females and offspring, have visited Mbeli Bai's all-you-can-eat vegetation buffet, Stokes and her colleagues have made astounding observations. They reversed the scientific community's belief that gorillas avoid water, and researchers discovered that gorillas use tools in the wild.

But all the while, to the north, east, and south of Nouabalé-Ndoki, trouble has been brewing. Where there had been no roads as recently as 1996, a network now runs into and through countless logging concessions. Experts fear the fate of the Congo will mirror the reality of West Africa's forests, 26 percent of which have been cleared in less than two decades. The United Nations says that from the 1980s through the early 2000s Africa lost more forest than any other continent.

In the north of the Republic of Congo, 90 percent of the landmass has been bought for cutting, and an estimated 60 percent of the entire Congo Basin has been sold to loggers, promising to split the wilderness wide open. In the Congo, logging is not just about cutting down trees. Logging interests, since they employ millions of Congo Basin residents (which amounts to only about 10 percent of the population), require infrastructure, including roads and towns. Roads bring poachers, and many species are hunted as pets, trophies, or for prized parts. Parrots, lizards, and crocodiles are succumbing, as are tons of elephants, whose ivory is still widely valued.

Logging has also swelled once-remote villages outside of Nouabalé-Ndoki, such as Kabo, Pokola, and Ouesso, into com-

Silverbacks, Congo

pany towns that are now filled with hungry people. Grumbling bellies turn to the rain forest for sustenance. "Logging brings with it people and roads, which place increasing pressure on the natural resources, including wildlife, and increase transport of bushmeat out of the forest and into urban centers where demand is high," says Stokes. "Bushmeat" is the term given to wildlife that is hunted illegally (in the case of endangered or threatened species), commercially, or from protected areas. The forbidden taking of duikers (forest antelopes), monkeys, buffalo, pigs, and highly prized great apes is skyrocketing. The harvesting of all these species is having untold effects on the Congo's biodiversity, including predators such as the golden cat, leopard, and crowned eagle that also subsist on them. Even in conservation areas, like national parks, illegal hunting is difficult to thwart because there are few rangers, and they're spread out over vast areas.

The United Nations Great Apes Survival Project estimates

that a staggering 1.1 million tons (2.2 billion pounds) of bush-meat per year is taken. They worry that much like with logging, Central Africa will follow West Africa's lead. In West Africa, forest antelopes and primates are flirting with extinction. If nothing is done to slow logging and hunting, the UN estimates that Central Africa will look the same as its western neighbors in as little as five years.

Experts know already that ape hunting is happening on a scale that the "critically endangered" (so called by the World Conservation Union, whose Red List highlights vulnerable species) populations cannot withstand. Primates simply do not reproduce as early or often as other forest mammals, putting them at much greater risk for extinction. "Great apes, like most forest-dwelling large mammals, occur at low densities across their habitat. The forests of Central Africa, their primary stronghold, are far less productive than other habitats," says Stokes.

Along with deforestation, Stokes is also concerned about other stresses on ape populations that may spell the end of the species. Experts say that the Ebola hemorrhagic fever virus has had a devastating impact on certain ape populations in Gabon and Congo over the past decade. Ebola is attacking some of the largest ape populations in otherwise protected zones, says Stokes. There is currently no vaccine or cure for Ebola, which targets both apes and humans.

Oil and natural gas development are also competing to get a footing in the Congo. Just west of Nouabalé-Ndoki, in Cameroon and Gabon, oil infrastructure, including roads, platforms, and pipelines, is replacing rain forest. A recent study headed by William Laurance of the Smithsonian Tropical Research Institute focused on an oil footprint in southeast Gabon. It found that similar to logging "inroads," roads for oil access provided hunters entry to areas not protected by the actual concession. Turning a formerly rigid rain forest into a year-round hunting ground is having dire consequences there.

"Our findings suggest that even moderate hunting pressure can markedly alter the structure of mammal communities in Central Africa," says Laurance.

In a similar manner, mining is also adversely affecting the Congo Basin and its inhabitants. The search for diamonds and coltan (a substance used in electronics) is also opening up areas once protected by their remoteness. Streams are also often diverted or dammed, greatly debasing waterways and a good portion of the land around them.

This ongoing damage is magnified by the political climate in some parts of the Congo, where experts simply have no idea how apes and their habitat have weathered years of civil strife and refugee crises. "There are many areas where we don't actually know how many apes are left," says Emma Stokes. "The Democratic Republic of Congo is a case in point. Vast and inaccessible areas, coupled with a decade of civil war, has meant that we have only the most general idea of important and endangered areas for apes.

"With all of these factors combined, given an ape population crash due to, say, Ebola or intense hunting pressure, it would take in the order of a hundred-plus years for a healthy population to recover. As human population growth continues to escalate rapidly across Africa, and previously remote forested areas and ape habitat succumb to logging and other exploitation activities, it is unlikely that we have a hundred-plus years in which to wait for such a recovery."

A dense, humid African forest without its great apes is not a healthy one. In their travels through dense bush, apes disperse seeds and lightly pack down vegetation, allowing in light and aiding the growth of those seedlings. Without apes, the forest will fail to replenish itself against the forces that seek to level it. And without the forest, great apes, the creatures with which humans share 96 percent of their genetic code, will become extinct.

The Congo, and great apes in particular, are not lacking local and international advocates who toil in beautiful, though sometimes brutal, terrain to ensure the survival of primates. The latest victory for them, and for the rain forest, came in late 2005 when leaders from the "range" states where apes live and international donors signed the Kinshasa Declaration in the Democratic Republic of Congo. The agreement requires that each nation devise a conservation plan to guard gorillas and their fellow apes. Such a commitment, provided it emphasizes policing poaching paths, could help. "In Central Africa, where apes are prized as food and where human population density is low, effective law enforcement of great ape populations, primarily in protected areas, but also outside, has proved to be the single most efficient means of ensuring their continued survival," says Stokes. Without that constant presence, both inside and outside parks and preserves, simply having conservation rules on the books will do little to save apes. "In spite of the fact that great apes are protected in all of their range states in Africa, there are still challenges," says Stokes.

Another tactic, aimed at diversifying the Congo's economic base and leveraging its biodiversity, is ecotourism. Right in Stokes's Nouabalé-Ndoki backyard, near the gorillas' social spot, Mbeli Bai, simple camps have been squeezed into otherwise unspoiled jungle. Travelers climb to the top of the three-story-high mirador above the swamp to gape at apes, which have become habituated to this human intrusion. In a park like Nouabalé-Ndoki, with a swollen population pressing in on its borders, there must be income possibilities to avert the need to hunt. In these areas, says Stokes, "community-based schemes, including ecotourism, have also met with some success." The operation not only helps to build a more sustainable living for locals, it also allows them to become stewards of their land and to manage the park for their children's future.

But these efforts, however grand their ideals, are still on too small a scale to shelter apes throughout the Congo Basin. Devoid of great apes, there may still be trees, but the rain forest may be muted, much like the Congo in Joseph Conrad's *Heart of Darkness*. "The reaches opened before us, and closed after, as if the forest had stepped leisurely across the water to bar the way for our return," he wrote. "We penetrated deeper and deeper into the heart of darkness. It was very quiet there."

MAASAILAND, KENYA

*On safari along elephant migration routes passing through native
Maasailand between Kenya and Tanzania*

IN JULY 2003, A GROUP OF AMERICAN TRAVELERS
climbed into their jeeps for a morning game drive through
Amboseli National Park's swampy wetlands. The rising sun cast
long shadows over the springs and marshes that dampen the dry
lake bed, and the resident wildlife started to stir. Elephants
waded in the shallows, a lioness yawned in the shade of acacias,
wildebeest dashed across the sprawling grasslands, and the click-
ing of camera shutters filled the air as the awestruck visitors
framed their shots against the backdrop of Mount Kilimanjaro.
It was a classic Kenyan safari experience, a few hours that might
have made the entire trip worthwhile. But these travelers hadn't
come to Kenya just to view its wildlife; they were there to
immerse themselves in a unique culture that is in decline.

The land that comprises Amboseli, several other wildlife
parks, and everything in between is called Maasailand, so named

for the Maasai people, who have inhabited it for centuries, if not millennia. Pastoralists who graze their cattle throughout the dry savanna and acacia woodlands of the low-lying Rift Valley, the Maasai subsist almost entirely on cow milk, meat, and blood. They measure their wealth by the size of their herds and have long shunned agriculture because cultivating land makes it unsuitable for grazing. Their intricate beaded jewelry and lively traditional dances have made the Maasai people icons of the nation's tribal heritage. Maasailand, their traditional territory, covers much of southern Kenya and northern Tanzania and is home to 80 percent of East Africa's wildlife—among them buffalo, rhinos, lions, leopards, and elephants, or the "Big Five" that have drawn outsiders to explore Africa on safari since the 1800s.

After the morning game drive, the group visited the community of Meshenani, where about three thousand Maasai villagers live just outside the park. In a two-room school hut made of mud and thatch, the Americans and the Maasai swapped stories of their daily lives—about the challenge of balancing work and family in the United States and about more elemental struggles in this part of Kenya, where the Maasai women, in their traditional red robes, must walk for miles just to fetch water. Not far from the school hut, the travelers saw an enormous hole where a hand-dug well had collapsed during a fierce rainstorm. "This thing was massive," says trip leader Kurt Kutay, owner of Seattle-based outfitter Wildland Adventures. "It was unbelievable that they could dig this out by hand." Because there had been no money for structural casings, the well had lasted only six months. Getting it working again and securing it properly would cost $6,000—nearly twenty times Kenya's average per capita income. "In the meantime," Kutay says, "women were walking twenty kilometers across open savanna over dangerous territory to get water."

This is a side of Maasai country that few tourists ever see. Far from the Nairobi markets, where crafty entrepreneurs peddle their famous beadwork, and the safari parks where smiling, spear-wielding tribesmen sell snapshots and trinkets to visitors returning from game drives, entire communities of rural Maasai are struggling to retain their rich culture and meet basic needs. The environment that these legendary herders and warriors have lived in harmony with for so long is failing to sustain them as commercial development, agriculture, and conventional tourism increasingly come into conflict with their traditional way of life.

The decline of Maasailand began at the turn of the nineteenth century, when British colonists brought smallpox and cattle plague. They then divided the central Rift Valley into concessions, claiming three fourths of the ancestral Maasai territory as their own. Much of that land was then farmed by white settlers, and the Maasai were confined to a "Southern Reserve" with inadequate dry-season rangeland. The reserve, despite its official designation, was vulnerable to illegal land-grabbing, and other tribes that had been displaced by the colonists encroached on the remaining Maasai territory. In the 1950s, groups of Maasai started seeking land titles and founding group ranches with the hope of improving grazing conditions, but many of those ranches have since fallen victim to subdivision and drought.

One of the greatest challenges to the modern Maasai is the safari industry. In the 1940s, Kenya and Tanzania began establishing national parks and game reserves to control hunting and glean income from foreign hunters. Parks were designated for game viewing and research; reserves were for game viewing, hunting, and traditional uses, which included limited access for the Maasai. When Kenya became independent in 1963, the new government recognized tourism as a cash cow and encouraged foreign development. Annual visits to Amboseli National Park grew 22 percent each year from 1965 to 1969. In the first thirty years after independence, the number of annual tourists to Kenya grew from 65,000 to 832,000. Today 80 percent of Kenya's visitors cite wildlife as the reason for their visit. The region's six largest national parks now cover five thousand square miles of what used to be Maasailand.

At the edges of those off-limits conservation areas, Maasai grazing has been restricted to smaller sections of land and is decimating the brush and interrupting migration patterns. Inside the parks and reserves, the development of tourism facilities has strained natural resources, and little has been done to encourage lodges to properly handle garbage and wastewater or to reduce firewood consumption. Industry guidelines meant to protect the fragile landscape are systematically ignored as safari guides, under pressure from wildlife-seeking clients, frequently drive off the designated roads and tear up the terrain in pursuit of up-close animal encounters and correspondingly large tips. Despite the fact that the Kenya Professional Guides Association recently began testing guides on game-park ethics and the Ecotourism Society of Kenya has developed a very basic lodge certification program, the world's most popular wildlife-watching destination is far from passing eco-muster. Because wildlife tourism is so lucrative, conservation policy is driven by economic factors; indigenous rights rarely come into play. Very little of the nation's tourism income ends up in Maasai hands, and what does is often hoarded by a small number of corrupt tribal leaders.

For these reasons, the Maasai living near the busiest parks and reserves have been forced into irreversible lifestyle changes. Many have sold their land titles and moved to the cities to take low-wage jobs. Others have recognized the marketing potential in their distinctive traditional garb and have turned themselves into tourist attractions. Visitors to the Masai Mara Game Reserve, the closest to Nairobi, encounter a very different Maasai than they would have met half a century ago. The classic red robes, spears, and beads have been reduced to costumes for the benefit of picture-taking tourists. There are few opportunities for a genuine cultural exchange.

That's not the case throughout Maasailand, however. In the Loita Hills, an extremely biodiverse, 127-square-mile forest east of Masai Mara and west of Amboseli, the Maasai community is poised to benefit from a different kind of tourism. Years ago, Frederique Grootenhuis and her husband, Jan, a wildlife veterinarian, moved here from Holland to help the local Maasai combat a cattle disease that threatened to wipe out their herds. After spending some time in this region, which is considered to be one of Kenya's last true wilderness areas, the pair realized that the Loita Maasai needed more than veterinary medicine; they needed a longevity plan. Borrowing from the model of a successful northern Kenya ecolodge called Il Ngwesi, where the local Maasai have hosted a steady stream of travelers since 1996, they set out to help the Loita community develop an entirely Maasai-run ecotourism business called Maasai Trails. They trained some guides to lead walking and donkey safaris through the forest, encouraging them to recognize their vast knowledge of native plants and wildlife as a valuable asset. Then they developed three routes that highlighted the glades, swamps, waterfalls, and overlooks of the Loita Naimina Enkiyio Forest. The result is much more rugged than the typical Masai Mara or Amboseli experience—partly because poor roads make the commute from Nairobi a seven-hour endeavor. But the lack of polish, Frederique Grootenhuis says, is part of its allure. "Loita is not a tourism destination as such yet, and so the Maasai are very unspoiled," she says. "They have their culture still intact."

Even so, there have been setbacks. Previous attempts by foreigners to protect the Naimina Enkiyio Forest have included plans to oust the Loita Maasai, an approach that, not surprisingly, has made community members wary. The success of Maasai Trails is partly contingent on the construction of a lodge, a project that has been held up by tribal leaders who distrust outsiders (and, by some accounts, fear that a successful community tourism venture could weaken their political clout). If those individuals grant permission to build the lodge, construction will begin almost immediately. "Then there will be jobs, then marketing can start, then Loita can become a selective tourist destination," Grootenhuis says. In the meantime, the pressure to log one of Kenya's last intact forests is on the rise. Without a management plan to provide a sustainable economic alternative, she says, an ecosystem that sustains forty thousand people— about 8 percent of Kenya's total Maasai population—could be destroyed within ten years. "If they lose their forest, then I could see that their springs and their swamp will dry up, and that is their lifeline. That would be a disaster." Along with carefully managed tourism, the Loita Maasai are implementing an animal health program to control outbreaks of East Coast fever, and they have started a commercial livestock business. "My dream is that the Loita Maasai become aware fast enough of the richness they have and the rights they have to benefit from their cattle and to benefit from their culture," Grootenhuis says. "And that they don't lose their respect for tourists nor for themselves, like has so clearly happened in the Mara."

Largely because of its proximity to Nairobi, the heavily traveled Masai Mara Game Reserve—where graceful gazelles sprint across a vast expanse of grassland along the murky Mara River, safari jeeps and other predators close behind—has sustained the bulk of the impact from poorly managed lodges and game drive operators. Amboseli, where tourism brought in $3.5 million in 2004, sees almost as many visitors. But unlike the Mara, Amboseli was, until recently, a national park. In September 2005, however, Kenyan president Mwai Kibaki, eager to win Maasai votes, demoted Amboseli to game reserve status and turned its management over to the local Olkejuado County Council. The local Maasai celebrated the decision as a victory for indigenous rights, but the change will almost certainly have negative environmental consequences as the mainstream tourism industry expands.

In Meshanani, the village at the edge of the reserve where the Wildland Adventures travelers saw the collapsed well, Amboseli's change in management is of little consequence. But the villagers have enjoyed one major improvement in recent years. The evening after the Americans visited, they gathered in the lobby of the Amboseli Serena Lodge to plan the well restoration. "It took awhile," Kutay says. "I remember seeing all the waiters in the hotel sticking their ears in, trying to hear these tourists talk about what they could do to support this community." After a lengthy and impassioned discussion, a couple from Seattle announced that they would take out a loan and wire the $6,000 needed for repairs, if the other travelers would raise funds to pay them back. The arrangements were made, the money was sent, and the women of Meshenani no longer have to risk their lives to fetch water.

"People want to give," says Kutay, who, like Grootenhuis, sees tourism as something of a panacea—95 percent of Wildland travelers donate money to conservation and community development programs in the places they visit, and they often maintain ties with the communities long after their return to the United States. "All we need to do as a company is create that opportunity when they're traveling," he says. "In recent years we've been designing trips to create those opportunities as much as possible."

MOUNT KILIMANJARO, TANZANIA

Kilimanjaro National Park

IN THE PAST DECADE, LEMA PETER HAS CLIMBED TO THE roof of Africa nearly a hundred times. Since he was nineteen he has accompanied hundreds of climbers, aged ten to seventy-eight, and it's still thrilling. "I just love being out there," he says. "Every time when I go back on the mountain it's new, even though I've been on the same route many times. I'm lucky to have that mountain there." Peter, a guide with Boulder, Colorado–based outfitter Deeper Africa and a member of the Mehru tribe, was raised in Arusha at the base of Mount Mehru, Africa's second-highest peak, just two hours from its lofty cousin, Kilimanjaro, which brushes the clouds at 19,340 feet.

Some say that the mountain in western Tanzania—a behemoth rising anomalously from the endlessly flat savanna—was given the name Kilimanjaro to describe its appearance. In Swahili, the most widely spoken African language, the moniker roughly translates as "shining mountain" or "the mountain that glitters." To the Maasai, it is Oldoinyo Oibor, or "White Mountain." Other linguists insist that it was named by the Wachagga (also called the Chagga) for its formidable nature. Legend has it that upon seeing Kili's snowy dome for the first time they curiously climbed it, or at least tried to. After failing to reach the top they referred to the mountain as Kelemakyaro, meaning (depending on whom you ask) "that which defeats," "a high mountain of God," or "that which is impossible for the bird, the leopard, or the caravan."

No matter what they called it, those who have gazed upon its girth for countless generations would likely not recognize what Mount Kilimanjaro is becoming. About ten thousand people now walk above its cloud skirt every year, among its improbable—and vanishing—glaciers, to look down upon the rest of the continent. Many fail to pay for their visit; still others leave their trash and waste behind. For a decade, locals like Peter have seen the impact from forces near and far, obvious and mysterious, and good and bad. "Being on the mountain for this amount of time, I've definitely seen a lot of changes just with my own eyes," he says.

The peak with the gleaming white cap is both geographical oxymoron—glaciers so near the equator!—and literary icon. Ernest Hemingway made its flakes famous in *The Snows of Kilimanjaro*, in which he exalted, "There, ahead, all he could see, as wide as all the world, great, high, and unbelievably white in the sun, was the square top of Kilimanjaro." Today Kili still appears like a mountain mirage, rising starkly from the rolling, dusty plains. When clear conditions permit, it can be seen from two hundred miles away. It is so massive—thirty-seven miles long, twenty-five miles wide, and over three miles high—that its placement here seems somehow accidental but profoundly special. With this backdrop, it's feasible that this could be the "cradle of humanity," as has been theorized—that something as major as humankind could have begun here.

The mountain is actually three volcanic peaks strung together—Shira, Kibo, and Mawenzi—forming a monolith. Its girth not only dominates the terrain but influences the weather and plant and animal life in the region. The climate on Kilimanjaro supports five extraordinary vegetation zones, with conditions from equatorial to arctic. A climber on the so-called everyman's Everest passes first across the toasted savanna, which averages eighty-five degrees Fahrenheit. The dryness dissipates into a thick band of tropical forest from roughly 5,900 feet to 9,100 feet, where most of the rain on Kilimanjaro falls. It's a foggy, wildlife-rich zone where leopards, elephants, monkeys, and a variety of game live, largely unseen, among fig, juniper, olive, and date palm trees. Kilimanjaro National Park begins here, at 8,850 feet, and continues upslope through a low alpine zone that is, again, completely different from the area beneath it. This zone is moorland, heath and heather with lumps of grass. Vultures, eagles, buzzards, and ravens may be seen overhead hunting mole rats. Next is high desert, from 13,120 to 16,400 feet, where moss and lichen blanket an otherwise barren, rocky landscape. Last is the summit region, which is entirely rock, snow, and ice, where light, white and blue, puts on a dazzling show.

Based on the best estimates, for twelve thousand years there has been ice on Kili—but a few decades of climate change will likely put an end to that. "The size of the glaciers has definitely decreased a lot and some of them have already disappeared," says Lema Peter. The world's top glaciologists and climatologists, who have drilled and prodded Kili's icy interiors, concur, and found that less than 20 percent of the peak's glaciers, which were first mapped in 1912, now remain. Some historical indicators suggest that the ice began receding as early as the 1850s and hasn't let up since.

In his expedition on the mountain in early 2006, Lonnie Thompson and his team from the Byrd Polar Research Center at Ohio State University confirmed their earlier prediction that the future of ice on Kili is not long. "Sure enough, not only are the glaciers continuing to retreat," says Thompson, "they are accelerating in the rate that they're disappearing." Since 2000 alone, seven to twelve feet of ice have been lost. That's why he's scrambling to sample Kili's glaciers before the atmosphere reclaims them. These ice cores, which are ideally as long as a glacier is deep, are hard-won with the use of a massive solar-powered drill, a technique that Thompson himself pioneered. (He was, in fact, the first person to drill an ice core above eighteen thousand feet and is said to have spent more time at that altitude, and higher, than any known mountaineer.) Air bubbles and dust particles in the samples reveal a climate timeline of weather patterns and geological events that is vital to understanding how climate is changing through time. Instances of climate change in Thompson's ice cores can often be substantiated by other means. He describes a telltale 1.2-inch dust layer, discovered among the 11,700 years of history locked in a Kili ice core that was drilled in 2001. "This dust layer represents a drought that impacted much of tropical Africa and was actually recorded in the written history from Egypt forty-two hundred years ago," says Thompson. "This massive drought may have contributed to the collapse of cultures from the Middle East to India."

For nearly thirty years, Thompson and several hundred fellow scientists, guides, and porters have been risking their lives in a race against climate change to retrieve these valuable clues. Kilimanjaro is the only place on the entire African continent where an ice core record can be gotten, and time is running out there. "These archives are disappearing because those glaciers will not be there," says Thompson. "You won't even be able to go out and get an archive on Kilimanjaro fifteen years from now."

Doug Hardy, a climatologist from the University of Massachusetts at Amherst who participated in the 2006 Kilimanjaro expedition with Thompson, has been watching the weather on Kili since 2000. During his latest trip he retrofitted some instruments at his weather station on the northern icefield on Kili's summit. The ice is melting so fast in some areas that keeping the weather station in one piece requires vigilance. On every other trip to the summit Hardy must chip out his climate gadgets from the ice and move them deeper. "Otherwise they'll melt out and tip over," he explains, much like the mummified antelope that the expedition came across recently at the summit, which had been encased in ice for hundreds of years.

For him the change in the glaciers since the last time he was there—less than a year earlier—was staggering. "Once on the top—particularly on the south-side glaciers, the ones right below the summit—the changes were extremely noticeable," says Hardy. "I had been there just eleven months before—in February 2005—and things had changed a lot. There was melting and collapsing of the vertical walls, in places where I had not seen collapses before. It just looked generally dirty, like it was wasting away." Hardy relates the rapid loss to the severe summer drought that Tanzania experienced from October 2005 through January 2006. The complete lack of snow falling on the peak kept the glaciers from growing. The other major shift that Hardy had noticed on Kili was a couple of years earlier when he returned to the mountain after a two-year absence. "From 2002 to 2004 I really saw dramatic changes. It was a real eye-opener," he says. "Just being able to look at glaciers and say, 'Wow, I remember that being bigger.'"

Lema Peter knows that feeling well. When he first started climbing, in 1997, the Furtwängler glacier, at 18,500 feet, used to drape from the summit to a crater below. "This glacier used to be hanging all the way to the crater rim itself and we used to walk for two hours across to go on the other side of the mountain," he says. "Nowadays we just cross over, because the whole hanging part is completely gone." At times the sight and sound of ice loss can be dramatic. On a recent stay at Crater Camp near Furtwängler, on top of the mountain's western breach, Peter had a rude awakening. "When we were camping up there we heard, in the middle of the night, these big chunks of glacier falling off," he says. "It's definitely a big loss that we're having on that mountain."

While the decline in ice on Kili is obvious to the senses, it's less clear what's really causing it and when the wasting will be complete. The dissolution of Kili's crown has become the poster child for climate change—time-lapse photos showing it melting like an ice cube in the Sahara have been widely distributed—but no one is exactly sure what force has been most instrumental to the melting. Warming temperatures are the likely culprit, as they are to blame for the meltdown of all other tropical glaciers. But Hardy says that Kilimanjaro is a singular place, and that pointing the finger at a rise in temperature alone is not enough. "There's a million ways in which there can be a link between global warming and the recession of glaciers on Kilimanjaro, it's just that we have not been able to characterize it very well," he says. He has been documenting conditions at the peak daily since 2000 in order to tell a more complete story of weather in the region, because up until that time, only anecdotal accounts existed. In the past several years he has seen a sharp increase in temperature on Kili's summit. "It's almost alarming to look at the trend over six years and see how much it's warmed," he says.

Still, Hardy resists pinning it all on a temperature increase. Precipitation change is at least equally responsible. Higher temperatures at higher elevations means rain falls instead of snow. No snow means no ice, no replenishment of lost glacial mass. "There's a big change for sure," says Lema Peter. "Back in the day, during the rainy season, we used to get snow from 11,300 feet and up, but nowadays, we might get a tiny bit, and within two hours it's already gone." Hardy has also seen signs of rain falling at high elevations that used to get only snow. "I saw some evidence [in 2005] that suggested that there had been some very heavy rainfall, instead of snow, very high up on the mountain, and that's exactly the kind of thing that we can expect to see from global warming. Even though we don't have this quantitative linkage between the loss of the ice and global warming, I'm certainly becoming more and more convinced that what we're seeing there is related to global warming, and to have a constant reminder of how humans are influencing the climate and the natural systems on earth, yeah, that's sad."

The total lack of precipitation recently—the area has been suffering a devastating drought for several years—has also fueled speculation that profound deforestation in the lush rain forests at the base of Kilimanjaro's south side over the past decade is wreaking havoc. Since trees tend to absorb groundwater and release it into the atmosphere, fewer trees means less water being released, which prevents clouds from forming and, consequently, rain or snow from falling.

Peter also worries that his steadfast, reliable mountain is losing stability as rock is released from ice and water drives it downslope. "The rockfalls have been increasing in some areas of the mountain," he says. "Now that the glaciers are going, there's a lot of erosion taking place." When he was last ascending the mountain on the Machame route, he could hear a lot of rock coming down from above him. "I think that's because the melting snow causes a lot of running water down the mountain and it's making all of the rocks loose," says Peter. "And you can see a lot of creeks, compared to how it used to be back in the day." While there may be more streams now, they will likely diminish, which also concerns Peter because they are his source of drinking and cooking water while climbing. "Water is going to be the big issue. A lot of campsites rely on water from the stream," he says. "It will become difficult to operate without them."

Peter is not alone in his concern for the changing conditions in his backyard. Local villagers recently voiced concerns to Hardy and Thompson over what the loss of glaciers and changing weather will mean for their water supply. While it's not yet known how much water reaches their villages from the glaciers—much of it actually evaporates into the atmosphere and never makes it downhill—Thompson is currently working on an answer to that question. It is almost certain, however, that residents rely heavily on water from the mountain for drinking, farming, and hydropower, and at times the situation is dire. "When we were there they started rationing electricity," Thompson says.

Tanzanian officials are also concerned about the attention that Kili is getting as an example for climate change. Tourism to Kilimanjaro National Park is the single greatest source of revenue for the Tanzanian government. "There's a real question of how many tourists will come there when the ice fields are no longer there," says Thompson. Tourism officials were so worried that they denied the scientific proof that Kili's glaciers are atrophying. "The minister of tourism was very upset and her initial response was, 'I don't believe the data that Dr. Thompson has produced," he says. "I told her, don't believe me, believe the people at the base of the mountain. There are families that have lived there for a hundred years. They'll tell you the same thing: the glaciers are disappearing."

Doug Hardy feels a glacial deficit would be a major visual loss. "It's an incredibly beautiful place to visit because you've got this contrast between the dark volcanic ash and the bright white of the glaciers," he says. "For me the glaciers are a big part of it. There's a sort of allure there. If the glaciers are gone from the summit of Kilimanjaro, that may impact the aesthetic experience. But that's making an assumption that it's a big deal for other people, and it maybe that's not true." Will mass tourism really evaporate along with the white peak? "Since that's the only highest mountain in Africa," argues Lema Peter, "I don't think it will affect the tourist flow."

Paradoxically, a drop in large-scale, unsustainable tourism on the mountain could benefit it. In the past couple of decades, Kili's reputation as a relatively easy summit got around. Today nearly twenty-five thousand visitors attempt to climb Kilimanjaro each year, up from fifteen thousand a decade ago. Hordes of tourists and porters have trekked up the most popular routes—the Machame and the Merangu, or "Coca-Cola," route—discarding along the way whatever they no longer cared to carry. As a result Kili's slopes began to look more like a landfill than a revered landmass. "It's too crowded in some of the camps, and that is causing a lot of problems," says Peter. "Local companies, these small companies, are not charging enough to be able to hire porters to carry their trash down. So they're burying their trash somewhere near camp." This jettisoned waste also includes substantial wads of used *karatosi ya choo*, a.k.a. toilet paper.

After several years of sporadic cleanup and ecological education (including a massive effort in 2002 when volunteers hauled fifteen tons of trash off the mountain), it is looking better, but not its best. "Still, if you go there today you wouldn't even notice that fifteen tons had been taken down," says Peter. "In some of these camps it's still really dirty. It's really disappointing." For years Peter and his colleagues have tried to teach other companies the "leave no trace" basics; they have even developed a portable bathroom that is hauled up and down the mountain, with all of its deposits.

But without better park rules and enforcement, it's difficult to keep the mountain clean. There is still no limit to the number of people one guide can lead, or any real litter enforcement. All rules, including those regarding payment, are on the honor system.

Last year, park officials said that they were so concerned about the declining ecology on the mountain that they doubled the national park fee, to about $60 per person, in pursuit of a low-volume, high-yield result. But that, says Peter, has done little to combat corruption that's inherent in the park's inner workings. "A lot of these tour operators who run trips through Merangu route and Machame route are local people, so these guys know each other, they know the park rangers, the park wardens," says Peter. "There was a lot of people sneaking in, taking clients in without paying park fees. Or you see someone has ten clients, and if you check on the permits, he only registered five people." Peter gets as angry as a charging elephant when he sees people disrespecting Kilimanjaro. "They know they're making money out of it but they don't know how to preserve it. They don't know that the future generation is going to need that mountain also."

The thought that people would cease to tap the mountain's mystique, or that its power would fade away along with its ice, is understandably heart-wrenching for Peter, because whether you reach the top of Kilimanjaro or merely catch a glimpse of it from beneath its sturdy shoulders, it brands itself on you. You may leave it, but it does not leave you. Months and decades after they've left here, travelers talk of dreams that revisit them time and again, in Africa's shades of green and gold, and of Kilimanjaro's turquoise tip.

TIMBUKTU, MALI

Sankare Mosque, Timbuktu

THERE'S A FESTIVAL THAT TAKES PLACE IMMEDIATELY
after the harvest in Timbuktu. Each year for centuries, people
have left behind their baking, weaving, farming, fishing, herding, studying, or praying to apply a new layer of mud on downtown buildings to fortify the city's ancient architecture. They
journey for days from northern Saharan villages, from Dogon
country in southeast Mali and from the western capital of
Bamako, several hundred miles away. During the festivities, even
members of the traditionally nomadic Tuareg tribe stay put temporarily to undo the damage that the dry, sand-laden winds have
wrought. It's a time for sweat, laughter, and feasts under the
early-summer sun.

The ceremony never fails to move Imam Musa Balde, founder
of the United States–based Timbuktu Educational Foundation,
whose ancestors resided in the vicinity of the historic city. "Chil-

dren go and get water to wet the earth, to make it mud and clay," he says. Women and men, old and young, pack the mucky reddish mixture onto the adobe houses, libraries, universities, and mosques—some nearly seven hundred years old—using the wood support beams that jut out from the structures as stepladders to reach building tops. "It's really an impressive celebration. If you have a heart pounding in your chest, you cannot help but be affected by it."

At the beginning of the twelfth century, Timbuktu was a simple Tuareg trading post, a well-stop on the trans-Saharan trading route that their ancestors, the Berbers, had been traveling since around 400 B.C. What had been frequented only by nomads following light footprints across the Sahara in camel caravans was settled by merchants and became the first great Muslim kingdom. In 1324, Kankan Moussa (Mansa Musa), emperor of the ancient state of Mali, made his famous pilgrimage from Timbuktu to Mecca with sixty thousand people, eighty camels, and four thousand pounds of gold (which he gave out along the way, no doubt fueling some of those notions of an über-wealthy Timbuktu). Caravans traveled south for a fortnight to reach Timbuktu from salt mines deep in the Sahara. At the time, salt, which was quite rare, rivaled gold in value. By 1330, Timbuktu was the center of African trade. Thus gold also passed through the city, as did kola nuts, ivory, leather, ostrich feathers, and slaves. Along with their trade wares, Arab merchants brought Islam.

Soon Timbuktu was not only the economic and cultural capital of West Africa but a religious and intellectual one too. During its golden age, from the fourteenth through sixteenth centuries, libraries, universities, and mosques, made of mud and logs, rose from the semiarid landscape. During the fifteenth century, books were actually the city's biggest money maker because they had to be hand-copied, an intricate task that was entrusted to Timbuktu's many scholars. African and Middle Eastern poets, writers, artists, and scholars crowded the city's prestigious universities, which in their heyday hosted twenty-five thousand students a year. Respect for the city and its offerings was then on par with Rome and Athens, and its population exceeded London's. "Timbuktu was the cradle of civilization, of knowledge and commerce, where people from all over the world could live together," says Balde.

But as meteoric and spectacular as Timbuktu's rise had been, its decline was just as precipitous. The growing Portuguese sea trade all but shut down the rough trans-Saharan trade route. A Moroccan invasion in the late sixteenth century (ordered by El Mansur, the sultan of Morocco, who had set his sights on Timbuktu's gold trade) dealt another blow. Under Moroccan rule, the city emptied out.

It was during this time that Westerners first landed in Timbuktu. The city had been rumored to be an exotic land where gold was as plentiful as the sand that blankets it. For the better part of four hundred years, Europeans had tried and failed to reach the fabled city, succumbing to brutal heat and defensive nomads. Early explorers were often intentionally misled or misguided by West Africans who feared, quite legitimately, that a cavalry might not be far behind a lone white traveler. Such a potential prize was Timbuktu that European nations competed to land their countrymen in the city first. In 1828, Réné Caillié, a poor French wine clerk seeking the ten-thousand-franc prize for finding Timbuktu, was the first to reach the city and return home to boast of his travels. Caillié's feat was accomplished by respecting the hostility for white-skinned travelers in the region. To blend in during his quest, he spent six months studying Arabic and the Koran, and physically disguised himself as a Tuareg. He draped himself in their traditional robes and head covering. For all of that work, Caillié was sorely disappointed when he finally reached Timbuktu. "The city presented, at first sight, nothing but a mass of ill-looking houses, built of earth. Nothing was to be seen in all directions, but immense quicksands of yellowish-white color," he wrote in *Travels Through Central Africa to Timbuctoo*, published in 1830. Europeans wondered if they had fallen victim to their own imagination. In his 1829 poem "Timbuctoo," Alfred Tennyson said, ". . . Wide Afric, doth thy Sun / Lighten, thy hills enfold a City as fair / As those which starr'd the night o' the elder World? / Or is the rumour of thy Timbuctoo / A dream as frail as those of ancient Time?"

Not finding a city paved with gold, the West wrote off Timbuktu. Following colonization by the French in 1893, it fell into further disrepair and ducked, once again, into relative obscurity. But Westerners had missed the point of why reaching Timbuktu was worth the trouble. Its real value is rooted in its multifaceted intellectual, political, and architectural history, which is still struggling to carry on. "Having been that type of place, obviously it should be a monument to the whole of humanity," says Balde.

To Westerners the name Timbuktu still conjures a remote, mysterious city of vast wealth. Its name is also used to suggest extremes of distance. In truth, the city is still remote, a state that has been both beneficial and detrimental. Its location far off the beaten path has allowed Timbuktu to retain much of its old-world vibe. But that has also made it easier to ignore the decline that the former African empire has been suffering. And now, due to environmental factors largely beyond the control of locals, Timbuktu is heading toward extinction.

The city is situated in the center of Mali on the southern edge of the Sahara desert. It's located in a semiarid zone called the Sahel, from the Arabic *sahil*, meaning the "shore" of the Sahara. To its south is a wetter, more fertile region. The Sahel, characterized by savanna and semidry grasslands, stretches from west to east across the entire continent, from the Atlantic coast to the Horn of Africa. The Sahel has long been the stomping ground of seminomadic people who farmed and grazed their animals there during the short but productive monsoon season. During the Sahel's dry season, when the hot and dusty harmattan winds blow in from the Sahara, the nomads move southward to greener pastures. But this immemorial migration dictated by the seasons has become highly unpredictable in recent years. As early as the 1970s, the Sahel was in the global eye when drought-induced famine took two hundred thousand lives. While conditions have improved somewhat, the drought was not anomalous.

The whole of the Sahel is now suffering greatly from desertification. The phenomenon now affects 70 percent of all drylands on earth. It's impacting parts of Asia and South America, but according to the UN Convention to Combat Desertification, it is hitting northern Africa hardest. Desertification in the Sahel is not an actual spreading of the Sahara south, burying still-fertile regions, but is instead a large-scale drying out of those fertile regions. It's both the result of agricultural overuse of the territory and of hotter, drier conditions that have persisted there over the past several decades. When the ground is stripped of vegetation and it doesn't get enough water, it simply blows away. That topsoil erosion is catastrophic to farmers and nomads alike in the Sahel, where the loss of what crops and grazing grasses did remain makes survival tenuous.

Few visitors have seen the effects of desertification as Patrick Gonzalez has. More than a decade ago, he walked 1,200 miles across Senegal's Sahel, stopping in 135 villages to gather data and local knowledge about the problem. Elders spoke of branches once heavy with cashews and trees plentiful enough for shade and firewood. Gonzalez, now a forest ecologist with the Nature Conservancy, has returned to the region time and again over the past eighteen years in his work with the US Geological

Survey, the US Agency for International Development, and the UN Development Programme. "I'm surprised, anytime I go back to the same places, at how much the tree cover continues to decline," says Gonzalez. He also compared his interviews with villagers to aerial photos and determined that from 1954 to 1989, tree species in that part of the Sahel had declined 33 percent. Gonzalez realized that three productive ecological zones—the Sahel, Sudan, and Guinean—had actually shifted fifteen to twenty miles south, where rain still falls. What happened to the modest rain that used to give life in the Sahel? The answer has only become clear in the past few years. "A lot of the precipitation seems to be falling over the ocean before it reaches land," Gonzalez says. Greenhouse gases trapped in the atmosphere are increasing ocean temperatures, which causes moisture-dense clouds to linger and never make landfall. While the locals don't cause desertification—that blame resides with industrialized nations that do not curb carbon emissions—they do exacerbate it in a few key ways. "The climate factors have driven the entire change. The human factors have intensified it," says Gonzalez. Cutting down trees for use as fuel is a major problem, as is grazing and farming until the faltering land is exhausted. Population growth is an additional strain.

The results of desertification are becoming evident across the landscape not only physically, as once-vast canopies of green disappear, but also socially and culturally. Nomadic tribes, such as the Tuareg, are being forced to set up shantytowns near cities like Timbuktu, which, historically, they've only visited. Competition for resources is causing tension across the Sahel as agricultural grains yield to grains of sand. Villagers, unable to survive in the manner of their ancestors, are also heading to urban centers. This influx is stressing cities' infrastructure; basic services like electricity, trash collection, and waste disposal are consequently overwhelmed.

Sorting building materials, Timbuktu

Much effort is being made on the part of Sahelians and international organizations to slow desertification. Agro-forestry, no-till farming, sand fences, and irrigation schemes are just a few of the ambitious actions being taken to preserve lives and livelihoods in an increasingly hostile climate. But experts agree that not enough is being done to keep pace with climate change. "With a lot of positive work, we can return the Sahel to a level of productivity to meet people's needs," says Gonzalez. "But if trends continue as they are, with climate change and population growth, I don't like to imagine how bad it could get."

Already Timbuktu is showing signs of severe strain. "It broke my heart when I saw that desertification was overtaking the city," says Balde. In recent years, locals in Timbuktu have been driven by poverty, fueled significantly by the hardships of desertification, to sell off some of the city's remaining riches, even hand-copied manuscripts and the carved wooden doors the city is famous for. "The sites are in such a precarious situation," says

Balde. He now brings delegations annually, not just to see the city, but to get their hands dirty. They help build schools, dig wells, and provide medical attention. Balde is inspired by Abdramane Ben Essayouti, imam of Timbuktu's largest mosque. "He is fearful that one day if we do not get up and begin to work on preserving and restoring it, it will no longer exist, and the next generation will blame us for that. It will be a shame if the next generation comes and finds these great monuments no longer in existence."

For anyone who's longed to say that they've been to Timbuktu and back, getting there from anywhere is a journey, not a trip. There are no paved roads to the city. The main transportation artery is still the Niger River, which zigzags its way across Mali for over a thousand miles. As the country has no coast and little rain, the river, which flows through three of Mali's five ecoregions (the Guinea savanna, Sudan savanna, and Sahel, but not the semidesert or desert areas), is its lifeline. Its fertile banks are densely cultivated for fruit, and it has West Africa's largest freshwater fish stock. The Niger River still links remote villages and remains key to Timbuktu's survival.

While some visitors do fly the 750 or so miles from Bamako to Timbuktu, flights are sporadic and unreliable (they're routinely overbooked and often canceled without notice). Besides, it seems sacrilegious to land so easily in a place that owes so much of its fame to people who struggled through sand and on water to reach it. By boat or Land Rover, travelers are more likely to catch a glimpse of the soul of Mali, which is best seen in the golden light of dawn or dusk and in the port towns clinging to the river. In Bamako you can hire a four-wheel-drive vehicle and driver to take you to the fabled city. It's expensive, but it's the best way to get a real sense of how far removed the former empire actually is. Not much compares to cutting across the dusty Sahel with few roads or signs, just scrub brush, some clay homes, and the horizon to head for. (Going it alone without a knowledgable navigator is ill advised, as bandits still roam the desolate landscape and mirages tempt travelers off course.) Boarding a boat in Bamako for the trip to Timbuktu can sometimes be a logistical hassle but is nonetheless another romantic, though far from luxurious, way to reach the city. Many Bamako-based tour companies will happily navigate the details of paying the right people the right amount for a river journey. The Niger is serviced by three types of craft: the pirogue, a slow, cheap, cramped, but authentic vessel; the pinnace, a long wooden boat painted with bright geometric shapes, which is a bit roomier and faster than the pirogue; and the steamer. When the river level is high enough, the Compagnie Malienne de Navigation takes hardy passengers toward Timbuktu at a quicker pace than on either pirogue or pinnace.

Korioumé is the nearest port to Timbuktu, which is about seven miles from the river's edge. Even though boats sometimes arrive there in the middle of the night, when they approach Korioumé, the sleepy boat awakens and the port buzzes with activity. Women balance baskets on their heads, often filled with fish or chickens they hope to trade. Plastic bags filled with ginger and hibiscus juices are sold. And Tuareg traders, resplendent in their traditional head-to-toe indigo robes (whose dye stains the skin, earning them the nickname "the blue men of the Sahara"), balance intricately woven carpet rolls atop their *tagelmoust*, or headwraps.

As the sky lightens over Timbuktu, some travelers feel that the city has had its day in the sun. Many of its monuments have been roughed up by time and the elements. But just as Rome's Colosseum and Athens's Acropolis are worthy places for mulling what transpired there, so is Timbuktu. And like Rome and Athens, Timbuktu remains a living, secular city. One can still walk through the messy maze of alleys in the city amid a buzz of students rushing to their classes or experience the quiet that follows the call to prayer five times daily. Its major university buildings and mosques are certainly degrading but remain proud and functioning. The main Djingareyber Mosque, big enough for two thousand followers to pray in, stills dominates the modest skyline after more than 650 years.

Still, the city does lack tourist infrastructure. This is at once a blessing and a curse. There's no Four Seasons, or anything like it. In fact only a handful of places are air-conditioned at all. But there are a few friendly restaurants, serving mostly rice with peanut sauce and local fish, and modest pensions, where the cost may not seem commensurate with comfort. And, as in most "developing" nations (a strange label for a place that was once as advanced as Timbuktu was), there is some trash and waste about. Relentless street hawkers will sell pretty much anything they imagine has souvenir value.

Take a stroll along its dusty streets and it's clear that locals work tremendously hard here—women knead and bake bread in outdoor clay ovens; herders endlessly drive goats, sheep, and cattle in search of decent grazing; and fishermen doggedly pursue their latest catch. Farmers close to the Niger harvest millet, maize, sorghum, and rice. Caravans of camels toting sweet, mild salt slabs from Saharan mines still arrive in the city, as they have for a thousand years, like mirages from the desert. To get a brief sense of trans-Saharan travel, visitors can even hire camels and head into the desert, where Tuaregs—who call themselves Tamasheq—will lay straw mats outside their tent and serve bitter tea from ceramic pots on silver trays. While it's one of the only truly touristy types of activity in the area, who could resist riding on camelback into the Sahara at sunset?

Timbuktu's economic capital is largely spent and much of its intellectual capital has migrated, but the city, like much of Mali, remains awash in so-called "social capital." Mali is often de-

scribed as a poor country—it is the fourth-poorest in the world—
that remains rich in people. Malians are, by and large, a proud,
passionate, diverse, and friendly lot. "And when you go to Timbuktu you will see that it's the best place to visit in Mali," says
Balde. "The people are so hospitable." Mali is still one of the
safest places on the continent to travel. Thirty or more African
languages and dialects are spoken, and while most locals speak
French, very few speak English. The country's deep musical roots
have spread internationally, from the slow, haunting melodies
of the Bambara people to the engaging, upbeat vocals of the
Malinke.

Timbuktu also still boasts an impressive number of scholars
and philosophers, and an astounding collection of ancient
manuscripts that would make any archivist ecstatic. More than
750,000 valuable volumes remain in the city, both in private col-
lections (which often amount to locals' steel storage trunks) or
at the Ahmed Baba Center, where 14,000 volumes are kept in
air-conditioned cases. The manuscripts, dense with flourished
Arabic calligraphy, include lessons in science, philosophy,
astronomy, math, governance, and—interestingly—peace. So-
called scholars of peace used to comb the area to sort out tension. "They used to go from region to region to solve problems
between people," says Balde. Perhaps the most remarkable thing
about Timbuktu is that tradition of tolerance, which lingers
today. Mali is still one of the only countries in the world (along
with neighbor Senegal) where democracy and Islam coexist and,
moreover, where other religious traditions dwell alongside
Islam. In Timbuktu, Jews, Christians, and Muslims lived harmo-
niously off and on throughout history. Today a small Christian
population and vibrant animist communities (as far as anyone
can tell, only Islamicized descendants of Jews remain) still worship peacefully in the vicinity of mosques.

There's an Islamic code that Imam Musa Balde reads every

day, from El Hadj Oumar Tall, a prominent nineteenth-century Timbuktu scholar: "Tragedy is due to divergence, and because of lack of tolerance. Glory be to he who creates greatness from difference, and makes peace and reconciliation." Balde says that it's these teachings, as much as the physical state of the manuscripts and buildings in Timbuktu, that need to endure. "Today, with the crises that we are having, the misunderstanding between Islam and the West, that legacy would be a vehicle to bridge the gaps between us," he says. But the likelihood of that succumbs to desertification a bit more each day. "You cannot put it into words how imperative it is for us to preserve this city. I believe that the cultural legacy of Timbuktu is the missing link for Africa to the rest of the world."

ASIA,
PACIFIC ISLANDS,
AND AUSTRALIA

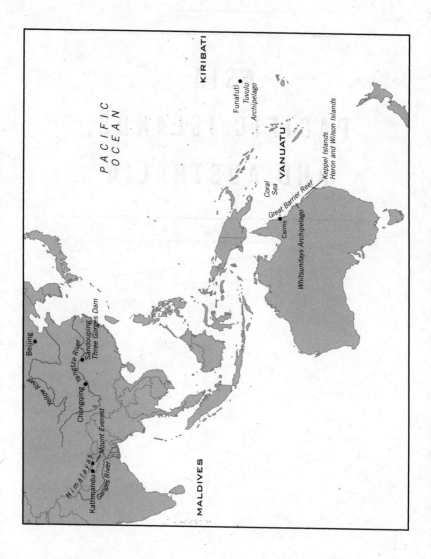

EVEREST NATIONAL PARK, NEPAL

Gokyo Ri, Nepal

ON MAY 29, 1953, SIR EDMUND HILLARY AND SHERPA Tenzing Norgay became the first men to summit the world's highest mountain. As they stood atop the 29,035-foot-tall peak, surrounded by the glistening ice formations and sinister crevasses they had conquered as they scaled Mount Everest's southern face, an elated Norgay waved his ice ax adorned with the flags of Nepal, Great Britain, the United Nations, and India against the clear blue sky, and Hillary snapped photographs of what he later described as "the whole world spread out below us."

More than half a century later, at eighty-six, Hillary undertook an even greater challenge: saving the very landscape that his photographs had helped make legendary. "The warming of the environment of the Himalayas has increased noticeably over the last 50 years," he wrote in a press release distributed to media outlets worldwide in July 2005. "This has caused several and severe floods from glacial lakes and much disruption to the environment and local people." Hillary hoped to convince UNESCO's World Heritage Committee to add Everest National Park to its danger list, a designation that would mandate worldwide government intervention. The park, which encompasses 443 square miles from the top of Mount Everest to the valleys to its south, has become increasingly pocked with glacial lakes that pose a flooding threat to the villages below.

As glaciers melt, they shed the layers of rocks and sediment that were trapped inside the ice, and the debris forms natural dams. Meltwater collects behind the unstable moraines until the pressure becomes too great, at which point the walls collapse, unleashing powerful floods of water, boulders, and mud. At least sixteen glacial lake outbursts have hit Nepal since 1935. The first to catch the attention of the international scientific community happened in 1985, when a large chunk of ice broke off from the Langmoche glacier and fell into the crescent-shaped Dig Tsho glacial lake. The impact wave toppled the 164-foot-tall moraine, pushing floodwater more than fifty miles through the valley. The lake emptied in less than six hours, releasing up to 350 million cubic feet of water in a thirty-five- to fifty-foot-tall surge. In addition to killing twenty people, the flood wiped out a new $1.5 million hydropower station, downed fourteen bridges, and destroyed a trekking trail to Everest Base Camp. Scientists with the United Nations Environment Programme and the International Centre for Integrated Mountain Development in Kathmandu have since predicted that twenty of Nepal's glacial lakes are filling so quickly they could breach their walls by 2009. If an earthquake strikes the Himalayas, dozens could burst at once.

In response to the pleas from Hillary and other international campaigners, the UNESCO World Heritage Committee set up a task force to investigate the issue. Should the group's findings lead to a danger list designation, governments around the world will be obligated to reduce greenhouse gas emissions to slow global warming. (How much that will actually change the behavior of individuals and nations is up for debate.) In the meantime, Nepali villagers can only watch and wait.

"The poor ol' people of Nepal, what do they contribute to global warming? I should think it's the square root of zero. But here they are, having to be confronted by climate change and in the worst possible position to be able to do much about it," says Roger Payne, a British mountaineer. In 2002, Payne organized an expedition with the UN Environment Programme and the International Mountaineering and Climbing Federation to highlight the impact of climate change in the Himalayas. The expedition set out to humanize the mass of climate change data that scientists had collected over the years, using laymen's observations to tell the story of global warming and its visible impacts on Everest. The team of seven included two filmmakers from Slackjaw Films, who later turned their footage into a documentary called *Meltdown: In the Shadow of Nepal's Lost Glaciers.* Their promotional materials urge viewers to "meet the Nepali people now, before they are washed away!" Sensational as it may seem, the prospect of thirty million tons of water leveling Khumbu Valley villages is not far-fetched.

Scientists began conducting regular studies of Nepal's glaciers in the 1970s. Since then they have found that two thirds are in rapid retreat, a trend they attribute to climate change. The glaciers in the Khumbu region near Mount Everest retreated one hundred to two hundred feet during the 1970s and 1980s, and the shrinking could accelerate. Like most high-altitude regions, the Himalayas are warming at a faster pace than lowland areas.

The Payne expedition began in Phakdingma, near the banks of the Dudh Koshi (Milk River), where Lama Sarky told the mountaineers of the disappearing snow and ice and the meltwater that has triggered devastating outburst floods in recent years. Unusually warm, damp weather followed the group to Namche Bazaar, where they acclimatized before setting out for the higher camps. Their goal was to summit 20,305-foot Island Peak, Mount Everest's neighbor in the mountainous Khumbu region. The peak was a symbolic choice. Used by Hillary and Norgay for reconnaissance and acclimatization before their Everest summit, Island Peak got its name because it appeared to float in a sea of ice. That ice has long since turned to water. "In '53 when they climbed Island Peak there was no lake, and now there is one a couple of kilometers long, five hundred meters wide, one hundred meters deep," Payne says of the Imja glacial lake. "Plus the mountain itself is becoming unclimbable because of the change of the glaciers."

As the mountaineers waited for their blood to thicken and for the gloomy skies to clear, they toured the Tengpoche monastery, where yet another lama spoke to them of outburst floods and changes in the weather. They left for Dingpoche the next day, trekking through the rhododendron forest to the open tundra, where they saw flood damage firsthand. Deep scars marked the western slope of Ama Dablam where water and debris had torn through in 1987. "I was surprised by the size of the scars on the walls," Payne says. "I'd walked past them before but I'd never thought of them as being caused by a glacial lake outburst flood." That sight gave the next day's journey beneath a series of large moraines a new intensity, as the mountaineers imagined being swept up in the wave of water and debris that could tumble down the mountain if a glacial lake breached its rocky barrier. "With the disappearing of the vegetation on the sides, one could then suddenly imagine this whole wall of water and rocks coming down," Payne says. "It was a scene I'd seen before, but when I was looking it at with these better-informed eyes, it really was quite dramatic."

Himalaya Mountains

Base camp was a small platform above a stream trickling from Imja glacier's terminal moraine. "If an outburst flood occurred to the Imja glacial lake, this would almost certainly be the exact spot where the moraine wall would burst," the climbers wrote in their expedition journal. They settled in, enjoying the views afforded by a cloudless day as they struggled with the thin air—the camp was above sixteen thousand feet. Then, nine days after they started, they reached the banks of the Imja glacial lake. Scientists at the UN Environment Programme and the International Centre for Integrated Mountain Development include this lake on their list of twenty that are in danger of an outburst flood. "At first sight the Imja glacial lake looks unremarkable; just another feature in very high mountain glaciated terrain," they wrote. "But the experts' reports of accelerated growth and instability, and the vast scale of the mountain walls and glaciers feeding the lake, make the risk to the densely populated valley below simply frightening."

Disastrous as the predicted outburst floods would be, the possible long-term implications of Nepal's glacial melt-off are even scarier. According to a 2005 WWF report on glacier retreat in Nepal, India, and China, 70 percent of the world's limited supply of freshwater comes from glaciers, and the demand for that water is on the rise as the global population grows. With the largest concentration of glaciers outside the poles, the Himalayas provide water to millions of people throughout Asia. When the flow from Nepal's shrinking glaciers starts to dwindle, rivers will begin to dry up, threatening the entire region's economy and, ultimately, its food supply. The greatest impact will be felt in Nepal, where the average citizen makes less than $4 per day and 76 percent of the population earns its income from growing jute, sugarcane, tobacco, grain, and other crops.

But the damage could extend far beyond Nepal's borders—water from the Himalayan nation's 3,252 glaciers, which trickles into its 6,000-plus rivers and rivulets, also feeds the Ganges, Indus, Brahmaputra, Salween, Mekong, Yangtze, and Yellow rivers. During the dry season, up to 70 percent of the Ganges's water comes from Nepal. A reduction in meltwater could reduce that river's summertime inflow by two thirds, causing widespread water shortages. "The rapid melting of Himalayan glaciers will first increase the volume of water in rivers, causing widespread flooding," said Jennifer Morgan, director of the WWF's Global Climate Change Programme. "But in a few decades this situation will change and the water level in rivers will decline, meaning massive eco and environmental problems for people in western China, Nepal, and northern India."

Four days after the mountaineers arrived at base camp, Payne and three others began their early-morning push to the Island Peak summit, plodding through the fresh powder that had dusted the glacial slopes during the night. It was overcast when they reached the peak at 10:30 A.M.—a fitting contrast to the bright and celebratory skies enjoyed by Hillary and Norgay atop Everest fifty years before.

Few visitors to Nepal will ever view the Himalayas from the vantage point of a four-mile-high peak. But it's possible to walk along a glacier in Everest National Park without learning technical climbing skills. Twice a year, adventure travel guides Karma and Wendy Lama take trekkers on an eighteen-day "Best of Everest" trip that covers some of the same terrain that Payne and his team explored (minus the nerve-racking jaunt beneath the stressed moraine). Karma Lama has been leading expeditions in the Himalayas since the early 1980s and has climbed some of Nepal's tallest mountains, including Lhotse and Island Peak. He and Wendy met while she was working as an ecotourism planner with the Mountain Institute, a conservation group working to advance mountain cultures and preserve mountain environments. The two founded their responsible adventure company, KarmaQuest, in 2000. This classic trekking route was one of their first itineraries.

After several days in transit, the trek begins at Lukla (9,200 feet) with a four-hour descent to Phakding (8,800 feet), where you can expect to be welcomed with home-cooked stew—one of the many perks of traveling with guides who have forged strong friendships over the years. After meandering along the Dudh Koshi to the historic Nepali-Tibetan trading center of Namche Bazaar (11,300 feet), you'll take a day to acclimatize before continuing on through the rhododendron forests to Tyangboche

(12,900 feet). On the fall trek you'll catch the Mani-Rimdu festival, where villagers come from all around to watch monks in elaborate ceremonial masks do traditional dances that convey Buddhist teachings. Two days later you'll reach Lobuche (16,400 feet), the site of an Italian research station where scientists study high-altitude ecology. This is where much of the data on glacial retreat originates. It's also the starting point for your peak-bagging day. From the top of Kalapathar (18,190 feet) you can look down on Everest Base Camp and the Khumbu glacier, and if the clouds cooperate, you'll catch a glimpse of Mount Everest's frozen peak. An optional side trip to Everest Base Camp (17,000 feet) takes you along the Khumbu glacier, where you can crunch your crampons on the endangered ice before starting the return trek to Lukla.

Every KarmaQuest trip that passes through Namche Bazaar includes a visit to the national park visitor center for a primer on responsible trekking, given by the Sagarmatha Pollution Control Committee, the region's conservation institution. Since Nepal opened its doors to outsiders in the 1950s, Western trekkers have flocked to its Himalayan trails by the hundreds of thousands. With them came an increasing demand for firewood that has wiped out large swaths of pine forest; a competitive market for labor that resulted in underpaid, dangerously ill-equipped porters; and so many ramen wrappers, oxygen cylinders, and other imported detritus that Everest became known in the 1980s as the world's highest garbage dump. Traveling responsibly means using alternative fuels, paying porters fair wages and making sure they're warmly dressed and well fed, and disposing of waste properly. "We feel that educating the visitors about the environmental impacts of tourism is really key to making sure that we and they are minimizing impacts on the environment. And also, the other side of responsible tourism is enlightening people to opportunities to benefit local people,"

Wendy Lama says. "Not everyone in the Everest region benefits from tourism—in fact, there are inflationary impacts that drive the prices of things up. So people need to understand when they're visiting there how to be responsible, how to treat people, how to treat the environment, and how to be aware when they're buying something or making a donation how tourism can benefit all aspects of the community."

Educating outsiders was a key component of the Payne expedition as well. On their return to Kathmandu, the mountaineers issued a report to the UN Environment Programme just in time for World Environment Day, the UN's annual effort to raise worldwide awareness about the issues affecting our planet. The report was not scientific in nature; it was simply a grassroots account of global warming and its toll on Everest's glaciers. "We were just mountain travelers observing something and trying to report it back to a wider audience for them to judge," Payne says. The conversations they recounted and the evidence they presented probably had a greater impact on public perception than any scientific data could. Among the more shocking revelations the team shared was an observation from Tashi Janghu Sherpa, president of the Nepal Mountain Association, who told the mountaineers that they would now have to walk two hours from Hillary and Norgay's 1953 base camp to find the edge of the Khumbu glacier. The famous ice that marked the start of mountaineering's best-known conquest had retreated more than three miles up the mountain. "It's only once you've been made aware that these events have happened in living history," Payne says, "that you look again with fresh eyes on the landscape you've seen before."

TUVALU AND MALDIVES

TUVALU TRANSLATES AS "EIGHT STANDING TOGETHER," which denotes the number of inhabited islands in the archipelago. The remote, delicate string of isles is made up of specks of land sprawling northwest across a 420-mile swath of the Pacific, just below the equator and halfway between Australia and Hawaii. These scraps of terrain are the peaks of huge underwater limestone reefs that formed over millions of years as the remains of marine life piled up on extinct volcanoes. So integrated are they with their ocean environment that when gliding along the water, it's hard to tell where the waves end and the crescents of golden sand begin. The archipelago's average elevation is just six feet above sea level. The combined landmass of all of Tuvalu's islands and atolls (which are made up of a cluster of small islets with a lagoon at their center) is a mere ten square miles, making it one of the smallest nations in the world.

Watching a Tuvaluan fisherman squint in the sun as he hoists a fresh dinner from a reed boat on Te Namo lagoon, or seeing salted fish drying on racks on Funafala beach, it seems like not much has changed in the two thousand or so years since these islands were first settled by humans. Almost all of today's 10,500 Tuvaluans are ethnic Polynesians, descendants of distant islanders on Tonga and Samoa. The first Europeans landed on the fragile archipelago in the sixteenth century, but it wasn't until 1877 that the British claimed them as the Ellice Islands, dethroning Aliki chiefs. The microcountry won back its independence in 1978.

Even today Tuvalu is a prototypical paradise—warm, sultry, and unspoiled by tourism. To a bird in flight, Funafati, Tuvalu's capital atoll, looks like a lasso of verdant green islets floating on an azure sea. Beneath the waves, striped and spotted tropical fish in shades of tangerine, lemon, and lime frequent forests of Day-Glo corals and sturdy mangroves. Lazy breezes rustle the fronds of tall, wind-bent coconut palms. Pale, velvety shores merge into patches of salt-tolerant ferns. On the west side of the atoll is a dense stretch of native broadleaf forest in the Funafati Conservation Area, where coconut crabs tiptoe on the sand, green turtles nest, and reef herons, terns, and bommies puncture the clear lagoon looking for lunch.

Opposite the reserve, to the east, is Fogafale, the widest part of the atoll, where *tamaliki*, or children, chase one another around coconut palms and pandanus-roofed huts. Nearby the buzz of the Vaiaku market, the whispered prayers at the *falekaupule*, or the hum of the ancient *fatele* chant might be heard. On the southern rim of Funafati Island is the *saute*, as it's known to the locals. To the fewer than one thousand tourists a year who find their way there, it's known as the "eighth wonder of the world." The saute is a postcard panorama of aqua tides lapping on pink sand where downy clouds merge with distant jade islets on the horizon. The notion of a tropical paradise could certainly have been first realized here.

Like all of its kin, Funafati (FUN in airport shorthand) has no freshwater streams, waterfalls, or mountains. Consequently Tuvaluans rely on shallow groundwater and rainfall for drinking and farming. For as long as anyone can remember, the islands have suffered occasional cyclones and king tides—the seasonal extreme high tides that can compromise their freshwater supply. These characteristics make Tuvalu—and the twenty-one other pancake-flat Pacific nano-nations—acutely vulnerable to climate variability.

Since the 1990s Pacific islanders have been noticing trouble in paradise. While all of the twenty-two petite Pacific island countries, with about seven million inhabitants total, are familiar with seasonally extreme weather events, they are not accustomed to the frequent and intense storms that have swept across their homelands as of late. As Teleke Lauti, Tuvalu's environmental minister, told the Hague in 2000, "The sea is our very close neighbor. In fact, on the island where I live, Funafati, it is possible to throw a stone from one side of the island to the other. Our islands are very low-lying. When a cyclone hits us there is no place to escape. We cannot climb any mountains or move away to take refuge."

In the past few decades, the number of people on South Seas islands affected by weather-related disasters, from flooding and cyclones to droughts, has risen by 65 percent. As weather phenomena like the complex and well-known El Niño Southern Oscillation (which have a great impact on the wind, sea temperature, and precipitation patterns in the tropical Pacific) become more variable, Pacific islands will be pressed to adapt to volatility. El Niño patterns are likely to bring more droughts to the western Pacific and torrential rain to the east.

In tiny Tuvalu and neighboring countries, the sea—which has been a constant companion for many generations—is beginning to beseige and frighten them. Until now, their land, these coral deposits upon which sand congregates and vegetation takes hold, has withstood the rise in sea level after the end of the last ice age. But now water threatens to overtake them. And the rains that have traditionally pounded their thatched and tin roofs now inundate their freshwater supplies, modest structures, and *pulaka* (a variety of taro) fields with surges of seawater. To the west, on islands that rely on rain for drinking water and subsistence farming, drought is also a growing problem. Throughout the region residents are anxious about their island existence. "We in Tuvalu live in constant fear of the adverse impacts of climate change and sea level rise," Maatia Toafa, Tuvalu's prime minister, told the UN General Assembly in 2004. The next year he reiterated his concern. "Living in a very fragile island environment, our long-term security and sustainable development is closely linked to issues of climate change, preserving biodiversity, managing our limited forests and water resources," said Toafa. "As witnessed world-over, a natural disaster like [a] cyclone, made worse by the effects of climate change, can have a devastating effect on economies and lives. For Tuvalu the effects are scary."

In the twentieth century, air temperature globally rose an average of one degree Fahrenheit. What seems a tiny temperature increase is deceiving, explains Gerald Meehl, a climate modeler at the National Center for Atmospheric Research in Boulder, Colorado. "The way that you see this slow, relatively small change in mean temperature is that the extreme events become more so," he says. That means that as air and water continue to warm over time they will persist in stirring up storms the likes of which have never been known.

Quality of life and, ultimately, their longevity on their home islands weighs heavily on the minds of low-lying island residents. Leaders of nano-nations in the Pacific and Indian oceans and the Caribbean Sea have spent the past several years pleading with, and occasionally suing, industrialized nations for relief from a crisis they did little to cause and can't mitigate alone. (While Tuvalu, like most island nations, emits greenhouse gases, its contribution is negligible. In total, Pacific islands are now responsible for 0.06 percent of all greenhouse emissions. In 1994, the last year for which there are records, Tuvalu had pumped five thousand tons of carbon dioxide into the atmosphere, and considering its recent focus on renewable energy, that number is expected to drop. By contrast, in 2004, the United States emitted 7.1 billion tons.)

Tuvalu's outcry and action (it has signed on to the 1997 Kyoto Protocol) have so far gone unanswered. Nevertheless, many island dwellers are still hopeful that they can hang on to their sovereign land and cultural identity by adapting to climate change. But realistically, there's only so much they can do. In early 2006, the highest tide in Tuvalu's history was recorded. Like on many areas of the islands, a foot and a half of seawater settled on palm-shaded Palagi Road. Waves carried boulders into classrooms (thankfully, the school had been closed). But Tuvaluans considered themselves lucky that this historic high tide, which was the result of a traditional high tide combined with the increase in sea level, rose beneath clear skies. Flooded-out roads and runways fared far better than they would have had the weather been rough. A storm of the kind that is increasingly likely under the new climate regime would have been catastrophic during such a high tide.

While they're recognizing the compounding dangers they now confront, the Tuvaluan leadership is admitting that its power is limited. At a UN climate convention several years ago a Tuvaluan delegate said, "Providing us with capacity building, adaptation, and other imaginative measures to mitigate climate change while refusing to institute domestic policy and political measures that will genuinely reduce global emissions is like treating us like the pig you fatten for slaughter at your eldest son's twenty-first birthday party." For example, they can ban the damage or taking of coral, whose reefs buffer shores from storm surges, but increasing water temperatures (which they can do nothing about) will continue to cause massive bleaching of coral.

In 2005, President Anote Tong of Tuvalu's northeastern neighbor, Kiribati, told the UN: "Given their small landmasses, there is a limit to the extent which populations of low-lying coral atolls can adapt." He addressed the UN in the same month that the Kiribati Meteorological Office reported king tides that drove seven- to twenty-six-foot waves inland for two solid days.

In his thirty-two-atoll country of ninety thousand souls they've been trying to steel themselves against the danger pounding their shores. I-Kiribati, the name for island residents, have been replanting depleted mangroves, adhering to stricter building codes that will minimize coastal erosion, and trying to better protect their freshwater supplies.

But in the wake of king tides (those traditional high tides) combined with frequent ferocious storms, island nations are facing yet another relentless force of climate change: sea level rise. Gerald Meehl says that while there's no set formula for precisely how air temperature affects sea temperature, one phenomenon is as clear as Funafati's crystal lagoon. He explains that greenhouse gases already "in the pipeline" would continue to affect weather and sea level even if carbon dioxide emissions were halted today. One recent study determined that if greenhouse gas emissions ceased today, Tuvalu, and other dots on the world map, wouldn't get any relief until 2100. "This is something that I think a lot of policymakers aren't aware of," says Meehl. "This idea has been around for a while, but there's this perception that if the problem gets bad enough, you can just put the brakes on— introduce measures to stabilize CO_2 concentration—and suddenly the problem just stops and everything's okay." Not so.

Another reason for this bleak projection is thermal inertia, the rate of expansion of water as it warms. Since water warms (and cools) much more slowly than air, oceans will continue to rise inexorably. Meehl says that while air temperature would stabilize in thirty to forty years if carbon emissions were stopped, the water temperature would continue to rise. "We're talking about warming up basically the entire volume of the ocean eventually," he says. "We're committed to long term sea level rise."

Predictions vary on the extent of sea rise in the coming decades, but most experts agree that the rate will accelerate. Researchers at the Australian Scientific Industrial Research

Organization say that in the twentieth century, oceans rose approximately 0.7 inches. By 2100, they expect that amount to nearly double, raising seas as much as 1.3 inches. As with temperature, a small number is more serious than it appears. Meehl explains that such estimates of ocean warming do not take into account how much seas will rise as a result of the melting of glaciers and ice sheets worldwide, another consequence of atmospheric warming. The Intergovernmental Panel on Climate Change, an international body composed of thousands of scientists from around the world, predicts that the total average global sea rise from both ocean expansion and melting ice could be as much as thirty-five inches by 2100. According to that worst-case scenario, most island nations would be nonexistent, or at the very least uninhabitable.

Despite the doomsday predictions, Meehl suggests that all hope for the islands is not lost. "The message that some people get that hear this information is, 'No matter what we do, warming is going to continue,' and that's the wrong message," he says. "The longer we wait, the worse the problem gets. Every day we're committing ourselves to climate change in the future. When you view it that way, it's not something that you should just give up on. It's something that should motivate you to do something about it sooner rather than later."

For islanders around the world who are already in harm's way, "sooner" is now. In Tuvalu their *motu* have gone missing. Motu, islets that lay beyond the coral reefs of their atolls, were a critical navigation tool for fishermen until they disappeared under rising water. Kiribati watched two of its uninhabited islands completely vanish beneath rising water in 1999. Both Tuvalu and Kiribati are already losing portions of their petite populations every year to New Zealand, which has begun accepting them as global warming refugees. Each year seventy-five Tuvaluans (a significant number in a population that's fewer than twelve thousand) and fifty I-Kiribati are allowed to emigrate. Tuvalu recently approached both Australia and New Zealand about eventually resettling all of its citizens. In Vanuatu, a nation of eighty-three islands southwest of Tuvalu, whole shoreside villages have been abandoned to escape rising water. In 2002, in what was described as the first instance of ecological displacement of an entire population, one hundred Tegua Island residents had to abandon their coastal village for the island's interior when violent storm surges tore through their homes.

While the situation is said to be worst in the Pacific, sea level rise is a global phenomenon. Across the world from Tuvalu, in another textbook tropical nirvana, lives and livelihoods are also in flux. The 1,190 islands and surrounding reef-rich waters that make up the Maldives—a nation roughly three hundred miles off the tip of southern India—subsist largely by growing and netting their food, and on tourism, which accounts for one third of their gross domestic product. Today, roughly 450,000 travelers per year, mostly Europeans, land there. Visitors gorge on mangoes and papayas hand-picked from local groves and float in placid fishbowl-like lagoons accompanied by gliding stingrays, darting dolphins, and paddling rare green sea turtles. (The Maldives' reefs are said to rival the Great Barrier Reef in diversity.) They take seaplanes from one island to the next, sampling their individual specialties: intricately woven grass mats on Huvadhoo; artistic lacquer work on Thulhaadhoo; sarongs, gold, silver, baskets, and jewelry on others.

Eighty percent of the Maldives is less than three feet above the surface of the jewel-toned waters that surround them, making more extensive tidal surges and accelerating coastal erosion potentially catastrophic. "The concept of 'coast' in the Maldives includes the total land area of each island," explains Faathin Hameed of the Maldives Ministry of Fisheries, Agriculture, and Marine Resources. For the three hundred thousand Maldivians on two hundred inhabited islands, climate change is already reality. The increasing unpredictability of tides and storms has led fishermen to all but abandon their *nakiy*, the age-old method of meteorological predictions made by examining stellar constellations.

All of the changes seem like a curse from the jinn, or evil spirits, but Maldivians are not giving up without a fight. Since 2004 the Maldivian government has been encouraging its lower-dwelling residents to relocate to higher parts of the archipelago as part of its Safe Islands project. The plan is to eventually consolidate the population onto five main islands, in order to better protect their safety and resources. Already twelve islands have been mostly abandoned and their residents moved to the capital, Male, around which multi-million-dollar protective barriers (financed by Japan) almost ten feet high, called "tetrapods," have been erected. The walls proved worthy during the 2004 Indian Ocean tsunami. The city, where 75 percent of the population lives, escaped major damage. Most of the islands were at least partially damaged by the waves, and at least eighty-two lives were lost. The economic effects were also devastating. While tourism is making a comeback, the event clearly showed islanders how a major drop in visitation could affect them in the long term.

The leadership of the Maldives hopes that its battle cry—which sounds a lot like those coming from Tuvalu, Vanuatu, and Kiribati—will be carried across the Indian Ocean and onto influential shores. "Now that you know a little bit more about the peculiar environmental vulnerabilities of the last paradise on earth," says their tourism ministry, "take a second look and see the fragility of our existence. And think about us, the people of Maldives. This is our home."

Those lucky enough, in the near future, to sink their toes into the salmon sands of Tuvalu's Funafati saute or laze in a hammock stretched between stately palms on Kiribati, Vanuatu, the Maldives, or any of the thousands of other luminous islands that bejewel our oceans may see them as Charles Darwin did when he cruised the South Pacific in 1835. At that time he was awestruck by the islands' vulnerable topography and remarked, "These low hollow coral islands bear no proportion to the vast ocean out of which they abruptly rise; and it seems wonderful, that such weak invaders are not overwhelmed, by the all-powerful and never-tiring waves of that great sea . . ."

YANGTZE RIVER VALLEY, CHINA

Endangered cottages on the Yangtze River

THERE'S A MORBID GUESSING GAME TRAVELERS PLAY when they're cruising on the Yangtze River toward the Three Gorges Dam. "Will that cottage be underwater?" "Yeah, I think so." "Those terraces?" "Definitely." It's a narrative that's been getting progressively more fatalistic since the world's largest hydropower project began flooding the valley in 2003, swallowing thirteen cities and hundreds of towns and villages, burying unknown numbers of archaeological relics, and forcing the relocation of nearly two million residents.

When the $29-billion-plus-dam is finished in 2009, it will be 1.3 miles long—more than five times the length of the Hoover Dam—and will generate 18,200 megawatts of electricity, about as much as eighteen nuclear plants. That will help feed the booming country's insatiable hunger for power and will expand river-based commerce in inland China. But it will also irreversibly alter the river valley between Chongqing and Sandouping, two cities that are about as far apart as Los Angeles and San Francisco. The water between them has already risen 298 feet and will soon be 62 feet higher, turning that stretch of the river into a 360-mile-long reservoir.

In Chongqing, the hilly metropolis that is the starting point for most tourist cruises on the Yangtze, you can visit the studio of artist Liu Zuozhong at the top of a hill in Eling Park. Liu spent most of his thirties and forties sketching the Yangtze between his hometown and the city of Yichan. When the government approved the Three Gorges Dam project in 1992, he devoted himself to memorializing that stretch of China's longest river in a mural, spending his life savings to complete *Thousand Miles Three Gorges* by 1995.

The finished work—328 feet long and 6.5 feet tall—is on permanent display at the small, cavelike museum outside his park studio, where he sells hundreds of smaller paintings, sketches, and booklets to passersby. In the mural, the region's ever-present mist hovers in the blue-tipped hillsides that surround the high rises and pagodas. Cruise ships, freighters, and sampans dot the chocolate milk–colored river, which narrows amid the mystical peaks that line the Three Gorges, the three towering limestone canyons carved millennia ago by the Yangtze, which runs 3,900 miles from the Tibetan Plateau to the East China Sea. Signs identify the counties and their numbers of "immigrants," residents who have been relocated. Dotted red-and-white lines mark the post-dam water level, below which lie acres of farmland and scores of pastoral dwellings.

Aboard a cruise liner, you can document the shrinking shoreline from the water. Nowhere is the geographical transformation more dramatic than within the Three Gorges. But ships traveling downriver from Chongqing take a full day to reach the first gorge and another to reach the dam. First you must endure a disheartening journey on an industrialized stretch of the river where construction projects line the banks, yellow streams of chemical waste flow directly from factories into the river, and the air and water are undeniably brown.

Then everything changes. Sweet-smelling orange blossoms announce the entrance to Qutang Gorge, where poplars, pines, and dense green scrub climb the cliffs, and mist hovers around the peaks that rise a few thousand feet above the water. The river is an immaculate emerald green—the penalty for littering here is 30,000 yuan (roughly $3,700), and garbage boats do daily rounds to skim any detritus from the surface.

On the steep hillsides of Wu Gorge, the second of the three, square white signs with black numbers climb the slope at two-meter intervals, marking where the water level will eventually top out. As striking as the limestone precipices are now, it's hard to suppress thoughts of how much more so they must have been when they rose higher above the river—and how much less so they will be when the water overtakes the white signs.

The third and longest gorge lies beyond the dam, on the other side of five cavernous ship locks that take several hours to pass through. Passengers crowd the decks to watch the eight-hundred-ton doors swing shut, the full force of the Yangtze behind them.

"Because of the construction of the Three Gorges Dam, everything is changing each day," says Li Da Wei, a river guide who has led travelers along the Yangtze for eighteen years. Before the flooding began, he traveled on foot, trekking on the tow paths that were used to pull river commerce vessels upstream until motorized boats made them obsolete. Now few of those tow paths remain, and Li does his guiding from a cruise ship.

Born in the metropolis of Chongqing, Li is a former air force pilot who had aspirations of becoming a Communist Party official until leading hikes on the Yangtze and interacting with "poor but happy" villagers made him reevaluate his priorities. "The government officials are so powerful, but I do not think they are very happy," says Li, who still wears a close-cut military hairstyle and an always-stoic expression. "I was born in the big city, but I prefer the country lifestyle today." From the deck of the *Victoria III*, a 156-passenger cruise ship, he points to a small remaining section of an old path on a slope in the twenty-eight-mile-long Wu Gorge. "That always reminds me of when we hiked it," he says wistfully.

Because of the dam, many of the villagers Li met have been relocated to places less suited to farming and have lost their livelihoods. "I feel a little bit sad about that," he says. He also worries about the deteriorating water quality in the Yangtze, from which his family and millions of others get their drinking water. Raw sewage enters the river at an estimated rate of 265 billion gallons per year. And the toxic substances once contained in the newly drowned cities are now underwater. When the river flowed freely, oxygenation helped flush out the pollutants. In the increasingly stagnant water, the filth just sits.

Despite his concerns, Li refuses to oppose the dam, arguing that what is good for China is good for its people. Westerners don't understand the Chinese mentality that values the society over the individual, he says. "We have a different culture, a different background, different traditions. We have a different understanding of human rights." Most Chinese are in favor of the dam, he says, because it will provide power, enhance commerce, and increase their economic opportunities by bringing more development and industry to the interior instead of keeping it concentrated on the coast.

From the vantage point of the river, it's apparent that not everyone agrees. Some scattered stone cottages that sit just above the present water line are still inhabited by residents who refuse to leave. ("It is sort of a headache for the government," Li says.) Higher on the hill, farmers who would rather take their chances by farming on unstable land than move to another region have built terraces on slopes so steep that a heavy rain could easily wash away their crops.

In 1992, the year the Chinese government approved the Three Gorges Dam project after decades of consideration, Beijing University sociologist Ding Qigang led a research team to villages that would be affected. A third of the villagers interviewed said they were unwilling to relocate. Since then, 13 riverfront cities and 140 towns have been reduced to rubble, and many of them have already been submerged. The "new cities," clusters of utilitarian gray-and-white concrete boxes, stand in stark contrast to the few old homes that remain.

Ding wrote an essay about his findings, which was published in the 1998 book *The River Dragon Has Come!* "All indications suggest that after inundation most rural resettlers will be left to cultivate inferior land and that their standards of living will indeed fall," he wrote.

The book is a collection of writings compiled by Dai Qing, an environmental activist and journalist who spent ten months in prison after the 1989 publication of her first book, *Yangtze! Yangtze!*, which lambasted the dam. That book surfaced shortly after the Tiananmen Square massacre, at a time when the Chinese government had zero tolerance for antiestablishment rhetoric. By the time the second book was published nine years later, the official attitude was somewhat more open. (Even so, many of the essayists wrote under assumed names.) In the essay Dai contributed to *The River Dragon Has Come!*, she wrote that China is "in the midst of a phase of 'uncontrolled' development where a sense of moderation and restraint are completely absent."

Future waterline markers, Yangtze River

Nearly a decade later, China's development has reached a frenzied pace as the government rushes to create a new and improved nation for the world to see during the 2008 Beijing Olympics. As high-rises replace historic *hutongs* and farmland gives way to factories, the Chinese joke that their national bird is the construction crane. And as the industrial growth continues to increase China's energy needs, plans have emerged for even more hydropower projects—including one on the Upper Yangtze at the 12,800-foot-deep Tiger Leaping Gorge that would create a 120-mile-long lake and displace as many as 100,000 people, and one in a nature conservation area on the

Nu River that would destroy the old-growth forest home of thirteen ethnic minority groups.

After Dai Qing's release from prison, she was forbidden to publish in China or speak in public for fifteen years. She broke her silence in 2005 with a talk at a Beijing bookstore, where supporters and party officials gathered to hear her mourn the fate of the Yangtze and hold forth on the shortcomings of hydropower. Calling the Three Gorges Dam "a mistake too big to correct," Dai admonished the government for ignoring the scientists who predicted in the 1980s that the dam would cause significant sedimentation. Now the murky river bears little resemblance to the Yangtze she remembers from her childhood, where she could see the riverbed from shore. "Nobody can save the Yangtze now," she said. Three years later, Dai remains under police surveillance.

The Three Gorges Dam may be the largest, but it's hardly an anomaly. China has been on a dam-building bender for more than half a century. Since Mao Zedong founded the People's Republic of China in 1949, the Chinese have built nearly twenty thousand major dams, far more than any other nation. The United States ranks second with 5,500 large dams, but the era of big dam building in America (and most of the Western world) ended two decades ago, as the negative consequences became apparent and people started to realize that hydropower isn't nearly as cheap or clean as they thought it would be.

In fact, large dams frequently cause more problems than they solve. Dammed river water has the potential to become a filthy haven for waterborne bugs. As it spreads out over land, it pushes the resident wildlife out of its native habitat and buries fertile soil; vegetation rots in the stagnant reservoirs, releasing greenhouse gases; and fish populations suffer as their migration patterns get cut off.

The story of the Chinese sturgeon is a favorite cautionary tale among dam critics. These half-ton monsters, thought to be 140 million years old, used to spawn near the Yangtze's headwaters and migrate to the sea. When the 1989 construction of the Gezhouba Dam made the upstream swim impossible, their population plummeted. Since then the government has gone to great lengths to protect the endangered fish, even creating a Chinese Sturgeon Institution to increase their numbers through artificial fertilization. Sturgeon no longer live above the dam.

Another ancient species, the Yangtze River dolphin, appears to have already fallen victim to the Three Gorges Dam. With its habitat irrevocably altered, the unusual river-dweller is now almost extinct.

The impact of large-scale dams on humans is even more daunting. According to the International Rivers Network, as many as eighty million people worldwide have been displaced because of hydropower projects. Most are poor farmers and indigenous people whose quality of life deteriorates significantly after they relocate. Those who stay, especially those who live and work close to shore, trust misguided promises of improved flood control that don't always take rising tributaries and sedimentation into account.

More alarmingly, dam failures have killed hundreds of thousands of people worldwide. China's most devastating breach happened in August 1975, when a typhoon drenched the central Henan province and caused the Banqiao Dam and sixty-one smaller dams to fail. At least twenty-six thousand people died in the floods as communities downstream were obliterated; the subsequent disease outbreaks and famine brought the death toll to more than two hundred thousand. Astonishingly, the disaster was kept a state secret for twenty years.

A breach at the Three Gorges Dam would be catastrophic. But experts worry much less about a dam failure than they do about landslides. As the reservoir rises over unstable riverside

DISAPPEARING DESTINATIONS

land, it creates the potential for slippage. Engineers have installed concrete slopes atop some danger areas to keep the dirt in place. Others remain unprotected. "Even a moderate geological disaster in the reservoir area can entail enormous human and property losses," geologist Fan Xiao wrote after a research trip to the Three Gorges region in 2006. Indeed, one month after the 2003 filling of the reservoir, a landslide occurred on the Qinggan River less than two miles from where it meets the Yangtze. The mass of earth caused sixty-five-foot waves that overturned twenty-two boats and wiped out three hundred homes. At least twenty people were killed. Though officials attributed the slide to heavy rainfall, independent researchers agreed the dam was partly to blame. Add the decreased land stability to the fact that two fault lines lie within fifty miles of the dam, and it's no wonder so many river watchers are holding their breath.

For now, the river valley and its tributaries are changing slowly, subtly. A farmer's cottage on the shoreline becomes a pile of rubble; a new bridge connects what's left of an old city to the new one on the opposite bank; a ship dock emerges on the shore of a tributary that not long ago was too narrow for anything wider than a peapod boat.

In 2009 onlookers will gather for the third inundation just as they did for the first two in 2003 and 2006. The water will rise to its final height over several eerie days. The Three Gorges, always magnificent, will become less so. And the dam will churn out power like never before, a symbol of a nation that is transforming itself at dizzying speed.

In 1996 Liu Zuozhong, the Chongqing artist who created the *Thousand Miles Three Gorges* mural, spent thirty-eight days on a solo hike in the Three Gorges, making sketches that will eventually become a second, more detailed version of the original mural. Now in his fifties, Liu holds court at his studio each day, occasionally breaking from his meticulous work to chat with visitors. Every so often they ask what has compelled him to spend so many years painting the Yangtze. "Three Gorges is the most beautiful view in the world, and now it is almost gone," he answers. "I have to do something for the next generation so they can remember the past."

GREAT BARRIER REEF, AUSTRALIA

Australia's east coast, Great Barrier Reef

RAY BERKELMANS WRAPPED UP THE SUMMER OF 2006 near the Tropic of Capricorn floating along the ancient rock and white-sand shores of the Keppel Islands on the southern end of the Great Barrier Reef. Berkelmans, a marine biologist with the Australian Institute of Marine Sciences and a lifelong coral reef devotee, had been out on the water for a couple of weeks seeing how the coral managed the long, warm summer. He didn't like what he saw. "Even before we dove in the water, you could look over the side of the boat and it's just white under there, which is most unusual," he says. The fans and folds, branches and bommies of coral, once resplendent in healthy shades of deep green and dense brown, had blanched into vast, ghostly coral forests. "Once you get in the water, it's so white, like someone's gone out and painted the whole reef," says Berkelmans. Coral is what he calls "thermally sensitive," meaning that when hot air causes ocean temperatures to rise, the coral suffers.

Australia's Great Barrier Reef, which stretches for over 1,250 miles along the northeast coast of Queensland, is said to be the only living organism visible from space. The reef, which is longer than the Great Wall of China, lies an average of forty miles off the coast and stretches east to the continental shelf. It's the largest reef system in the world and is actually made up of 2,900 reefs and several hundred continental islands and cays. The Great Barrier has more than four hundred types of coral in three categories: fringe, which hugs the mainland and island coasts; ribbon, which consists of long, continuous "streamer" walls in the north; and platform, the most common type, which appears off the edge of the continental shelf, sometimes in clusters over four hundred feet high.

Although there's public access to parts of the Great Barrier Reef Marine Park all along the reef, most people take day trips from the central coast cities of Cairns and Port Douglas and the Whitsunday Islands. Mass tourism operators take out hundreds of people at a time on high-speed catamarans from there, which means that 85 percent of reef peepers only see about 10 percent of the Great Barrier, leaving the northern and southern ends largely unexplored. The lesser-known southern departure points of Heron and Wilson islands, where some of the best snorkeling spots are just footsteps from front porches, are between fifty and sixty miles off the coast of the southern mainland city of Gladstone (750 miles south of Cairns). Both islands offer reef and ecology walks to overnight guests (no day-trippers allowed), and on Heron Island, the thick *Pisonia* forest is a birder's bliss. Visitors between October and May could be joined by spawning turtles (note that Heron Island, which is a wildlife sanctuary, is closed in February for bird nesting). And on a full moon in late November or early December, night divers may catch the mysterious and massive reef spawning, tantamount to an annual coral orgy and oft described as an underwater blizzard.

While most people miss the spawning spectacle, nearly two million people snorkeled, dived or peered through a glass-bottomed boat at the coral mammoth in 2005, generating over $5 billion for the Australian economy. Humans have been gaga for the Great Barrier Reef since the 1890s, when pleasure cruises first left Cairns for Green Island, seventeen miles off the coast (and roughly six hundred miles north of the Keppels). In the fifty or so years that followed, visitor numbers rose but were confined to the coast. By the late 1970s, faster boats had come on the scene, allowing for extended trips up to nearly twenty-five miles offshore. In the early 1980s, visitor numbers began to skyrocket by 30 percent per year. In the past decade, the gains have slowed, but numbers continue to rise. Traveler infrastructure has met the demand. There are now 800 permitted outfitters operating 1,500 boats on the reef.

While the astronauts who saw the Great Barrier Reef from space called it a "great white scar upon the earth," most people know it as a natural wonder of the world without equal. It is, of course, made up of vast coral communities, but also mangroves, sea grass, sandy islands, and sponge gardens whose colors even Crayola couldn't replicate. The Great Barrier Reef is also believed to be the epicenter of earth's marine biodiversity. Among the species that breed there are the endangered herbivorous dugong, or "sea cow," and the humpback whale. The tropical waters that surround the 135,136 square mile Great Barrier Marine Park, the earth's largest World Heritage Site, are frequented by dwarf minke and killer whales, and hammerhead and whale sharks. The world's largest black marlin and the giant Maori wrasse, or Napoleon fish, share the surf with 1,500 other kinds of fish. Six out of seven of the world's species of marine turtles, including the giant green loggerhead, nest there among crustaceans, anemones, sponges, and marine worms. Hundreds of bird species nest on the reef's cays and islands.

To understand what endangers the Great Barrier Reef, says Berkelmans, it helps to know that coral is a sensitive creature, a skeletal animal with algae growing within its tissue. A single coral colony is composed of thousands of individual coral polyps, which, like pixels in a photo, combine to form the entire image of the reef. Algae living symbiotically within coral photosynthesizes sunlight, feeding the coral and giving it its color. Healthy reefs are rich green, brown, and yellow. Berkelmans has known Keppels reefs in full bloom and attests to them being some of the finest coral on the Great Barrier Reef. "You'd think that it's too cold and really the reefs are struggling, compared to the northern reefs, but the corals are so abundant down there," he says. Coral in the southern reefs grow two to three times larger and grow faster and more extensively than their northerly cousins. "They get to enormous sizes compared to the corals farther north," says Berkelmans. "It really is an extraordinary place. Coral cover is somewhere between sixty and eighty-five percent, which is absolutely amazing to look at."

But that's all changing. The Keppels bleached first in 1998 and then again in 2002 and 2006. The main cause of this bleaching on the Great Barrier Reef is the heating of the Pacific Ocean. According to the Australian Bureau of Meteorology, 2005 was the country's hottest year on record. That banner year was followed by Queensland's warmest-ever summer in 2006. (It was a bit cooler in the summer of 2007 but was still far above average.) When coral is stressed, which happens easily because it thrives only within a narrow temperature range, it begins to shut down. In an effort to survive, its resident algae release toxins, forcing the coral to expel them. Without their algae lifeline, sickly reefs drain of color, sometimes first exhibiting a pastel or fluorescent hue on their way to "bleached" white. Where and when coral will bleach is impossible to predict. "Bleaching is one of these events that's patchy; you have it here and you don't have it there. It's all due to local and regional weather patterns," says Berkelmans.

Bleaching isn't necessarily a death sentence for coral. In fact, most Keppel reefs recovered from the bleaching events in 1998 and 2002, in which nearly all of their coral turned white. Unlike the less-flexible northern Barrier Reef, the Keppels were long known for their ability to bounce back from large-scale bleaching. But the impact of the long hot summer of 2006 seems to have been especially harsh. "It's resilient. We've seen it come through a couple of bleaching events," says Berkelmans. "Not quite this time, though." Upwards of 30 percent of Keppels coral has moved beyond bleaching and is already dead. "It's just far too many days at relatively high temperatures, more than what they're used to. It's more than the corals can cope with," he says. Berkelmans, a world expert in coral bleaching, worries that every hotter-than-average year could deliver another fatal blow. "Now we're finding that 'unusually warm summers' are happening more often," he says.

Preservation efforts on the Great Barrier Reef have thus far focused on local issues. When the reef began to show signs of decline several years ago, Australian officials scrambled to halt it with a flurry of new policies, declarations, and fees. As natural systems go, the Marine Park now enjoys Fort Knox–like protection (at least on paper) against many of the forces that were once believed to be the greatest threats to the Great Barrier, including pollution and its many ills. Wastewater, farm outwash, and pollution, loaded with "nutrients" from (mostly tourism-related) development on the mainland and twenty-seven of the Barrier Reef's islands, had been throwing off the complex and delicate balance of the reef. While these nutrients are ideal for algae, they can be fatal to coral. Algae blooms were consuming coral and blotting out other rich marine flora and fauna. Such nutrient concentrations had quadrupled from the mid nineteeth century to the end of the twentieth century. The implementation of the Reef Water Quality Protection Plan in 2004 has resulted in modest improvements.

Nutrient loads are still suspected of hastening outbreaks of the notorious "crown of thorns," one of coral's deadliest foes. This blight overtakes coral, either by wounding and scarring it or by releasing digestive enzymes that consume its tissue outright, leaving behind only a skeleton. A series of outbreaks from 1966 to the present has threatened the integrity of the entire reef. "Crown of thorns have eaten the coral cover down from fifty to ninety percent of some reefs," says Berkelmans. "It takes those reefs a good ten years to recover from that." Other crown facilitators include sea temperature rise, loss of predators, and overfishing. Unsustainable commercial and recreational fishing using long-line and trawling techniques also did plenty to devastate parts of the reef on its own. The targeting of key predators, like snapper and grouper, destabilized the reef's ecological balance. Thankfully, in 2004 the "no-take" portion of the reef was increased from 5 percent to 33 percent, allowing fish populations to begin to recover.

At one time, the increasing pressure on the reef from the multi-billion-dollar tourism industry was another concern. Irresponsible boaters, mindless of the damage their propellers and one-ton anchors could do, were a problem, as was the sheer number of tourists touching, kicking, and standing on the reef. But collaboration between the Marine Authority and the reef outfitters, who now educate their millions of clients, has gone a long way to safeguarding the gentle giant of a reef.

One such outfitter is David Hutchen, who's spent twenty-five years on the reef, based in the Whitsunday archipelago (about halfway between Green Island and the Keppels). In the fourteen years that his company, Fantasea Cruises, has been touring the Hardy Reef, Hutchen estimates that it has brought 1.5 million

Coral, Great Barrier Reef

travelers to see it. He says that over time, there has been grow-ing concern by travelers about keeping the reef healthy. "Those people are all intimately interested in the reef. They question everything we do," says Hutchen. He says that his guides "lec-ture" the boatloads of tourists on the basics of reef dos and don'ts in an effort to minimize the effect of so many sunscreen-slick snorkelers. "Don't sit on it or stand on it. Just look at it," says Hutchen.

All outfitters, including Hutchen, who is on three govern-mental panels, obviously have a vested interest in minding the reef. "We all look at the coral, and we all have customers who want to look at the coral," says Hutchen. "We preach to each other about protecting it all day, every day. We're doing a bloody good job. If you look, you'll see that the reef is alive and well." Like many tour operators, Fantasea is also active in a program called Bleach Watch, monitoring a specific area of the Great Barrier for signs of stress. Hutchen took an additional step when, in consort with the Australian Institute of Marine Sciences, he installed a radiometer on one of his boats in order to take daily water temperature readings. The institute's Berkelmans says, "We have an awful lot of industry that is dependent on the reef. All of Queensland basically depends on it. It's in all of our interests to have a healthy reef."

The combined regional stresses of tourism, development, water quality, and fishing are by no means moot, but they are now being actively managed. If aggressively enforced, policies to lessen the impact of these issues may buy some time for the greatest of reefs. But the gravest threat to the reef is much harder to mitigate. "While [the reef] might be able to manage things locally, like runoff, point-source pollution, visitation, and extraction from fisheries, climate change is not something that she can manage locally," Berkelmans says. "It's something that we have to manage as a global society." The only way to lessen the effect that greenhouse gases are having on the earth's atmosphere and ocean temperatures is to satiate our thirst for energy in less polluting ways. But, says Berkelmans, "There's really been no incentive for change."

The effects of lesser-understood global climate change phenomena are more daunting still. Joanie Kleypas, a marine ecologist and geologist with the National Center for Atmospheric Research in Boulder, Colorado, has spent several years looking at the effect of the oceans' absorption of carbon dioxide on marine life. A recent study led by Kleypas concluded that since 1980, oceans have absorbed roughly one third of human-supplied carbon dioxide. Increased carbon dioxide storage leads to a process of ocean acidification, in which carbonate ions are sabotaged. Without those ions, corals suffer a kind of osteoporosis and are greatly impeded in developing and solidifying their skeletons. The less of that carbonate ion you have available, the fewer blocks you have available for building the skeleton," says Kleypas. Since acidification is chronic and its effects are less immediate than bleaching, it's been an uphill battle to draw attention to it.

Kleypas equates the reef's condition to that of a patient with both pneumonia and cancer. "You're going to treat the pneumonia first, but it doesn't mean you're not going to treat the cancer," she says. Kleypas, who spent three years studying the reef out of Townsville, shudders to consider what will become of the Great Barrier if climate change is not arrested. "It's one of the healthiest reef systems we have. They've done a great job of protecting it. But this is an awful thing that's really going on in the oceans, and everything tells us that it's not good for organisms." Kleypas says that if global warming was the only threat to the reef, some of it might be salvaged, but add acidification, and the chances of that lessen greatly. "You take the most pristine reef out there and it's hit by both warming and acidification—it's pretty hard to predict which one is the most threatening, but I know in the long term that it won't survive acidification," she says. "There may be some coral but there'll be no reef."

The potential loss of the Australian icon is practically inconceivable for Kleypas. "The reef is remarkable. I was so in love with it. It just becomes part of you," she says.

It's just as unthinkable for Ray Berkelmans, who got a startling glimpse of the reef's possible future in July 2006. He went up to do some diving in the Coral Sea, about halfway between Australia and New Caledonia. He and his team were assessing the mortality of coral that had been hard-hit by bleaching in 2002, and they saw, for the first time, that most of it had not recovered. Berkelmans estimates that 97 percent of the coral on the plateau where he was diving is dead. "It is so remote and so pristine out there, but that pristineness is of no help at all when it comes to climate change," he says. "This is kind of an eye-opener for us on the Great Barrier Reef." The prognosis for Australia's reef given by its bleaching experts is not good. "Their projections say that by 2050 or so we'll be seeing coral bleaching events every year and there'll be major, major reductions in coral cover by then," says Berkelmans. "This is what we're doing to our beautiful reefs. This is our paradise that we're letting slip by."

In the meantime, when friends come to visit Fantasea's Hutchen in the Whitsundays, he'll still load them onto one of his company's high-speed catamarans and take them out to Hardy Reef. There, in one of the world's seven natural wonders, gardens of lush coral bloom just below the surface of the transparent surf. Hutchen guides his friends away from the hundreds of other visitors floating and flapping about to secret gardens. He leads them over five-foot-wide green and purple clams and past anemones swarming with garish clownfish. "It's quite wonderful to see," says Hutchen. "I can't wait to get out into the water and do it again."

ACKNOWLEDGMENTS

WE DOUBT THERE IS A FINER EDITOR THAN EDWARD Kastenmeier, whose pen graced our manuscript with such tactful precision that his improvements didn't hurt a bit. Thanks, too, to the patient and diligent Timothy O'Connell and the eagle-eyed Aja Pollock.

We are indebted to our early visionaries and advisers, Christine Testolini, Dawn Davis, and Jim Ballard; to the Redmond family, who so graciously opened up their Idaho retreat for a co-author summit; and to the friends and colleagues whose assistance and moral support we could not have persevered without: Seth Ames, Jason Arth, Amy Asman, Shantel Beckers, Christie Botelho, Dorothy Boudreau, Deirdre Campbell, Alex Cohen, Rachel Duchak, Aimee Durfee, Frances Figart, Bert Forbes, Monica Foster, Nicole Friederichs, Sofia Gelpi, Justin Grune-wald, Jessamyn Harris, Alison Jaffe, Greg Knipe, Jenn Knudsen, Brian Mohr, Jeanné Mutziger, Sonya Nitschke, Rafael Pesantes, Elizabeth Pierce and family, and Aerin Wilson.

The support and enthusiasm of the family members who cheered us on for reasons that (they insist) transcend shared DNA and marital vows was immeasurable: Scott Bisheff, Robyn Hansen, Mark and Terri Lisagor, Adam Lisagor, Suzan Paras, and Ellen, Alison, Andrew and Eric Baukney.

Few of these words could have been written without the patience and conviction of the scientists and conservationists who spent countless hours confirming facts and explaining complex concepts. Likewise, the people who awoke to changes in their own backyards and took the time to tell us about it. Thank you all for your strength, for answering our call to truth, and for giving us cause for hope.

Finally, to the travelers who understand their role as protectors of, not just visitors to, these special destinations, we offer thanks and solidarity.

ILLUSTRATION CREDITS

APPALACHIA
Hawks Nest State Park: Steve Shaluta/West Virginia Department of Commerce
Highland Scenic Highway: Steve Shaluta/West Virginia Department of Commerce

ARCTIC NATIONAL WILDLIFE REFUGE, ALASKA
Mountains and Meandering Creeks, Arctic National Wildlife Refuge: US Fish and Wildlife Service
10-02 area of Arctic National Wildlife Refuge: US Fish and Wildlife Service

MOUNT RAINIER AND THE CASCADES
South Sister from the Cascade Loop Highway: Bert Forbes
Mount Rainier from Mount St. Helens: Jon Major/US Geological Survey

CASCO BAY, MAINE
Outer Green Island, Casco Bay, Maine: Karen Young/Casco Bay Estuary Partnership

THE EVERGLADES, FLORIDA
Pinelands in Everglades National Park: Gary M. Stolz/US Fish and Wildlife Service
Snowy egret in Everglades National Park: Gary M. Stolz/US Fish and Wildlife Service

GLACIER NATIONAL PARK, MONTANA
Avalanche Lake, Glacier National Park: Heather Hansen
Glacier National Park: James C. Leupold/US Fish and Wildlife Service

GREAT SMOKY MOUNTAINS NATIONAL PARK
Great Smoky Mountains National Park: National Park Service

NAPA VALLEY, CALIFORNIA
Sonoma: © Jessamyn Harris
A vineyard in Sonoma: © Jessamyn Harris

OAHU, HAWAII
Mokulua Islands from the Oahu mainland, Hawaii: Jamie Lisagor
Lanikai Beach, before seawall construction: Mokulua Guides

THE RIO GRANDE
Rio Grande near Taos, New Mexico: Kimberly Lisagor
Rio Grande near Embudo, New Mexico: Mario Malvino

YELLOWSTONE NATIONAL PARK
Grand Canyon of the Yellowstone, Yellowstone National Park: US
    Geological Survey
Norris Geyser Basin, Yellowstone National Park: Heather Hansen

HUDSON BAY, MANITOBA AND NUNAVUT
Hudson Bay, Canada: Gerald Ludwig/US Fish and Wildlife Service

INSIDE PASSAGE, BRITISH COLUMBIA
Inside Passage: Neil Rabinowitz
Inside Passage: Nimmo Bay Resort

BIOLUMINESCENT BAYS, PUERTO RICO
Vieques: Nicole Friederichs
Vieques: Nicole Friederichs

ROATÁN, HONDURAS
Bear's Den, Roatán, Honduras: Ian Drysdale © 2007
Sea lilies, Roatán: Karl Stanley

TURKS AND CAICOS ISLANDS
Sea oats on West Caicos: Kimberly Lisagor

AMAZON BASIN
Yasuní National Park in the morning, Ecuador: Seth Ames
Hypsiboas fasciatus, Yasuní National Park, Ecuador: Seth Ames

AYSÉN, PATAGONIA, CHILE
Río Baker Valley, Aysén, Patagonia, Chile: Brian
   Mohr/EmberPhoto.com
Río Baker, Aysén, Patagonia, Chile: Brian Mohr/EmberPhoto.com

GALÁPAGOS, ECUADOR
Bartolomé Island, Galápagos: Heather Hansen

MACHU PICCHU, PERU
Urubamba River and Machu Picchu: Heather Hansen

THE ALPS
Ski resort near the Matterhorn: Arthur Pierce
The Matterhorn: Arthur Pierce

CANARY ISLANDS, SPAIN
Pico Viejo, Teide National Park, Tenerife: © UNESCO/J. Pestano

DANUBE RIVER AND DELTA
Fisherman, Danube Delta: © UNESCO/Bruno Cottacorda

DEAD SEA, ISRAEL, PALESTINE, AND JORDAN
The Dead Sea, Israel: © UNESCO/Leah Lourier
Kayaker on the Dead Sea: Dor Kayak

VENICE, ITALY
Venice: © UNESCO/Dominique Roger

CONGO BASIN, CENTRAL AFRICA
Navigating the Congo Basin: Bert Forbes
Silverbacks, Congo: Mark Attwater/UNEP

MAASAILAND, KENYA
On safari along elephant migration routes passing through native
   Maasailand between Kenya and Tanzania: Photo courtesy of
   WildlandAdventures.com

MOUNT KILIMANJARO, TANZANIA
Kilimanjaro National Park: © UNESCO/Christoph Lübbert

TIMBUKTU, MALI
Sankare Mosque, Timbuktu: © UNESCO/T. Joffroy
Sorting building materials, Timbuktu: © UNESCO/T. Joffroy

EVEREST NATIONAL PARK, NEPAL
Gokyo Ri, Nepal: Bret Meldrum/KarmaQuest Ecotourism and
 Adventure Travel
Himalaya Mountains: Bert Forbes

YANGTZE RIVER VALLEY, CHINA
Endangered cottages on the Yangtze River: Kimberly Lisagor
Future waterline markers, Yangtze River: Kimberly Lisagor

GREAT BARRIER REEF
Australia's east coast, Great Barrier Reef: © UNESCO/Jim Thorsell
Coral, Great Barrier Reef: © UNESCO/Jim Thorsell

APPENDIX A

RESPONSIBLE TRAVEL RESOURCES

Ecotourism Australia (ecotourism.org.au)
GPO Box 268 Brisbane,
Q. 4001 Australia
+617 3229 5550

EndangeredPlaces.com

Green Globe 21 (greenglobe21.com)
GPO Box 371
Canberra, ACT 2601
Australia
+612 6257 9102

The International Ecotourism Society (ecotourism.org)
1333 H Street NW
Suite 300, East Tower
Washington, DC 20005
(202) 347-9203

Planeta.com

Responsibletravel.com
4th Floor, Pavilion House
6 The Old Steine
Brighton, East Sussex BN1 1EJ
England

Sustainable Travel International (sustainabletravel.com)
PO Box 1313
Boulder, CO 80306
(720) 273-2975

Tourism Concern (tourismconcern.org.uk)
Stapleton House
277–281 Holloway Road
London N7 8HN
England
+44 (0) 20 7133 3330

Travelers' Philanthropy (ecotourismcesd.org,
    travelersphilanthropy.org)
Center on Ecotourism and Sustainable Development
1333 H Street NW
Suite 300
Washington, DC 20005
(202) 347-9203

The VISIT Initiative (yourvisit.info)
European Centre for Eco Agro Tourism
PO Box 10899
1001 EW Amsterdam
The Netherlands
+31 20 6630479

APPENDIX B

THE ALPS

International Commission for the Protection of the Alps
 (cipra.org)
Im Bretscha 22, FL-9494
Schaan, Switzerland
+41 423 237 4030

Alpine Initiative (alpine-initiative.ch)
Herrengasse 2, PO Box 28-6460
Altdorf, Switzerland
+41 (0)41 870 97 81

World Wildlife Fund–Austria (panda.org)
Alpine Programme
Innsbruck, Austria
+43 512 573534 25

AMAZON BASIN

Amazon Watch (amazonwatch.org)
One Hallidie Plaza, Suite 402
San Francisco, CA 94102
(415) 487-9600

Save America's Forests (saveamericasforests.org)
4 Library Court SE
Washington, DC 20003
(202) 544-9219

APPALACHIA

Appalachian Center for the Economy and the Environment
  (appalachian-center.org)
PO Box 507
Lewisburg, WV 24901
(304) 645-9006

Ohio Valley Environmental Coalition (ohvec.org)
PO Box 6753
Huntington, WV 25773
(304) 522-0246

ARCTIC NATIONAL WILDLIFE REFUGE, ALASKA

The Gwich'in Steering Committee
  (gwichinsteeringcommittee.org)
122 First Avenue, Box 2
Fairbanks, AK 99701
(907) 458-8264

Defenders of Wildlife (savearcticrefuge.org)
333 W 4th Ave., #302
Anchorage, AK 99501
(907) 276-9453

AYSÉN, CHILE

Ecosistemas (ecosistemas.cl)
José M. Infante 1960 Ñuñoa
Santiago, Chile
(562) 494 02 33 or (562) 458 4776

CODEFF Aisén (aisenreservadevida.cl)
12 de Octubre #288, 2° piso
Coyhaique, Chile
(562) 067 234451

BANKS ISLAND

Climate Action Network (climateactionnetwork.ca)
412-1 Nicholas Street
Ottawa, Ontario, Canada K1N 7B7
(866) 373-2990

International Institute for Sustainable Development
(iisd.org/communities)
Community Adaptation and Sustainable Livelihoods Project
161 Portage Avenue East, 6th Floor
Winnipeg, Manitoba, Canada R3B 0Y4
(204) 958-7700

BOREAL FOREST, LAPLAND, FINLAND

Greenpeace International (greenpeace.org)
Ottho Heldringstraat 5
1066 AZ Amsterdam
The Netherlands
+31 20 7182000

Reindeer Herders' Association (paliskunnat.fi)
Koskikatu 33 A 1
PL 8168, 96101
Rovaniemi, Finland
(016) 331 6000

CANARY ISLANDS, SPAIN

Asociación Tinerfeña de Amigos de la Naturaleza (atan.org/en)
Calle Santo Domingo, 10
Apartado de correos 1015
38080 Santa Cruz de Tenerife
Spain
(34) 922 279 392

Ecologistas en Acción de Canarias
  (ecologistasenaccion.org/canarias)
C/ Senador Castillo Olivares 31
Las Palmas de GC
Spain
(34) 928 362 233

MOUNT RAINIER AND THE CASCADES

Climate Impacts Group (cses.washington.edu/cig/)
Center for Science in the Earth System
Joint Institute for the Study of the Atmosphere and Ocean
University of Washington, Box 354235
Seattle, WA 98195
(206) 616-5350

David A. Johnston Cascades Volcano Observatory
  (vulcan.wr.usgs.gov)
Columbia Tech Center
1300 SE Cardinal Court, Bldg. 10, Suite 100
Vancouver, WA 98683
(360) 993-8900

CASCO BAY, MAINE

Casco Bay Estuary Partnership (cascobay.usm.maine.edu)
PO Box 9300
Portland, ME 04104
(207) 780-4820

Friends of Casco Bay (cascobay.org)
43 Slocum Drive
South Portland, ME 04106
(207) 799-8574

CHACALTAYA, BOLIVIA

Institut de Recherche pour le Développement (ird.fr)
213, rue La Fayette
75 480, Cedex 10
Paris, France
33 (0)1 48 03 77 77

National Program on Climate Change (pncc.gov.bo)
Mercado Street Nbr 1328
Edif. Mariscal Ballivián, Mezannine
La Paz, Bolivia
(591) 222-002-06

THE CONGO, CENTRAL AFRICA

Programme for Conservation and Rational Utilization of
    Forest Ecosystems in Central Africa (ecofac.org)
Batterie 4—Face groupe scolaire Gros Bouquet 2
BP 15115
Libreville, Gabon
(241) 732-343

Wildlife Conservation Society (wcs-congo.org)
Development Office
Bronx Zoo
2300 Southern Boulevard
Bronx, NY 10460
(718) 220-5090

DANUBE RIVER AND DELTA

Regional Environmental Program for Central and Eastern
    Europe (rec.org)
Ady Endre út 9-11
Szentendre, Hungary 2000
36 2650 4000

European Rivers Network (rivernet.org)
ERN-SOS Loire Vivante, 8 rue Crozatier
43000 Le Puy, France
33 471 02 08 14

World Wildlife Fund (panda.org)
Danube-Carpathian Programme
2A Dimitrie Cantemir Boulevard
Block P3, Entrance 2
Apartment 32, Sector 4
Bucharest, Romania 040241
40 21 335 25 74

DEAD SEA, ISRAEL AND JORDAN

Friends of the Earth Middle East (foeme.org)
PO Box 840252
Amman, Jordan 11181
962-6-5866602/3

Global Nature Fund (globalnature.org)
International Foundation for Environment and Nature
Fritz-Reichle-Ring 4
D-78315 Radolfzell, Germany
+ 49 (0) 77 32-99 95-80/-85

EVEREST NATIONAL PARK

International Centre for Integrated Mountain Development
   (icimod.org)
GPO Box 3226
Khumaltar, Kathmandu, Nepal
+ 977 1 5525313

WWF Nepal Program (wwfnepal.org)
PO Box 7660
Kathmandu, Nepal
+ 977 1 4434820

EVERGLADES, FLORIDA

Earthjustice (earthjustice.org)
111 South Martin Luther King Jr. Blvd.
Tallahassee, FL 32301
(850) 681-0031

Friends of the Everglades (everglades.org)
7800 Red Road, Suite 215K
Miami, Florida 33143
(305) 669-0858

GALÁPAGOS

Galápagos Conservancy (galapagos.org)
407 North Washington Street, Suite 105
Falls Church, VA 22046
(703) 538-6833

World Wildlife Fund, Ecuador (panda.org)
Edif. Fundacion Natura Piso 2 Avenida Republica 481
Quito, Ecuador
593 2 25033 85

GLACIER NATIONAL PARK/FLATHEAD VALLEY

Flathead Coalition (flatheadcoalition.org)
PO Box 394
Columbia Falls, MT 59912
(406) 862-6722

National Parks Conservation Association (npca.org/
  northernrockies)
Glacier Field Office
214 W. Second St.
PO Box 4485
Whitefish, MT 59937
(406) 862-6722

GREAT BARRIER REEF

Heron Island Research Station (marine.uq.edu.au/hirs)
Centre for Marine Studies
University of Queensland
Great Barrier Reef via
Gladstone, Queensland 4680
Australia
(61 07) 4978 1399

ReefED (reefed.edu.au)
Great Barrier Reef Marine Park Authority
PO Box 1379
Townsville, Queensland 4810
Australia
(61 07) 4750 0700

GREAT SMOKY MOUNTAINS NATIONAL PARK

Appalachian Voices (appvoices.org)
703 W. King Street #105
Boone, NC 28607
(877) APP-VOICE or (828) 262-1500

National Parks Conservation Association (npca.org/southeast)
Southeast Regional Office
706 Walnut Street, Suite 200
Knoxville, TN 37902
(865) 329-2424

HUDSON BAY, CANADA

Inuit Circumpolar Conference (inuitcircumpolar.com)
170 Laurier Avenue West, Suite 504
Ottawa, Ontario K1P 5V5
Canada
(613) 563-2642

Natural Resources Defense Council (savebiogems.org/polar)
40 West 20th Street
New York, NY 10011
(212) 727-2700

INNER AND OUTER BANKS, NORTH CAROLINA

North Carolina Coastal Federation (nccoast.org)
3609 Highway 24 (Ocean)
Newport, NC 28570
(252) 393-8185

INSIDE PASSAGE, BRITISH COLUMBIA

Bluewater Network (bluewaternetwork.org)
311 California, Suite 510
San Francisco, CA 94104
(415) 544-0790

The British Columbia Environmental Network (ecobc.org)
2474 Bowker Ave.
Victoria, BC V8R 2G1
Canada
(250) 361-1876

Campaign to Safeguard America's Waters
 (earthisland.org/c-saw)
Box 956
Haines, AK 99827
(907) 766-3005

MACHU PICCHU, PERU

World Monuments Fund (wmf.org)
95 Madison Avenue
New York, NY 10016
(646) 424-9594

MAASAILAND, KENYA

Maasai Environmental Resource Coalition (maasaierc.org)
2020 Pennsylvania Avenue NW #136
Washington, DC 20006
(202) 785-8787

MOUNT KILIMANJARO

Climate Institute (climate.org)
1785 Massachusetts Avenue NW
Washington, DC 20036
(202) 547-0104

Porter Assistance Project (sherpafund.org/porter)
International Mountain Explorers Connection
PO Box 3665
Boulder, CO 80307
(303) 998-0101

OAHU, HAWAII

Sierra Club, Hawaii chapter (hi.sierraclub.org)
PO Box 2577
Honolulu, Hawaii 96803
(808) 538-6616

Surfrider Foundation, Oahu chapter (surfrider.org/oahu)
(808) 531-SURF

PUERTO RICO

Fideicomiso (fideicomiso.org)
PO Box 9023554
San Juan, Puerto Rico 00902
(787) 722-5834

The Vieques Conservation and Historical Trust (vcht.org)
Calle Flamboyán #138
Vieques, Puerto Rico 00765
(787) 741-8850

RIO GRANDE

American Rivers (americanrivers.org)
1101 14th Street NW, Suite 1400
Washington, DC 20005
(202) 347-7550

Amigos Bravos (amigosbravos.org)
1608 Isleta Boulevard SW
Albuquerque, NM 87105
(505) 452-9387

Middle Rio Grande Water Assembly (waterassembly.org)
PO Box 25862
Albuquerque, NM 87125
(505) 797-4306

ROATÁN, HONDURAS

The Coral Reef Alliance (coral.org)
417 Montgomery Street, Suite 205
San Francisco, CA 94104
(415) 834-0900 or (888) CORAL-REEF

WWF Centroamérica (wwfca.org)
Apartado postal 629–2350
San Francisco de Dos Ríos
San José, Costa Rica
+ 506 234 7638

TIMBUKTU, MALI

Timbuktu Educational Foundation (timbuktufoundation.org)
PO Box 222
Alameda, CA 94501
(510) 748-9033

TURKS AND CAICOS ISLANDS

Turks and Caicos National Trust (nationaltrust.tc)
PO Box 540
Providenciales, Turks and Caicos Islands, BWI
(649) 941-5710

TUVALU/MALDIVES

Pacific Regional Environment Programme (sprep.org)
PO Box 240
Apia, Samoa
685 21929

Seacology (seacology.org)
2009 Hopkins Street
Berkeley, CA 94707
(510) 559-3505

VENICE, ITALY

Venice in Peril (veniceinperil.org)
Hurlingham Studios, Unit 4
Ranelagh Gardens
London SW6 3PA
England
44 (0) 20 7736 6891

YANGTZE RIVER VALLEY

International Rivers Network (irn.org)
1847 Berkeley Way
Berkeley, CA 94703
(510) 848-1155

Three Gorges Probe (threegorgesprobe.org)
225 Brunswick Avenue
Toronto, Ontario M5S 2M6
Canada
(416) 964-9223

YELLOWSTONE NATIONAL PARK

Public Employees for Environmental Responsibility (peer.org)
2000 P Street, NW Suite 240
Washington, DC 20036
(202) 265-7337

Sierra Club Grizzly Bear Project (sierraclub.org/grizzly)
PO Box 1290
Bozeman, MT 59771
(406) 582-8365

Buffalo Field Campaign (buffalofieldcampaign.org)
PO Box 957
West Yellowstone, MT 59758
(406) 646-0070